STUDIES ON ETHNIC GROUPS IN CHINA

Stevan Harrell, Editor

STUDIES ON ETHNIC GROUPS IN CHINA

ON THE MARGINS OF TIBET

Cultural Survival on the Sino-Tibetan Frontier

Åshild Kolås and Monika P. Thowsen

UNIVERSITY OF WASHINGTON PRESS

Seattle and London

THIS PUBLICATION WAS SUPPORTED IN PART
BY THE DONALD R. ELLEGOOD INTERNATIONAL
PUBLICATIONS ENDOWMENT.

Copyright © 2005 by the University of Washington Press
Printed in United States of America
Designed by Pamela Canell
12 11 10 09 08 07 06 05   5 4 3 2 1

University of Washington Press
P.O. Box 50096, Seattle, WA 98145
www.washington.edu/uwpress

Library of Congress Cataloging-in-Publication Data
Kolas, Ashild.
On the margins of Tibet : cultural survival on the Sino-
Tibetan frontier / Ashild Kolas and Monika P. Thowsen.
    p. cm. — (Studies on ethnic groups in China)
Includes bibliographical references and index.
ISBN 0-295-98480-5 (alk. paper)
ISBN 0-295-98481-3 (pbk. : alk. paper)
    1. Tibet (China)—Civilization.
        I. Thowsen, Monika P.
        II. Title.   III. Series.
DS786.K695 2005   951'.505—dc22   2004021640

The paper used in this publication is acid-free and 90 percent
recycled from at least 50 percent post-consumer waste. It meets
the minimum requirements of American National Standard for
Information Sciences—Permanence of Paper for Printed
Library Materials, ANSI z39.48-1984. ⊗ ◉

CONTENTS

APPENDIXES

PREFACE AND ACKNOWLEDGMENTS

The study on which this book is based was conducted under the auspices of the Research Project on Tibetan Culture in China, initiated by the International Peace Research Institute, Oslo (PRIO), and funded by the Norwegian Ministry of Foreign Affairs. The Research Project on Tibetan Culture in China was developed in 1996 after preliminary contacts had been made in China through the Ethnic Affairs Research Center of the State Ethnic Affairs Commission. During the autumn of 1997, further dialogue was initiated between PRIO and the Institute of Nationalities Studies (INS) of the Chinese Academy of Social Sciences (CASS). Project director David Phillips first met with INS representatives during a preparatory trip to Beijing and Lhasa in November 1997.

In March 1998, INS delegates visited Oslo and signed a Memorandum of Understanding on the implementation of scholarly research between PRIO and the INS. The delegates were invited to attend the seminar "Trends in Tibetan Culture" (23–24 March 1998) and discuss their cooperation on the project. A representative of the Ethnic Affairs Research Center also participated in the seminar. The delegates from CASS were Sun Yu (foreign affairs secretary in charge of Europe at the CASS main office), Professor Hao Shiyuan (director of the INS), Chen Jingyuan (director of the Department of Visual Anthropology, INS), and Guo Yang (editor in the Publications Department, INS).

Before the agreement was signed, an International Advisory Board was established in order to help ensure the scholarly quality of the project. The advisory board was chaired by Thommy Svensson, initially in his capacity as director of the Nordic Institute of Asian Studies, Copenhagen. The other

members of the advisory board were Dru Gladney (professor of Asian stud-
ies, University of Hawaii at Manoa, and dean of academics, Asia-Pacific
Center for Security Studies, Honolulu), Samten Karmay (director of
research, Centre National de la Recherche Scientifique [CNRS], Paris),
Robert Thurman (professor, Columbia University, New York), and Jens
Braarvig (director, Network for University Cooperation Tibet-Norway,
Oslo). The advisory board held its first meetings during 21–27 March 1998.
We would like to express our gratitude to all the members of the board for
reading our reports and manuscripts and for their advice and close atten-
tion to our work throughout the research process.

During the summer of 1998, Åshild Kolås made an initial research trip
to Dechen (Diqing) Tibetan Autonomous Prefecture (TAP) in Yunnan for
the purpose of assessing research methods and access to necessary data. The
evaluation was positive, and valuable data were collected during the trip.
Based on this experience, Åshild Kolås and Monika P. Thowsen undertook
similar research trips to Tibetan areas in Sichuan, Gansu, and Qinghai. They
conducted five months of fieldwork in the areas under study, which are all
officially designated as at least partially Tibetan autonomous areas. Kanlho
(Gannan) TAP, in Gansu, and Ngaba (Aba) Tibetan and Qiang Autonomous
Prefecture, in Sichuan, were visited in March–April 1999; all the Tibetan areas
in Qinghai were visited in July–August 1999; and Kandze (Ganzi) TAP, in
Sichuan, was visited in April–May 2000. The results were written up during June–November 2000, and the International Advisory Board reviewed
the first drafts during 25–26 November 2000 at a workshop in Paris. Very
little new data was added after that date.

At PRIO, Dan Smith and David Phillips oversaw the work at various stages,
and Henrik Syse provided guidance in his capacity as leader of the PRIO
Program on Ethics, Norms, and Identities, which eventually headed this
project. Heidi Fjeld was a project research assistant during the year 2000. Karl
Ryavec (Department of Geography, University of Minnesota-Minneapolis)
provided us with digital maps of the areas under study, showing the borders
of administrative units down to the village district level and, for some areas,
the location of towns down to the township level. Heidi Fjeld then completed
the data on the location of towns and registered place-names in Tibetan and
Chinese. These place-names were drawn from indexes produced in China
and, in some cases, from large-scale prefecture maps collected on-site.

This book has benefited from the questions and commentaries of Heidi
Fjeld and several other PRIOites, particularly fellow researchers in the Ethics,
Norms, and Identities program. Odvar Leine provided important library

assistance. Credit is also due to Tashi Nyima, a Tibetan born and raised in Tibet, who worked as a project consultant from July 1998 to December 2000; his ideas and suggestions have been invaluable. A number of Tibetologists and Sinologists supplied important input to the project, either as active participants in meetings and seminars or through personal communications. Members of the Board of the International Association for Tibetan Studies were invited to Norway to discuss the project in January 1998. Those who participated were Per Kværne (University of Oslo), Samten Karmay and Anne-Marie Blondeau (CNRS, Paris), the late Michael Aris (University of Oxford), Ernst Steinkellner (University of Vienna), Martin Brauen (University of Zurich), Helga Uebach (Bayerische Akademie der Wissenschaften, Munich [now at the Bavarian Academy of Sciences, Munich]), Janet Gyatso (Amherst College, Massachusetts [now at Harvard University, Cambridge]), and Elliot Sperling (Indiana University, Bloomington). Others who contributed their comments and criticisms include Janet Upton, Tsering Shakya, Axel K. Strøm, Anders Højmark Andersen, Ellen Bangsbo, Rinzin Thargyal, Hanna Havnevik, Koen Wellens, Mette Halskov Hansen, Harald Bøckman, Katrin Goldstein-Kyaga, Stevan Harrell, Lorri Hagman, and Dawa Norbu as well as several anonymous readers.

The opinions and interpretations presented in this study are those of the authors alone. In particular, it should be noted that the INS researchers who accompanied us were there as facilitators and not as co-researchers. Due to their limited involvement, they are in no way responsible for the outcome of the research, nor do we know whether they share any of the views published in this book. Nevertheless, we would like to express our gratitude to the INS researchers and staff who helped make this study possible. We would also like to thank all the others who assisted us in so many ways during our trips to the field. We did not identify our interviewees by name, and in the case of politically sensitive statements, we actively disguised the identity of our sources. We do, however, wish to emphasize that without the contributions of all the people we encountered during our travels, this book could never have been written.

A NOTE ON TRANSLITERATION

We transcribed Chinese terms in pinyin and generally gave Tibetan terms a more readable romanized transcription in the text. The correct spelling of these terms using Tibetan characters can be found in the glossary. In the notes, we also transcribed Tibetan terms according to Wylie's system of transliteration. Names of monasteries were given a readable phonetic romanized form in the text, with transcriptions according to Wylie sometimes given along with the Chinese name of the monastery when available. We regret that in a few cases we were not able to find the proper Tibetan name of a monastery in our Chinese-language sources, and in such cases we provide only the Chinese name.

For place-names, we use the Tibetan name in a romanized form and give the most common transliteration from Chinese in parentheses the first time the name appears in the chapter. The proper Tibetan transcriptions (according to Wylie) are in appendix 5. The romanized forms and Wylie transcriptions of all Tibetan county names are those used by the Amnye Machen Institute. Maps are bilingual, using romanized Tibetan forms (not Wylie's) and pinyin Chinese.

After careful consideration, we concluded that it would be impractical to use Tibetan place-names without providing the Chinese equivalents. This is because the Tibetan names do not appear in any available Chinese maps or in any other published Chinese sources and are sometimes not even used by the majority of those living in the locality. Tibetan place-names are becoming obsolete in many of the areas under study, which is in itself another aspect of the problem discussed in this book.

ON THE MARGINS OF TIBET

GANSU

Tsochang (Haibei)
TAP

Pari (Tianzhu) TAC

Tsonub (Haixi)
M & T AP

Amdo

Malho (Huangnan)
TAP

QINGHAI

Haidong
Prefecture

Tsolho (Hainan)
TAP

Tsonub (Haixi)
M & T AP

Jyekundo (Yushu) TAP

Golok (Guoluo)
TAP

Kanlho (Gannan)
TAP

Ü-Tsang

Ngaba (Aba)
T & Q AP

Kandze (Ganzi)
TAP

Kham

SICHUAN

Mili (Muli)
TAC

Dechen (Diqing)
TAP

YUNNAN

Map of Tibet Autonomous Region

Introduction

For centuries, the margins of the Tibetan Plateau have been sites of cultural interaction. The frontier towns on the edge of the Plateau were meeting places for people who were known by a variety of different labels, among them those identified as Tibetans and others identified as Chinese or Han. After the so-called Peaceful Liberation of Tibet by the People's Liberation Army in 1950, the former frontier areas on the margins of Tibet were fully incorporated into the Chinese state as autonomous prefectures in four Chinese provinces: Gansu, Qinghai, Sichuan, and Yunnan. This book deals with issues of cultural survival in these areas.

The founding of the People's Republic of China brought significant changes to all the Tibetan areas, but new policies were first carried out in the areas outside what eventually became known as the Tibet Autonomous Region (TAR; Ch: Xizang Zizhiqu). In the late 1950s, the Tibetan monastic clergy and other landowners came under attack as all agricultural land was redistributed and subsequently turned into communes. The Cultural Revolution (1966–76) later targeted all expressions of traditional culture, including religion. Starting in 1979, in the aftermath of the Reform period, religious expressions were again permitted. This led to what many writers have termed a religious revival among Tibetans.[1] However, despite policy changes initiated during the early 1980s, the articulation of Tibetan identity is still a contentious issue in China, particularly since the survival of Tibetan culture has become a key matter of disagreement between China and the rest of the international community.

The issue of cultural survival in Tibetan areas has become heavily politicized in recent years as Tibetan exiles and Tibet support groups have increasingly linked their political agendas to the protection of cultural rights in Tibet. When criticizing China's human rights record in Tibet, they argue that Tibetans in Tibet are denied religious freedoms. They also question the ability of Chinese authorities to provide proper educational facilities for Tibetans, and many claim that the Tibetan language is being overtly suppressed in the Chinese school system. The Tibetan government-in-exile further contends: "What China terms 'Tibetan cultural development' boils down to the production and dissemination of literature, films, songs, etc., in praise of the new socialist Tibet and denouncing traditional Tibet as a dark, barbarous, brutal and backward society."[2] Finally, these groups argue that cultural survival should be linked to issues such as sustainable development, environmental degradation on the Tibetan Plateau, and ethnic and racial discrimination. They also contend that the large-scale in-migration of Han to Tibetan areas is a result of Chinese policies designed to dilute Tibetan culture by making Tibetans a minority in their own country.

Chinese authorities claim that, on the contrary, they have removed the fetters of "feudal exploitation" by emancipating Tibetan cultural and economic life. From their point of view, they have created a modern Tibetan society in which religious freedom is protected by the constitution and faith is a personal affair rather than a consequence of the theocratic rule of the Tibetan clergy. The Chinese government is also proud that it has introduced modern secular education in the Tibetan areas and views its role as one of helping Tibetans progress by providing them with technological and scientific knowledge and teaching them Chinese. Official Chinese statements further assert that the Tibetan language and literature have been protected and developed through the introduction of new technologies such as broadcasting, modern printing techniques, computer software, and fonts in Tibetan. Authorities categorically dismiss the claim that in-migration of Han to Tibetan areas or other aspects of their development policies have had detrimental effects on Tibetan society or culture. Rather, they argue that Chinese policies have tremendously improved social and cultural conditions in the Tibetan areas, especially since the beginning of the Reform era.

Two documents published in 2000 offer a clear illustration of the disagreement: a white paper from the Chinese government on the development of Tibetan culture and a response to this white paper from the Tibetan exile government. The Chinese white paper credits China's beneficial government policies for what it describes as improvements in Tibetan culture during the last four decades and claims that "what the Dalai clique is aiming at is nothing but hampering the real development of Tibetan culture." Comparing the "development of Tibetan culture" with the elimination of the "dictatorial system of feudal serfdom and theocracy" in medieval Europe, the paper argues that the past decades of Chinese rule have led to the emancipation and development of Tibetan society and culture:

> The development of Tibetan culture in the last four decades and more has been achieved in the course of the same great social change marked by the elimination of feudal serfdom under theocracy that was even darker than the European system in the Middle Ages. With the elimination of feudal serfdom, the cultural characteristics under the old system, in which Tibetan culture was monopolized by a few serf-owners were bound to become "extinct," and so was the old cultural autocracy marked by theocracy and the domination of the entire spectrum of socio-political life by religion, which was an inevitable outcome of both the historical and cultural development in Tibet. Because without such extinction, it would be impossible to emancipate and develop Tibetan society and culture, the ordinary Tibetan people would be unable to obtain the right of mastering and sharing the fruits of Tibet's cultural development, and it would be impossible for them to enjoy real freedom, for their religious beliefs would not be regarded as personal affairs. However, such extinction was fatal to the Dalai Lama clique, the chief representatives of feudal serfdom, for it meant the extinction of their cultural rule. Therefore, it is not surprising at all that they clamor about the extinction of traditional Tibetan culture.[3]

In its response, the Tibetan exile government describes this white paper as "yet another attempt to hide China's repressive policies of cultural genocide in Tibet":

> Tibet—a distinct nation with a rich cultural heritage—has a recorded history of over 2,000 years and, as verified by archaeological findings, a civilization dating back over 6,000 years. From very ancient times, especially since the advent of Buddhism in the seventh century, Tibet developed as an extraordinary treasure house of culture. However, since the destructive Maoist campaigns of Communist China's "democratic reforms" began in 1958, Tibet has been reduced to a cultural wasteland, where even the survival of the Tibetan language is in question. . . . From the 1980s, Tibetan literacy and arts have enjoyed a minor revival in the hitherto cultural wasteland of Tibet, thanks to the efforts of the Tenth Panchen Lama and Tibetan patriots. Nevertheless, it must be stated that what survives today is only a fraction and reflection of

what once flourished in this rich cultural reservoir on what was once the "Altar of the World." Certainly, the traditional social structure in Tibet did not meet all the expectations and aspirations of the populace. However, this 2.5 million square kilometer nation preserved a vast treasure of culture with every spiritually minded Tibetan serving as its protector. China is the sole destroyer of this heritage. And this destruction continues. Beijing has claimed to be the political representative of Tibetans for 45 years. With the 21st century it now lays an additional claim to be the protector of Tibetan culture.[4]

These two important documents not only present contradictory "facts" about Tibetan culture but also differ radically in their conceptions of what Tibetan culture is or should be. One of the major points of disagreement concerns religion's role as a marker of Tibetan identity and, from the perspective of the Chinese Communist Party (CCP), the role religion should be allowed to play in the shaping of a modern Tibetan society. We will examine the contradictory claims of Chinese authorities and Tibetan exiles in the following chapters in order to discern their conflicting views on almost every aspect of Tibetan cultural life, particularly on religion, language, and the "development" or "preservation" of Tibetan culture.

Our aim in this book is to investigate current conditions for expressions of Tibetan culture as defined by those who are debating its preservation. The area under study comprises the Tibetan autonomous areas that lie outside what is known in China as the Tibet Autonomous Region. The study is based on fieldwork and interviews conducted in all these prefectures during the years 1998–2000. The geographic delimitation was chosen for pragmatic reasons and also because these areas are little studied, are of particular interest as Tibetan areas that have become part of Chinese-majority provinces, and constitute the margins of the Tibetan cultural area. As such, they are subject to a heavy influx of settlers, traders, and transient laborers, making cultural issues particularly salient.

Although we have tried to provide a comprehensive discussion of the prominent issues within current debates on Tibetan culture, in this book we concentrate on the revival of monastic life in Tibetan monasteries, the teaching of Tibetan language in schools, the use of Tibetan in the media and in publishing, and other expressions of Tibetan culture, primarily those that are government endorsed. In addition, we address socioeconomic issues as an important contributor to ethnic tension and as an aspect of cultural survival in its own right.

The influx of settlers, traders, and transient workers has been identified as a significant problem for the survival of Tibetan culture. Since the 1950s, Chinese authorities have been resettling Han on "reclaimed" land previously used by nomadic herders. Authorities also fenced grasslands and settled nomadic families, built roads, extracted minerals and timber, and constructed hydroelectric power plants throughout the Plateau, claiming that these programs are helping Tibetans develop. New policies implemented as part of the Develop the Western Region (Ch: Xibu Da Kaifa) campaign aim to increase the pace of this development by improving infrastructure and bringing in foreign capital to further advance the extraction of natural resources from the Tibetan Plateau and neighboring regions in western China. The results of these policies are as yet difficult to predict, but if they fail to benefit Tibetans, they will undoubtedly contribute to ethnic tension in all the Tibetan-inhabited areas.

SOME THEORETICAL ISSUES

The purpose of this project was initially defined in terms of providing information on Tibetan culture. However, the concept of culture is not as distinct today as it once was and therefore deserves some clarification. In addition to the various interpretations by Western social scientists of the term "culture," the interpretations of Tibetans and Chinese should also be considered. The different meanings of "culture" have implications that will be investigated further in the following chapters.

Basically, two established ways of understanding culture can be identified in Western social science and popular discourses. One perspective ties culture directly to the way of life, and sometimes even the way of thinking, of a group of people. The other perspective understands culture as the expressions of a group of people, such as language and literature, architectural styles and decorations, religious ceremonies, arts and crafts, folk songs and dances, cuisine and costumes, and games and festivals, and particularly those expressions that serve to define and promote the identity of the group.

Within contemporary social science, especially in the field of anthropology, ideas of a simple relationship between society and culture have long been questioned, and the concept of ethnicity has been differentiated from that of culture. Culture is no longer a zone of shared meanings but one of disagreement and contest, and the study of culture has in many cases become the study of the *politics* of culture and the invention of tradition.[5] To sum up a long and complex debate, the concept of culture in anthropology and related disciplines has evolved from that of something shared, or "public," to something contested, or "unequally distributed," and constructed, or invented.[6] The very notions of culture and identity have been questioned, and a number of writers have criticized the use of the culture concept.[7] The criticism includes the role of the anthropologist or ethnologist in constructing culture, defining the "other" ethnic group, maintaining that "otherness," and making the "otherness" seem self-evident.

It has also been pointed out that many Third World elites have adopted a cultural nationalist discourse that reiterates early anthropological talk about culture as something that coincides with a particular people.[8] In Chinese social science, there is a similar assumption that ethnicity is based on shared culture, or the sharing of objective cultural traits, along with shared origin. The boundaries of a culture are basically assumed to be coterminous with the boundaries of an ethnic group, and ethnography thus describes the culture of a particular group. One talks about Tibetan culture as the culture of the Tibetan people, with both "culture" and "people" referring to discrete, clearly defined entities.

Contemporary Chinese discourses on culture have certainly been influenced by ideas that can be traced back to what is now considered outdated Western social science. These ideas have also found their way into the Tibetan language. However, both Chinese and Tibetan languages left their marks on the terminology and added further meaning to the concepts we translate as culture. In the Chinese term for "culture," *wenhua, wen* refers to writing and *hua* is a verbalizer. The term literally means to make cultured, to civilize, or to educate. One often speaks of someone who is educated by saying that he or she has *wenhua*. The most commonly used Tibetan term for culture, *rig gnas*, similarly describes someone as knowledgeable, much in the same sense as the English word "cultivated." The kinds of knowledge indicated by the term *rig gnas* are the "five great fields of knowledge" (T: *rig gnas chenmo nga*) studied in the monasteries: language, logic, arts and crafts, medicine, and spiritual realization. However, Tibetans sometimes use another term, *rig gzhung*, which is more comprehensive and more abstract than *rig gnas*. Whereas *gnas* means area, place, or field, *gzhung* means way or path.

We have found that the term "culture" is widely used among social scientists in China, including Tibetans, and is also recognized by the general public, although the sense in which it is used often differs from that intended by the European or American social scientist. What is interesting in this context is not so much how Sino-Tibetan views differ from Euro-American ones but rather how these views give rise to different ways of understanding culture, and Tibetan culture in particular. We do not set out here to decide which characteristics or cultural markers differentiate Tibetans from other ethnic groups. Rather, our study takes as its point of departure how the label "Tibetan" is defined in practice by those who use the term in local contexts. This local usage includes a wide range of implicit and explicit definitions of Tibetanness assumed by the staff of research institutions, officials in various government departments, education professionals, and other people to whom we talked during our fieldwork. The focus is thus on the ascription and use of various signifiers or markers of Tibetan identity, such as language, literature, and oral traditions; elements of lifestyle, such as clothing and diet; typical forms of economic organization; and spirituality and religious rituals.

In China, stereotypes of what it means to be a Tibetan are created in the popular media, school textbooks, and research publications. These publicly transmitted stereotypes provide a frame of reference as people relate them to their own experiences and use them to build their own worldviews. Our study is descriptive rather than definitive in that it is based on these different ways of understanding Tibetanness and does not provide an in-depth investigation of how the stereotypes are re-created and are sometimes challenged. Although we do not specifically address the issue of what it means to be a Tibetan, we do reflect on the consequences of categorizing something as Tibetan. In this sense, we are concerned with the different ways in which the terms "Tibetan" and "culture" are understood and the implications of the label "Tibetan." This means that for analytical purposes, we understand culture as symbolically constructed and reinvented and therefore subject to constantly changing interpretations, which means it is inherently contestable. The culture we are talking about, then, is neither a commonly held system of norms and values nor a shared structure of meanings. It is formed in debates about identity and in political processes through which government policies and even the legitimacy of the state are being challenged.

This book deals with cultural politics and contemporary debates about Chinese policies. As such, it necessarily examines those implicit definitions of culture, and those meanings of Tibetan culture in particular, that are held in common by the participants in these debates. We begin with the common ground of understandings by which certain definitions of culture have been more or less accepted although the conditions for maintaining or preserving this culture are fiercely contested. We also examine the limits of this common ground and the disagreements on what Tibetan culture actually implies or should imply.

Our goal here is not to contribute to scholarly debates or analyses of the concept of culture but to investigate the concerns of those who are debating Tibetan culture. Our working definition of culture thus reflects those meanings that are part of current debates on the preservation of Tibetan culture, and our focus is on the core issues of the debates. These include policies on religion and the conditions for continuing monastic traditions, education and the teaching of Tibetan language in schools, the cultural development work of Chinese government departments, and the economic policies that affect the maintenance of traditional subsistence lifestyles in the areas under study.

No matter how we define culture, it has become increasingly obvious that we live in a world where it is virtually impossible for any culture to survive in isolation, unaffected by economic globalization, tourism, and television broadcasting. As Richard Madsen observed, even when indigenous peoples in relatively isolated villages practice rituals and customs that have been "preserved from the past," they can never do so with the matter-of-factness of the era before roads, telephones, and the Internet, not to mention modern methods of political control.[9] While we question the notion of unchanging cultural traditions, however, it is also important to question change and examine the ways in which, at different times and under different circumstances, change takes place.

As mentioned, notions of cultural preservation are featured in the political arguments of both Tibetans in exile and Chinese authorities. In these discourses, the dilemmas of modernization and cultural change are carefully hidden. Obviously, modernization in any form entails cultural change, and whatever one's understanding of culture, cultural survival involves a series of difficult choices, including balancing the need for modernization with the need to preserve cultural traditions. Reports on Tibetan culture issued by both the Tibetan exile government and the Chinese authorities fail to acknowledge these problems. Statements from the Tibetan government-in-exile tend simply to attack Chinese authorities for the negative effects of modernization on Tibetan culture, while statements from Chinese authorities uncritically emphasize the positive aspects of modernization. Reports from Chinese government sources typically advertise economic progress, improved healthcare facilities, industrialization, urban construction and housing development, and the building of dams and hydroelectric plants and at the same time allege that Tibetan culture has been thriving since the establishment of the People's Republic of China. They argue that both traditional and modern art forms and media have flourished and offer as examples folk-dance and opera performances, modern art exhibitions, museums, modern Tibetan literature, publishing, radio and television transmission, and scientific research on Tibetan medicine. In fact, when Chinese authorities describe how Tibetan culture is being developed, one of the most pronounced features of the alleged development is the use of new technology and "scientific methods," which is considered wholly positive and entirely unproblematic in terms of cultural preservation. Chinese media propagate the idea that traditional Tibetan culture is essentially backward and in need of modernization, as elucidated in the Chinese white paper on Tibetan culture:

> The [Tibetan] people's modes of thinking and concepts are bound to change with the changes of the modes of production and life in Tibet. During this process, some new aspects of culture which are not contained in the traditional Tibetan culture but are essential in modern civilization have been developed, such as modern scientific and technological education and news dissemination. The fine cultural traditions with Tibetan features are being carried forward and promoted in the new age, and the decayed and backward things in the traditional culture that are not adapted to social development and people's life are being gradually sifted out. It is a natural phenomenon in conformity with the law of cultural development, and a manifestation of the unceasing prosperity and development of Tibetan culture in the new situation. To prattle about the "extinction of Tibetan culture" due to its acquisition of the new contents of the new age and to its progress and development is in essence to demand that modern Tibetan people keep the lifestyles and cultural values of old Tibet's feudal serfdom wholly intact. This is completely ridiculous, for it goes against the tide of progress of the times and the fundamental interests of the Tibetan people.[10]

The Western world is not without its own essentialist stereotypes of Tibet and Tibetans, which commonly revolve around the image of Shangri-la. The tendency to conceptualize Tibet and Tibetan lifestyles as a utopian ideal has been explained by some as a reflection of Western attitudes about our own societies and the need to find alternatives to consumerism.[11] Tibetans are thus recast as a spiritual people living in harmony with nature. Such stereotypes should be countered because they are romantic and in many ways unrealistic and because they obscure the difficult challenges Tibetans face when trying to find a balance between preserving and developing their ways of life.

This problem has also been recognized by several Tibetan exile critics, such as the writer Jamyang Norbu. For instance, in an article published in the exile magazine *Tibetan Review,* he criticizes not only the Western media for creating Shangri-la stereotypes of Tibet but also Tibetans for re-creating those stereotypes for commercial aims. He argues that we should avoid "calling on people in underdeveloped societies to live passive, traditional and ecologically correct lifestyles—and not emulate the wasteful lifestyles of people in Western consumer societies."[12]

It may be fruitful to examine the changing economic and social roles of cultural expressions and their relationship to particular ways of life under distinct natural and social conditions. We should also be aware, however, that assessments of the traditional and the modern are not value-neutral but are essentially political statements. This is the case whether modernization is defined as positive or negative and whether tradition is seen as an obstacle to development or as something precious that must be protected.

In addition to issues of modernization and cultural survival, one should also consider the politics of culture itself. In speeches and news reports, Tibetan culture has been systematically put to ideological use by Chinese authorities. For instance, in 1996, Tibetan culture was declared non-Buddhist by the CCP secretary in Tibet Chen Kuiyuan. The secretary gave a speech describing Buddhism as a foreign culture and praising the song "Emancipated Serfs Are Singing" as an example of healthy and useful national culture.[13] One of the most interesting points made by the Tibetan exile government in its answer to the Chinese white paper is that the Chinese government is promoting a new socialist Tibetan culture that portrays traditional Tibetan society as "dark, barbarous, and backward." According to the Tibetan government-in-exile, this has resulted in the development of two cultures, "the traditional spiritual culture of Tibet and the communist-nurtured 'campus culture,' which is neither Tibetan nor Chinese." Furthermore, the knowledge of this shallow campus culture may help a person make a living as a poet, writer, translator, journalist, or administrative clerk under the Chinese government, but "it does not empower him or her to further the development of Tibetan culture."[14] We will return to this issue in the following chapters.

In the course of developing and refining our project methodology, it was necessary to take a critical look at the complexities of cultural survival, and of culture as a contested concept, and find operational ways of dealing with our topic. With the quantifiable data, we thus confined our investigation to some relatively easily defined aspects of what might be termed "cultural production" rather than trying to study culture as such. This selection in itself assumes a particular understanding of culture. Specifically, it gives prominence to the importance of language and religion. However, we based much of our analysis on a more inclusive understanding of culture, emphasizing the strong connections between cultural expressions and culture as a way of life. In this view, culture includes livelihoods and means of subsistence. Cultural survival depends on the sustainability of these means of subsistence, which are linked to the natural and social conditions essential for their existence. This does not mean that livelihoods remain unchanged, only that the conditions required for their practice must continue to exist.

In Western countries, a popular contemporary image of Tibetan culture is that of the "vanishing civilization." According to the Tibetan exile researcher Tsering Shakya, "The politics of Tibet have been reduced to the question of the survival of a civilization, which is on Death Row. It is no longer a question of whether it can be revived or saved. The implicit assumption is that it cannot be saved; commentators are busily writing a 'Requiem for Tibet' and predictions of 'The Last Dalai Lama.' Therefore, the politics of Tibet are seen as how to preserve a dying civilization, whether it is better to preserve it in jam jars or museums."[15]

When culture must be preserved in a museum, is it still "authentic" culture? Who judges the authenticity of Tibetan culture? Does it matter whether a Tibetan—or a Han, or a Western academic—does the documenting, collects the samples, and sets up the exhibits? What about the different opinions among Tibetans about what it means to be a Tibetan today? Whose opinions are most valid? And if we define Tibetan culture as a way of life, who has the right to tell Tibetans that they should preserve that way of life? These are some of the disquieting questions that must be posed, although the answers may be difficult, if not impossible, to find.

ISSUES AT STAKE

The revival of Tibetan monasteries and the use of the Tibetan language have been the focus of much of the debate about Tibetan culture, in China as well as internationally. Religion and language are widely acknowledged by Tibetans, both within and outside China, as essential aspects of Tibetan culture. Tibetan Buddhist literary heritage, traditions, and institutions are commonly regarded as the core of Tibetan civilization. The rush to rebuild monasteries and revive religious traditions since the early 1980s is thus a matter not only of personal conviction but of asserting and strengthening group identity. While the Tibetan language is seen as an important medium for the transmission of Buddhist teachings, the preservation and development of the Tibetan language is also regarded as significant in its own right, as a vital aspect of cultural survival. The suppression of Tibetan religion and language that took place during the Democratic Reforms of the 1950s and the Cultural Revolution (1966–76), and the new understanding of ethnic identity introduced through China's minority policies have contributed to the recognition of Tibetan Buddhism and the Tibetan language as principal markers of Tibetan identity.

Monastic Reconstruction

In this study, we investigate the issue of monastic reconstruction in terms of the number of monasteries and nunneries that have been restored since the period before the first CCP campaigns and how many monks and nuns have joined these monasteries and nunneries. We also examine possible restrictions on the restoration of monasteries and the admittance of monks and nuns. Government funding for the restoration of monasteries has been widely publicized, but who has actually provided the funds for rebuilding monasteries and supporting monks and nuns, and under what circumstances does the state contribute to monastic reconstruction or financial support for clerics?

Tulkus (reincarnated lamas) are highly revered by Tibetan Buddhists and thus play a key role in all Tibetan areas. They are in many ways the keepers of Tibetan cultural traditions. For the government, tulkus are important as respected informal leaders of Tibetan communities and potential mediators between the authorities and the Tibetan people at large. For these reasons, tulkus are often appointed to the People's Congress or the Chinese People's Political Consultative Committee (CPPCC) at all administrative levels, are made leading members of the Buddhist Association, or even enter the ranks of government officials. Consequently, the process of recognition and approval of new tulkus is strictly regulated by the authorities in charge of religious affairs. A major issue thus concerns official mechanisms of controlling the tulkus and absorbing them into state institutions. To determine whether there are restrictions on the restoration of tulku lineages, we analyzed the number of tulkus today as compared to their numbers in the 1950s.

One of the critical issues regarding the practice of religion is the contemporary limitation on religious freedom. What are the limits for lay Tibetans, and how are monasteries controlled? The revival of monastic life is not just a question of reconstructing monastery buildings and admitting new monks. It also includes the revival of religious ceremonies, crafts such as butter sculpture and mandala making, religious music and performing arts, painting, astrology and divination, medical practice, woodblock printing, and various branches of Buddhist studies and practices. Have government regulations influenced the revival of monastic life? What have been the general conditions for the revival of religious traditions after twenty years of disruption?

For some Tibetans, monastic education is a compelling alternative to the state educational system, which implicitly transmits ideas of the cultural inferiority of ethnic minorities. Monastic education is a source of pride for Tibetans who value what they understand as their own cultural heritage. Yet, many educated clerics promote secular as well as religious education. Monastic leaders and tulkus have established foundations to provide financial support to local schools and even to build private schools that combine religious and secular education. Whereas Chinese media often emphasize the contradictions between religious practice and economic progress in Tibetan areas, and by extension the conflict between monasteries and schooling, there are important links between monastic and secular education.

Education

In addressing the topic of public education, we focus on both the teaching of Tibetan and the use of Tibetan as the language of instruction in schools for Tibetan children. The availability of such teaching is in itself a complex issue and includes not only whether there are schools teaching Tibetan or in Tibetan but also the cost of schooling, admittance procedures and examination requirements, access to boarding, living conditions in dormitories, and the quality of teachers. We further assess the extent to which these schools are actually within reach of Tibetan children. Interrelated issues are the perceived use of education by parents, career opportunities after graduation, and problems faced by students who attended schools that teach in Tibetan when they reach higher levels of the educational system.

A core problem concerns the balance between Tibetan and Chinese in bilingual schools and which language is used in teaching. Although many educators argue that Tibetan students who are taught in Tibetan achieve far better results than do those who are taught in Chinese, others emphasize the problems these students face when they continue their studies in Chinese. The extent of failure among Tibetan students who compete in exams with native speakers of standard Chinese (Mandarin) is an impor-

tant factor to consider. There has been ongoing discussion among educators in China as to whether it is better for Tibetan children to learn Chinese
from the beginning of their schooling or to be taught in Tibetan. Among
those who favor teaching in Tibetan, some have argued for extending the
approach to higher levels of education and expanding the use of Tibetan
to more subjects and fields of study.

The explicit role of education in China is to promote the idea of a unified
motherland and develop patriotic citizens. By infusing such ideals as patriotism and love for the motherland and placing a heavy emphasis on Chinese
values and traditions, schools may be contributing to the assimilation of
ethnic minorities. At the same time, it is difficult to imagine how the Tibetan
language could survive, as a viable written language at least, without being
taught in these same schools. In the face of these realities, the educational
system plays a highly ambiguous role in terms of its influence on Tibetan
culture.

RESEARCH DESIGN

Fieldwork for this study included making systematic observations on-site,
photographing sites, gathering information through informal communication, and developing contacts with local research institutions engaged in
Tibetan studies. We carried out research in twenty-five counties covering
all the Tibetan areas under study and collected primary source materials
such as lists of religious sites, county history publications, statistics on education, and samples of teaching materials from schools, bookstores, and
publishing houses.[16] Key interviews were semi-structured and open and were
conducted with county, prefectural, and provincial government officials,
schoolteachers, religious and educational specialists, school and university staff, researchers and staff of cultural institutions, monastic leaders,
and monks and nuns. Other interviews were unstructured. We conducted
approximately ninety interviews with government officials in various departments and units and at least as many other key interviews.

For our investigation of the rebuilding of religious sites and the practice
of religion, we visited about forty monasteries and nunneries and numerous other religious sites. We interviewed local community experts on the
history of religious sites in the area and obtained information on the historical background and current situation at each site. Claims were verified
through systematic observation of religious practice, and standardized
questions assured that comparable data were gathered. We interviewed

officials in local religious affairs departments and others involved in implementing religious policies. County and prefectural "local histories" (Ch: *difangzhi*) also provided basic information about the number of monks and the geographic distribution of monasteries and religious sites in each county. The data from these and other written sources were compared with corresponding data gathered on-site, from interviews with officials in the religious affairs departments, and from documents acquired from these departments.

For our research into education in Tibetan, we visited a total of forty-five schools and colleges, interviewed teachers, administrators, and educational specialists, and observed educational practice where possible. We collected samples of teaching materials, school curricula, and other relevant written materials. Assessments include official educational programs as well as locally managed grassroots educational facilities designed and run by local Tibetans. We visited schools at all levels (primary, middle, vocational, college, and university), including boarding schools in herding areas and village primary schools in agricultural areas; most were visited without prior notice. Statistical data were collected in interviews with leaders of the prefecture education departments and include detailed information on the total numbers of schools and students and the numbers of bilingual schools and students at all levels, by county. Interviews with local school staff supplemented the figures provided by government officials and gave us more detailed information about the actual situation.

We used two basic types of literary sources: works in the field of minority studies and works that draw on statistical materials. Some remarks must first be made about "minority studies" or "ethnology" (Ch: *minzuxue*) in China. Ethnology is institutionally and intellectually tied to the practice of "nationalities work" and minority policy.[17] The discipline still leans heavily toward Marxist evolutionist theory, rooted in the works of Friedrich Engels and Lewis Henry Morgan.[18] Issues such as the negotiation of identity, cultural commoditization and globalization, the social construction of culture and ethnicity, and the politics of historical and ethnographic writing have so far been more or less ignored. This means that the theoretical approach of Chinese scholars differs markedly from contemporary Western approaches.

Even more can be said about the use of official Chinese statistics. During fieldwork, we were told that government officials in China commonly have three or four documents on each topic, for various uses, which give widely disparate figures. The credibility of these documents is rarely checked by outside agencies. In some cases, officials may not even be aware of which document contains the correct information. By all accounts, Chinese statistical materials are notoriously unreliable. As Graham Clarke pointed out, China has a system of administration that depends on local interpretation and implementation of central commands and initiatives.[19] In most areas of China aside from the eastern seaboard, this includes survey work. Furthermore, direct lateral linkages among counties or provinces are weak, there is no independent cross-checking for accuracy, and the primary allegiance of officials who carry out data collection is to the local administration.

As a result of these and other inadequacies in surveying and data collection, statistics generally are riddled with errors. Politically motivated distortions could make data on production and income levels particularly unreliable. Common survey errors include discrepancies in the use of terminology and interpretation of categories, reclassification of categories over time, obvious data entry errors, inaccuracies and inconsistencies in recording, mistakes in aggregation and simple calculation, and sampling biases.

We tried to counteract some of these problems by linking wider statistics to case studies. One strategy we used in interviews was to repeat the same questions at all administrative levels and then compare the figures supplied by the different levels. Prefectural figures were compared to county figures, and county figures to figures collected at a particular site. This strategy at least revealed those figures that were clearly unreliable. A question remains, however, as to which of the different figures are more accurate. When figures are exactly the same for two levels, this may indicate either that they are accurate or that they have been drawn from the same source.[20]

One might ask, then, if Chinese official statistics are so unreliable, why refer to them at all? First, we unfortunately did not have the resources necessary to collect all of our statistical data. Second, there are no independent statistics available. Third, in order to confirm or contradict supposed facts, the facts must first be available, which means that further research on these areas will benefit from any baseline reference data, if only for the sake of replication. The data presented here are, as of this writing, not easily obtained outside of China, at least for researchers who do not read Chinese. It is therefore an additional aim of this volume to make basic data on these under-researched areas more widely available. Finally, even unreliable statistics can be useful, if read with an understanding of which distortions to expect. For instance, since China introduced compulsory nine-year education, we know that the goal for any government education bureau is to have 100 percent of school-age children attending school. If an education bureau reports a rate of 85 percent school attendance, we should expect the actual figure to be no more than or anywhere below 85 percent. Thus, the data presented here should not be understood as factual but should be read with these considerations in mind.

Two main methods were used on-site: observation and interviews. Observation is not always as simple as it seems. Efficient observation depends on the experience and background knowledge of the researcher. This background knowledge can also create blind spots. One expects to see something, and as a result, that is what one sees. Taking this logic to an extreme, it is possible to say that one cannot claim to know something just because one has observed it. Interviews also presented a range of difficulties. Although one of the authors is fluent in Chinese and the other has studied Central Tibetan, the great majority of interviews required some degree of interpretation. This was especially significant when interviews were conducted in a Tibetan dialect (Khamba or Amdo-ke) or a local dialect of Chinese. Even with good interpretation, answers to seemingly simple questions, such as "How many monks are in this monastery?" or "How many rooms are in this school?" may be inaccurate. For example, we once spent more than two hours interviewing a monk in a monastery. Our first question concerned the number of monks in the monastery, and we were given an apparently straightforward answer: five monks. After completing a long list of other questions, we spent some time discussing the ritual calendar of the monastery. At that point, it became clear that we had come in the middle of the summer holidays, when most of the monks were at home with their families. We went back to the first question about the number of monks and finally managed to find out that the number of monks ordinarily staying at the monastery was about eighty. In addition to interpretation problems, there is the obvious problem of accuracy in responses. Most people are rarely compelled to be totally accurate and cannot be expected to provide precise information, especially hard figures.

Even simple questions about religious and minority issues were highly sensitive matters. This is why we never asked people for their names or other personal information. Although officials rarely accompanied us on our visits to religious sites, we did not interview monks or nuns if officials were present. Visits to monasteries and many schools were made without prior notice, and most school visits were unaccompanied. We traveled with a letter of introduction from our host institute, the Institute of Nationalities Studies (INS), a department of the Chinese Academy of Social Sciences, and were accompanied on fieldtrips by an INS researcher who acted as our guide and translator. Despite this, since most sites had never received foreign researchers before, many of those interviewed were obviously ambivalent, and some may have felt uncomfortable disclosing information to foreigners. It is difficult even for a Chinese citizen to obtain information from the Chinese bureaucracy, since officials usually do not see it as a responsibility to provide information to the general public. There is simply no precedent for openness.

Among the most basic data we wanted to gather were the number of monasteries that have been rebuilt and the number of monks, nuns, and tulkus today as compared to the early 1950s. Although we consulted a number of Chinese sources, our most important sources are our own interviews. We interviewed officials in the religious affairs departments in most of the prefecture governments and in many counties.[21] In addition, we visited a number of monasteries and interviewed monks in most of them. We interviewed officials at the provincial government level in Sichuan and Qinghai for the purpose of obtaining overall figures.[22] We further cross-checked this information with written sources and with our own findings from the same areas. On Gansu and Qinghai, our main written source is Pu Wencheng's work on Tibetan Buddhist monasteries in the two provinces, which lists and briefly describes more than 800 Tibetan monasteries.[23] This book also lists the Tibetan name of every monastery. Another source is Ran Guangrong's book on Tibetan Buddhist monasteries in China, which gives a general overview of the Tibetan autonomous areas of the four provinces and includes chapters on the TAR and Inner Mongolia.[24] We also used other available monographs and compilations about specific areas, such as Dechen (Diqing), Golok (Guoluo), and Kandze (Ganzi).[25] Finally, we looked for relevant information in a large number of prefecture and county histories published during the 1990s.

Our main English-language source has been Steven D. Marshall's and Susette Ternent Cooke's study *Tibet Outside the TAR*. This extensive survey is a very good source of detailed background information on most of the counties we researched, although it has some significant geographical gaps and lacks substantial information on religious or educational institutions. In addition, since the authors worked undercover, the type of data to which they had access is very different from our material. We hope our study will update and complement their work.

METHODOLOGICAL PROBLEMS

During our research, we encountered a number of challenges. For instance, it was extremely difficult to estimate how many monasteries existed in the areas under study before destruction of religious sites began in the late 1950s. The names of monasteries in Tibetan and in Chinese are often completely different, which makes it difficult to use old Tibetan sources such as those kept by the Tibetan government-in-exile. Published sources in Chinese, which tend to use the Chinese names of monasteries, do provide information on the current situation. Among the various Chinese sources, however, several give substantially different figures, on both former and current numbers of monasteries, nunneries, monks, nuns, and tulkus.

Authorities in charge of religious affairs keep a detailed account of different categories of monks, but these categories may not be identically defined. Historical records often describe different categories of "religious personnel" (Ch: *zongjiao renyuan*), such as tulku, *geshe* (monk who has acquired the highest degree in the Gelugpa study program), abbot (*khenpo*), lama, and *draba* (monk). When different sources list past and current figures, the definitions of categories may differ, and categories may therefore be confused. In addition, it is often unclear which categories are included in the total figures.

Various sources also define monks and nuns differently. Written sources often provide detailed information on the numbers of monks, ordained monks, lamas, monks with a *geshe* degree, abbots, tulkus, etc., without noting which of these are counted as monks. This makes it difficult to know whether the numbers should be combined. Some sources use the term "religious personnel" without noting how many of these are considered monks. Should monks in Tibetan Buddhist traditions such as Nyingmapa, which allows monks to marry, be defined as monks? "Practitioners of magic" (T: *ngagpa*) may or may not be counted as monks, since they usually dress like monks but are permitted to marry. And if a monastery is defined as a place where monks live, are religious professionals considered monks when they live in a monastery? We noted particularly contradictory information on the numbers of Nyingmapa monks and monasteries.

It is worth mentioning that prior to the establishment of the People's Republic of China in 1949, 10–50 percent of all monks were known to live outside monasteries.[26] Some were itinerant storytellers, and some monks and, more commonly, nuns lived at home as dependents of the head of household. It is unclear whether the percentages cited above include *ngagpa*, who even today roam the countryside telling fortunes. In several of our interviews, we were given information on "private monks and nuns," "monks and nuns living at home," and "traveling monks and nuns." These individuals were occasionally included in the statistics on monks and nuns. We suspect that some of these monks and nuns were not accepted at or were expelled from monasteries and nunneries. However, some of them may be living outside monasteries and nunneries for the same reasons as in former times. It is difficult to know how monks and nuns are registered and statistics are gathered, and how the procedures differ from one area to the next. The number of monks and nuns who live outside of monasteries today, permanently or temporarily, is particularly unclear.

The current system of registering monks creates other ambiguities. Since the authorities are trying to maintain strict control over the numbers of monks, detailed accounts are kept, using a number of different categories. Whereas traditionally monks never retired, today monks above a certain age "retire" (Ch: *tuixiu*), although they may continue to live in the monastery. If retired monks are living in monasteries, it is unclear what their retirement means except that they are no longer counted as monks in official statistics. Similarly, one must be at least eighteen years old to become a monk or a nun. Those under this age are sometimes not reported or are reported as other than monks or nuns. As one county government official explained: "Those under the minimum age are there to help elderly monks or to learn a craft." It is sometimes unclear whether monks under the age of eighteen are even included in the statistics. Another problem was brought to our attention by local government officials in charge of keeping records of monks and nuns. These officials complained that their job was made more difficult when monks are registered in a monastery in their county but are living in a monastery in a different county. The monastery where the monk is actually residing would of course have similar problems in deciding how to account for him.

At present, authorities in charge of religious affairs set quotas for the acceptance of monks and nuns into monasteries or nunneries. These quotas are very often exceeded, and when officials are asked about the number of monks or nuns in a monastery or nunnery, they sometimes give the quota figure rather than the actual figure. The figures collected by the prefectures and provinces are based on reports from each county, and we learned in local interviews that the religious affairs departments keep at least two accounts of the number of monks. One figure represents the number of monks living permanently in each monastery, and the other indicates the quota of monks allowed to reside permanently in the monastery. These two figures often vary greatly, and it is not always clear which figure is being presented. Visits to local monasteries revealed further complications. We visited monasteries with up to 100 percent more resident religious personnel than were reported by local authorities.

The same statistical problems apply to nuns. In addition, we regret the shortage of exact information on nuns available from any sources, written or oral, from many of the areas we visited. Little was known about the number of nuns in the 1950s, and the impression we gained from interviews with county governments is that there may be more nuns than are reported by the prefectural governments. This is probably due to the large number of nuns living outside nunneries. For instance, in Derge (Dege) County, authorities in charge of religious affairs informed us that the county currently had only one nunnery with 23 nuns. In addition, we were told, approximately 300 were practicing as nuns but living at home. These 300 were not included in the statistics. If the situation is similar in other counties, statistical figures for nuns are even more problematic than those for monks.

Statistics on tulkus are even more complicated. One problem is that tulkus often live outside their original monasteries or even outside the country. In addition, tulkus may not be monks, and some sources classify tulkus as monks while others do not. When counting tulkus, some count lineages (both living and deceased tulkus), whereas some count only the living. In some instances, only officially accepted tulkus are counted, and they may be but a fraction of the tulkus who are recognized within monasteries and local communities. Our information indicates that there may be a substantial number of these "self-appointed" (Ch: *zi ren ding de*) tulkus, as they were termed in one of our interviews.

As simple as it may seem, counting monasteries is a difficult matter. In some interviews, authorities in charge of religious affairs identified inconsistent definitions of a monastery as the reason for the smaller number of monasteries at present compared to before 1958. Authorities explained that some old records of monasteries might have included household shrines and small temples for the mountain gods, offering sites where buildings of any kind had been constructed, tulku residences, and so forth. We were further told that the government now uses a much narrower definition, with "monastery" designating a place where monks reside, and describes other places of worship as "religious sites" (Ch: *zongjiao huodongchang* or *zongjiao huodongdian*). Despite these claims, authorities in some areas reported that there were more monasteries in the late 1990s than in the 1950s. In these cases, there was no mention of changing definitions at all. It is obviously very difficult to judge whether the reported redefinition of the term "monastery" is really a problem for record-keeping or is instead a convenient excuse for the authorities.

Of course, old records might be inaccurate in a number of ways. For instance, the three great Lhasa monasteries—Ganden, Sera, and Drepung—had ideal numbers of monks (Ganden, 3,300; Sera, 5,500; and Drepung, 7,700). The true number of monks may have once resembled these figures but would naturally have fluctuated. Other monasteries may also have reported such ideal figures, which could well have found their way into historical records. Another source of confusion might be the identification of some monasteries as "branch monasteries" (T: *dgon lag*) and some as mother monasteries.[27] It is not inconceivable that records of monasteries may occasionally have counted only the mother monastery. The monks in branch monasteries may also have been counted as belonging to the mother monastery. Today, however, monasteries are officially regarded as equal in rank, although the distinctions are still very much alive in the minds of local people.

Rebuilding a monastery and accepting monks require government permission. In a number of cases, monasteries were rebuilt without permission because people became tired of waiting. These illegal monasteries are sometimes not counted in official statistics simply because officials are reluctant to admit they exist. Ironically, this results in figures on restored monasteries that are too low. Finally, there are great variations in the way people define "restored" or "reconstructed," which might cover any action from complete reconstruction to a few minor repairs.

In researching education, we were interested in knowing how many Tibetan children have the opportunity to learn Tibetan and how many are taught with Tibetan as the language of instruction. We wanted to know the number of Tibetan children who actually attend school. The question of school attendance is politically sensitive, since the central government has decided that nine years of education should be compulsory throughout China. In some of the areas under study, even a three-year education was unavailable to a majority of school-age children, and in counties where herding is the predominant livelihood, we found that official enrollment rates were as low as 28 percent. Despite this, in other counties with very similar conditions, government officials reported enrollment rates as high as 90 percent.

Local governments sometimes receive funding from higher levels of government based on student enrollment and may offer incentives to parents to enroll their children or sanction them if they fail to do so. In addition, although enrollment and attendance are two different matters, local officials may apply the terms "entrance rate" (Ch: *ruxuelü*) or "enrollment" in different ways, for example, to refer to the number of children registered in school compared to the school-age children in the area, the number of school-age children who attend school regularly, or the number of school-age children who complete primary school, defined as either four or six years of schooling. Due to these and other problems, accurate information on school attendance is very difficult to find.

The language of instruction is a less politically sensitive question but may be difficult to determine for other reasons. One of the officials we interviewed, a former teacher, provided the following illuminating description: "The teachers are bilingual and the pupils sometimes even have two sets of books, one in Chinese and one in Tibetan. Sometimes the teachers write on the blackboard in Chinese and explain in Tibetan; in other situations they might teach in Tibetan and explain in Chinese. Homework might be given in Tibetan, but exams can be taken in either language."

This seems to be the practice in many of the areas we visited. It is obviously difficult, even for the teachers, to decide exactly what the language of instruction is. School staff and officials define this differently. In addition, we visited schools classified as Tibetan language that had parallel classes in each grade taught in Tibetan and in Chinese. In some of these schools, only one third of the pupils were taught in Tibetan.

As with monasteries, defining a school is not as easy as one might expect. We were told that the number of schools in a county was unclear, since officials did not know whether to include teaching stations or "point schools" (Ch: *dianxiao*), which may not have permanent buildings at all. We were told of one school that held class in a dry riverbed, where pupils sat on rocks, and of another that conducted teaching in the "prayer house" (T: *mani khang*). School hours and days may also be irregular, and as officials do not go out to inspect very often, they may not know how many of the schools are functioning on a regular basis. Many point schools are bilingual, which then makes the number of bilingual schools uncertain. Along with the unclear definition of a school, our sources often were also not sure about whom to count as a student or a teacher. For instance, during interviews, we sometimes realized that preschool pupils might be included in the total number of students and that administrative staff might have been counted as teachers.

Since all schools in China should (and the great majority do) teach

Chinese, we have defined a bilingual school as one where two languages are taught, for our purposes, Tibetan and Chinese. This is also the common understanding of the term among educators and officials in charge of education. However, some officials tend to be imprecise and equate "minority education" (Ch: *minzuban*) with "bilingual" (Ch: *shuangyu*) education. In minority areas, "*minzu* schools" (Ch: *minzu xuexiao*) are intended to provide educational opportunities especially for ethnic minority students, but this does not mean that all students in such schools are necessarily ethnic minorities. In one case, we were informed that the definition of a *minzu* school was that at least 65 percent of the students belong to a minority ethnic group. In other cases, we were told that even fewer of the students in such schools actually are minority students. In addition, it is very common for *minzu* schools to teach only Chinese, and we found a number of cases in which *minzu* schools in Tibetan areas did not teach Tibetan at all.

As mentioned above, government officials tend to exaggerate enrollment rates, including at bilingual schools, which means that attendance figures might also be too high. Another serious problem is a tendency to exaggerate the number of bilingual schools. In addition, a school's classification as bilingual gives no indication of how many students are taught Tibetan or the number of hours per week they study Tibetan. During fieldwork, we came across schools in which Tibetan was taught only above the fourth grade or only to an experimental class. In these schools, the pupils were studying Tibetan two to four hours a week, while Chinese was taught up to eleven hours a week.

Another problem is the lack of specific data on the percentage of students who are Tibetans. On the one hand, as noted above, Han students sometimes attend *minzu* schools in quite large numbers, and there are also strong indications that Han children generally attend school more frequently than do Tibetan children, particularly above the primary school level. On the other hand, Han are more restricted by the "planned reproduction policy" (Ch: *jihua shengyu*), commonly known as the one-child policy, than are Tibetans and other minorities, who are usually allowed more than one child. In the case of parents employed by the government, the limit is generally two children, whereas farmers and herders are usually allowed up to three children. Because we relied solely on demographic figures, we unfortunately were not able to take these added factors into account.

The demographic figures cited in this book are drawn primarily from national censuses, which are considered the most accurate sources. The most recent national census was conducted in November 2000, but the source material for this book is based on the latest census data available at the time of writing, the 1990 national census. Although more than ten years have passed since then and the population has increased, we mainly need to know the percentage of Tibetans living in an area, not the actual number. As many critics have pointed out, however, this is exactly where official statistics may be the most unreliable because of inconsistencies in who is and is not counted as residing in a particular area when the census is taken. Among the groups not counted, Han are believed to constitute the great majority. The most important groups not counted in the national census are members of the armed forces and temporary migrants, defined as those living in a locality for less than a year and continuously absent from their place of registered residence. We also included demographic information from the 1990 census for the sake of comparing different areas according to ethnic composition and discerning variations in conditions for the reconstruction of monasteries and the teaching of Tibetan in schools. We have thus tried to substantiate the effects of Han versus Tibetan majorities in the population.[28]

USE OF TERMINOLOGY

As already mentioned, we use the term "bilingual school" to refer to a school where Chinese and a minority language are taught. Both the terms *minzu zhongxue* (*minzu* middle school) and *Zangwen zhongxue* (Tibetan middle school) were used by some of our sources to refer to bilingual middle schools as opposed to "standard middle schools" (Ch: *putong zhongxue*). The difference between the terms appears to be that *minzu* schools are for minority students, in this case Tibetans, although they are often taught in Chinese with Tibetan language as an additional subject, while Tibetan schools use Tibetan as the language of instruction. We use the terms "*minzu* school" and "Tibetan school" as they are used by our sources but note that different criteria for each are applied from place to place.

Minzu in Chinese generally refers to "minority ethnic groups" (Ch: *shaoshu minzu*). This is explained in more detail in chapter 1. When we use the term *minzu* in this study, it is drawn directly from a particular source and follows the usage of that source. When we refer to these minority ethnic groups in our own discussions, we prefer to use the term "ethnic minority" or "minority." The use of the term "minority" in reference to Tibetans has been protested by some who see it as inappropriate for political reasons. As used in this study, the word "minority" is not politically motivated but merely expresses that the particular ethnic group is in the minority in

a county, prefecture, province, or China as a whole. In other cases, however, Tibetans are the majority group within an area and are then referred
to as the Tibetan majority.

We have chosen to refer to the Chinese majority population as "Han,"
although this is also a politically charged term. Some might accuse us of
transmitting the view that the Han are only one of many Chinese peoples
and that all ethnic minorities are equally Chinese. The term "Han" also creates the impression that there is such a thing as a homogenous Chinese
nation, effectively disguising large variations within the majority Chinese
population in terms of language, way of life, customs, and religious traditions.[29] Several scholars have in fact noted that the term "Han *minzu*" is a
recent invention,[30] although it emphasizes the connections between the
present-day inhabitants of China and their ancestors in the ancient Han
dynasty (206 BCE–220 CE).[31] Despite these disagreements, we use the term
"Han" as it is used in China today, to categorize the majority of Chinese
who are not recognized as members of a minority ethnic group.

1 / The Setting

Contemporary Tibetan cultural politics is linked closely to the politics of ethnic and national identity. In order to understand the context for this cultural politics, we need to know something about the history of China-Tibet relations. The very concept of Tibet and the Tibetan identity has evolved through this historical relationship and has at the same time been reiterated through Chinese and Tibetan history-building projects.

For centuries, China's ethnic minorities have encountered various civilizing projects, informed by different ideologies that were adopted in turn by Chinese authorities and European colonialists.[1] These processes, described by Stevan Harrell as "cultural encounters," are crucial to the negotiation of Han as well as Tibetan identity. Since the People's Republic of China was established, its policies have had an especially deep impact on the expression of cultural and ethnic identities by the indigenous communities in China and on the very meaning of those identities. The revival of minority cultures in China, including Tibetan culture, should be understood in light of these and other historical circumstances. The issue of Tibetan cultural survival in China is also inextricably linked to the broader controversies and international concerns over Tibet.

This chapter outlines the background of these debates, including the history of the areas under study, which is tied to the disagreement between Tibetan exiles and Chinese authorities over the very definition of Tibet, the dispute over Tibet Major or Greater Tibet. It provides an overview of the ideological standpoint of the Chinese Communist Party (CCP) on the ethnic minority question, CCP efforts to classify the ethnic minorities of China, and the administrative system that has been set up to govern these areas.

DEFINING THE AREAS UNDER STUDY

Chinese histories claim that Tibet has been part of China for more than a millennium and that it was "peacefully liberated" by the People's Liberation Army (PLA) in 1950, one year after the People's Republic of China was established. However, Tibetans who fled to India and Nepal and formed a government-in-exile under the leadership of the Dalai Lama have different views. They argue that the so-called peaceful liberation was a military invasion of an independent country.

Another contentious issue is the definition of Tibet as such. The Chinese government formally established the Tibet Autonomous Region (TAR) as late as 1965, after the Dalai Lama had taken refuge in India in 1959. By then, the authorities had already established Tibetan Autonomous Prefectures and Counties within four bordering provinces—Gansu, Qinghai, Sichuan, and Yunnan—covering an area almost the size of the TAR itself. According to national census figures, well over 2 million Tibetans, more than half of all Tibetans in China, live in these Tibetan areas outside the TAR.

The Tibetan government-in-exile holds the view that the rightful territory of Tibet encompasses all the areas recognized by China as Tibetan autonomous regions and not just the TAR. According to Tibetan exiles, "We have only to glance at the map of Asia to see Tibet clearly marked off by encircling mountain chains." They further argue that after the PLA brought the whole of Tibet under its control, the Chinese Communists "began to pursue their colonial policy of 'divide and rule' by dividing Tibet and distorting the facts of Tibetan history."[2]

Representatives of the Chinese state are equally adamant. For instance, in one of its white papers on Tibet, the State Council argues: "The Dalai Lama clique has . . .contended that geographically Tibet extends far beyond the boundaries of today, including areas inhabited by the Tibetans in Sichuan, Qinghai, and other places, making a total population of six million. This so-called Tibet Major is merely a conspiracy hatched by imperialists in an attempt to carve up China."[3]

"Tibet" is a European name. Tibetans call their country Bod (Ch: Tubo or Tubote) and commonly divide it geographically into the "three regions" (T: *chol kha gsum*) of Ü-Tsang, Kham (Ch: Kangba), and Amdo. Several nineteenth-century Tibetan sources refer to the three regions of Tö or Ngari, Ü-Tsang, and Domed.[4] In these sources, Domed designates the lower parts of Tibet and includes Amdo and Kham. In contemporary China, however, Xizang, which is often translated into English as "Tibet," refers solely to the territory of the TAR. The TAR covers Ngari, Ü-Tsang, and western Kham, while Amdo and eastern Kham are incorporated in the provinces of Gansu, Qinghai, Sichuan, and Yunnan.

Writers outside China sometimes make a distinction between political and ethnographic Tibet, with political Tibet being the area under the political control of the Dalai Lama on the eve of the Communist era and ethnographic Tibet consisting of the areas inhabited by Tibetans and dominated by Tibetan culture.[5] Although political Tibet is commonly described as corresponding largely to the TAR, the exact boundaries of both areas usually are not identified. This is not surprising, since the nature of political control in the region before the establishment of the People's Republic of China was very different from that of today, as were the ways in which people identified themselves. The areas outside political Tibet were the frontier areas between Tibet and China dominated by local chieftains and warlords, sometimes in a zone of conflicting interests and often outside the control of any regime.

A HISTORY OF CHINESE-TIBETAN RELATIONS

In Imperial China, the world was basically divided between the "civilized" Chinese and their "uncivilized" neighbors, among whom were the nomadic peoples of the grasslands. In early Chinese records, the peoples inhabiting the plateau and mountain areas to the west of the Chinese Empire were called Tubo (Ch: Tufan) and Qiang. Records from as early as the Han dynasty (206 BCE–220 CE) describe imperial expansion into the highlands and attacks on nomads as far west as the Amnye Machen mountain range in what is today known as Golok (Guoluo) Prefecture in the modern province of Qinghai.[6] In the early sixth century, the Yarlung dynasty emerged in central Tibet, and by the eighth century it had become an empire. The "Yarlung kings" (T: *btsan po*) sent their soldiers into Chinese areas, attacking and occupying the Tang capital of Chang'an (now Xi'an) in 763. A settlement negotiated in 729 established boundary markers 320 *li* (160 kilometers) east of Siling (Xining).[7] The name Bod then became associated not only with the core area around Lhoka and the Yarlung Valley in central Tibet but with the entire mountain region controlled by the Yarlung kings. After another agreement with China in 821–22, the Tibetan Empire gradually declined, as did the Tang dynasty (618–907).[8] Several centuries later, at the time of the Yuan dynasty (1271–1368), Mongolian tribes entered the northern parts of the Tibetan Plateau, but not until the seventeenth century were the north-eastern areas of today's Qinghai incorporated into the Qing empire (1644–1911).

The years 1723–28 mark a turning point in the political history of the border areas. In 1723, Mongolians and Tibetans in the Kokonor area revolted against increased Qing control. The revolt was harshly suppressed, and the Kokonor area was incorporated into the Qing empire, which meant that taxes were paid directly to Qing officials rather than to monasteries or Mongolian overlords.[9] Between 1720 and 1728, the Qing sent three armies to Lhasa and for the first time established a protectorate in Tibet. A border stone was erected at Bum La, the pass between the Drichu (Yangzi River) and the Dzachu (Mekong River), and the watershed between the two rivers demarcated the boundary.[10] The areas west of the watershed were administered from Lhasa, while the territories to the east were administered by native chiefs under the supervision of the governor of Sichuan. At the present time, the border between the TAR and Sichuan follows the Drichu.

During the late eighteenth century, Qing armies were sent to save Tibet from invading Gurkha forces.[11] From the beginning of the nineteenth century, however, the Qing dynasty gradually lost influence in Tibet, particularly with the onset of the Opium War in 1840. In northern Amdo by the end of the nineteenth century, Qing forces controlled a corridor of land north of the Machu (Yellow River) and eastward from Xining to Gansu, in today's Haidong Prefecture. As for the areas south of the Machu, symbolic incorporation, by way of rewarding local leaders for tribute, was reinforced with occasional military incursions.[12]

Despite this nominal control, there was not much evidence in the late nineteenth century of Chinese settlement in Qinghai south of the northern bend of the Machu near Xining.[13] The Sun and Moon Ridge, together with the trade market at Thongkor (Huangyuan), west of Xining and east of Qinghai Lake (Tso ngön), divided the highland pastoral and agricultural areas until 1949.[14] Today this line marks the border between Tsochang (Haibei) Tibetan Autonomous Prefecture (TAP) and Xining Municipality. The areas outside "political Tibet" were in general very remote and inaccessible, and in present-day Jyekundo (Yushu) and Golok TAPs, for instance, the state was unable even to send in postal couriers during the Republican period (1912–49).[15] After the founding of the Nationalist state, Amdo came under the control of the Muslim warlord in Xining, Ma Bufang, who became notorious for his brutality.

With the decline of the Qing dynasty, a Nyarong chieftain, Gonpo Namgyal, initiated a military campaign to seize control of most of the local polities of Kham. The Lhasa administration sent a Tibetan army to defeat Gonpo Namgyal in 1863 and thus regained control of the areas that had been taken over by Sichuan in 1725. However, by the end of the nineteenth century, after subsequent military campaigns by Chinese armies, the states of northern Kham were under Lhasan authority with those in southern Kham (Lithang and Bathang) loosely supervised by the Qing governor-general of Sichuan.[16]

In 1904, the British sent troops from India to Lhasa for the purpose of forcing the Dalai Lama to negotiate a trade agreement with British India. In the same year, the Chinese undertook an incursion into Kham that lasted until the end of the Qing dynasty in 1911. The campaign was led by Zhao Erfeng, special commissioner in charge of the Yunnan-Sichuan frontier. By 1910, most of the autonomous polities of Kham had become districts under the authority of Chinese magistrates, colonies were being established in Bathang and Dzayül, and Zhao's troops had reached Lhasa, leading to the flight of the thirteenth Dalai Lama to India.[17] In order to recruit settlers to colonies in Bathang and Dzayül, Zhao issued proclamations promising to give settlers land, cover their travel expenses, and provide oxen, plows, and seed, which they could pay for over a three-year period.[18] Zhao was killed only a year later, however, and the Qing dynasty ended. The Chinese immediately lost control of Pome and Dzayül,[19] while the garrisons in Kham withdrew or deserted after being attacked by Tibetan forces. Tibetan forces subsequently regained control of most of Kham. Despite the establishment of a nominal province, Xikang, in Kham during the Republican period, only nine of Zhao Erfeng's thirty-one magistrates still existed in 1931.[20]

During the Simla Convention (1913–14), British, Chinese, and Tibetan officials attempted to reach an agreement on regulating the borders between British India, China, and Tibet. The final agreement was signed and ratified by Britain and Tibet but not by China.[21] As proposed by the British representative, the agreement established the territories of Outer and Inner Tibet. Outer Tibet was recognized as suzerain and Inner Tibet as sovereign Chinese territory. Outer Tibet coincided approximately with what is now the TAR and Jyekundo TAP in Qinghai. Inner Tibet included what is now Dechen (Diqing) TAP in Yunnan, Kandze (Ganzi) TAP in Sichuan, Ngaba (Aba) Tibetan and Qiang Autonomous Prefecture in Sichuan, Golok TAP in Qinghai, and areas in western Qinghai north of Jyekundo TAP. The Tibetans relinquished areas north of the Amnye Machen mountain range and the Tawang district in India's North Eastern Frontier Area region, also known as Arunachal Pradesh, and the so-called McMahon line was established. This proposed boundary between Tibet and India is a matter of dispute between China and India today.

The Simla Convention was initiated by British colonial authorities and should be understood in light of the ongoing Great Game in Central Asia, with the two great powers Russia and Britain each trying to expand its authority and China seeking to maintain its imperial influence. The last imperial dynasty in China, the Qing dynasty, had ended in 1911, and the British wanted to take advantage of unstable conditions to establish Tibet as a buffer zone in Central Asia. In order to do this, it was important to agree on the border between Tibet and China, which previously had been marked only by border stones at strategic points and never delineated on maps. In fact, fairly accurate maps of Tibet did not exist until British cartographers assembled geographical data collected by British soldiers, colonial government officials, and agents.

In looking at the history of European cartography, one can see that as Europeans began to explore and conquer, maps became scientific instead of cosmological. The same process took place in China, where modern cartography developed as an important tool of the Republican and later the Communist government. During the 1950s, Chinese authorities continued the systematic mapping of the Tibetan Plateau while defining the present-day administrative divisions and creating the current system of Tibetan autonomous areas.[22] As this occurred, all Tibetan place-names were sinicized, and many villages were given completely new Chinese names.

THE "TIBET QUESTION"

The questions of how to define Tibet and which areas to include as Tibetan are an aspect of the broader controversy over the status of Tibet in international law. The roots of this controversy go back at least to the days of the British Empire and the Great Game in Central Asia, but it was not until 1950, when the PLA marched through Kham on its way to "liberate" Tibet that the question of Tibet's status as a sovereign state actually gained relevance. This was due not only to the military power of the PLA and the expansionism of the Communist Chinese rulers but also to the new significance of the concept of statehood engendered by the recently established United Nations (UN).

In October 1950, the PLA crossed the Drichu and defeated the strategically important city of Chamdo. Chinese radio broadcasts announced that the "peaceful liberation of Tibet" had begun. Tibetan leaders in Lhasa real-

ized that Tibet was finally being invaded, and in desperation, they turned
to the West—Great Britain, the United States, and the United Nations—
for help.

The United Nations responded by debating whether to present the invasion of Tibet to the UN General Assembly. The British Foreign Office initiated a legal inquiry into whether Tibet was eligible to appeal to the United
Nations, since the UN Charter stipulates that the appealing party must be
a state. The foreign office concluded that Tibetan autonomy was sufficiently
well established to consider Tibet a state as defined by the UN Charter.
Nevertheless, in the UN debate that followed, the British representative rec-
ommended that no action be taken, arguing that they "did not know
exactly what was going on in Tibet, nor was the legal position of the country very clear."[23] There are several reasons for this apparent contradiction
on the part of Great Britain. First, the British had decided to allow the newly
independent India to take the lead in formulating policies toward its neighbors. The British thus would have supported a resolution against China on
the Tibet issue if India had initiated such a resolution; however, India was
under strong pressure from China not to do so.[24] Second, Britain feared
that a resolution against China could be enforced only by armed action,
which neither Britain nor the United States was prepared to undertake. The
result would have been a loss of prestige for the United Nations.[25]

While these debates were taking place in Europe and the United States,
the PLA invaded Kham and advanced toward Lhasa. After all their requests
for assistance had been denied, the Dalai Lama and his government had no
other option than to negotiate with the Chinese. Under the leadership of
the governor of Chamdo, Ngabo Ngawang Jigme, a Tibetan envoy went to
Beijing to open a dialogue with the Chinese government. In May 1951, the
Tibetan delegates signed the so-called Seventeen-Point Agreement on the
Peaceful Liberation of Tibet.[26] The agreement stated that the existing
Tibetan political system, including the status and functions of the Dalai
Lama, would remain unaltered, that religious freedom would be protected
and the income of the monasteries would remain unchanged, and that the
spoken and written language and the education of Tibetans would be devel-
oped "step by step in accordance with the actual conditions in Tibet." It
also declared that the local government of Tibet should actively assist the
PLA in its efforts to enter Tibet and "consolidate the national defenses." [27]

Despite the fact that the Seventeen-Point Agreement was extorted from
the Tibetans under military pressure, the international community considered the issue of Tibet's status to be basically settled. The Tibetan lead-

ership had apparently accepted Tibet's status as a Chinese province, leaving little to discuss. However, when the Dalai Lama officially denounced the agreement upon arriving in India in 1959, the status of Tibet again became an international issue. It became clear that if Tibet were recognized as having been an independent state in 1949, the Chinese Communist action was then an invasion and occupation of a foreign territory and not an internal Chinese affair. Moreover, the invasion would violate the section of the UN Charter prohibiting the use of force against the territorial integrity or political independence of any state. In order to gain support, the government-in-exile thus had to convince the world that Tibet had been a legitimate state according to the accepted definition: having a permanent population, a delimited territory, a government, and the capacity to enter into relations with other states.

The attempt to apply the criteria of modern statehood to the pre-1950 situation in Tibet has served to complicate the issue rather than bring it closer to a solution. Before 1950, Tibetan Buddhism essentially defined the political unit of Tibet. Tibet was the religious land, the polity based on and legitimized by religion as expressed in the concept of "king as protector and patron of religion" (T: *chos rgyal*) and the "dual religious and secular system of government" (T: *chos srid gnyis ldan*). In Amdo and Kham in particular, the larger monasteries were not only important religious and trade centers but also administrative centers. The political system was epitomized by the crucial status of the Dalai Lama as political leader and, in his sacred role, protector deity of Tibet. It is not certain, however, that the political unit thus defined by religion was understood as a state in the present-day sense of the word, nor were the boundaries of this political unit clearly demarcated. In Tibet, as in Benedict Anderson's "dynastic realm,"[28] populations were subjects, not citizens, the ruler derived his legitimacy from divinity, not from populations, and political units were defined by their centers, not by legally established borders.

None of the world's governments has officially recognized Tibet as an independent nation, but there is currently a broadly held international view of Tibet as an oppressed country under Chinese domination.[29] A number of state leaders have called for a dialogue between the Tibetan government-in-exile and the Chinese government. Chinese leaders have claimed that they will meet with the Dalai Lama and his representatives as soon as he stops calling for independence and announces that Tibet is part of China. However, even though the Dalai Lama has stated repeatedly, since launching the Strasbourg Proposal in the European Parliament in 1988, that he is no longer striving for Tibetan independence but is instead seeking what he has termed "real autonomy" within the Chinese state, Chinese authorities still refuse to enter into formal negotiations. Through the Chinese press, they continue to condemn the Dalai Lama for leading a "clique of separatists who are relentlessly trying to split China."[30]

Whereas the Tibet issue has been dominated by historicist arguments, in recent years the importance and validity of historical evidence concerning Tibet's legal status have been called into question. After all, ideas of legitimate government and the responsibilities of the state have evolved only within recent decades, and it is during this period that Tibet support groups and Tibetan exiles began to criticize China's human rights record in Tibet and revealed serious cases of politically motivated persecution and systematic suppression of dissent. They also exposed widespread poverty and illiteracy among Tibetans, pointed out China's failure to protect the environment, and noted that exploitation of nonrenewable resources on the Tibetan Plateau has not benefited Tibetans. Finally, they brought to center stage of the debate the problems of large-scale in-migration to Tibetan areas, ethnic discrimination, and "cultural genocide." The Dalai Lama and others have called for a referendum on the status of Tibet among Tibetans within and outside China and insisted that the Tibetan people have the right to decide their own destiny, including their system of government and political affiliation.

THE CONCEPT OF *MINZU* AND THE IDENTIFICATION OF "NATIONALITIES"

China's system of autonomous areas rests on the concept of "ethnic groups" (Ch: *minzu*) and the understanding that specific discernible areas of China are inhabited largely by ethnic minorities that are distinguishable from the majority Han population by distinct, shared cultural traits. The Chinese term *minzu* can mean the inhabitants of a country or the different ethnic groups within a country. The term *Zhonghua minzu*, which refers to the Chinese nation, relies on the first sense of the term and was introduced as a concept by Chinese Nationalists seeking to overthrow the Manchu-ruled Qing dynasty at the end of the nineteenth century.[31] In common parlance, the second sense of *minzu* has become equivalent to "minority groups." "Ethnology" or "minority studies" is translated as *minzuxue,* derived from the Japanese *minzokugaku.*[32] One of the basic tenets of Chinese Marxist social science is the idea of stages of social forms, in which "minority ethnic groups" represent less advanced stages in the evolutionary system. The supposed primitiveness of the minorities typically is contrasted with the modernity of the Han ethnic group. As a consequence, the "more advanced" Han are seen as responsible for helping their less fortunate compatriots to develop.

This "mission to civilize the natives" should be all too familiar from the justifications offered for European colonialism.[33] The roots of Chinese minority studies, so closely connected to political ideology, can in fact be found in Europe and the United States. Lewis Henry Morgan's *Ancient Society* and Herbert Spencer's *Principles of Sociology* were among the first sociological works translated into Chinese in the first years of the twentieth century.[34] Morgan's theory of social evolution subsequently became the cornerstone of Chinese ethnology.[35]

After the founding of the People's Republic of China, Chinese ethnographers were faced with the task of redefining the concept of ethnic minority in Communist terms and identifying the ethnic minorities of the new nation. Joseph Stalin's theory of national identity and Friedrich Engels's reworking of Morgan in *The Origin of the Family, Private Property, and the State* were of theoretical importance.[36] The "*minzu* identification project" (Ch: *minzu shibie*) was initiated in the early 1950s when local groups were invited to submit applications for the status of *minzu*, resulting in more than 400 applications.[37] Teams of researchers began fieldwork and detailed studies in 1953. By 1965, a total of fifty-four minority ethnic groups were officially recognized.[38] Researchers used criteria defined by Stalin to determine *minzu* status: a common language, a common territory, a common economy, and a common psychological nature manifested in a common culture.

Whatever the definition of culture, one can obviously find very pronounced cultural differences within the borders of China. At the same time, it is important to recognize that the characterization of ethnic markers and the categorization of ethnic groups were undertaken by ethnologists working in state-sponsored academic institutions. Some of the most influential construction of ethnic culture has thus taken place in institutes and academies that are carrying out ethnographic research. During the first decades of the People's Republic of China, ethnographic research was conducted almost exclusively by Han scholars, but this began to change in the 1980s, when Tibetan and other minority students and researchers gained access to resources through various academic institutions.[39] There is now an educated Tibetan elite of cadres, professional artists, writers, and scholars who are engaged in Tibetan studies, albeit within the disciplinary and ideological framework outlined by policy makers.[40]

Ironically, the *minzu* identification project, together with the preferential policies accorded minorities, may in some cases have reinforced ethnic identities that were almost forgotten.[41] In addition, in a number of cases people complained that they were denied a separate ethnic identity and, in their opinion, wrongly classified with an unrelated group. Others charged that separate identities were created for people who feel that they actually belong to a single group.[42]

One can find examples of both situations among Tibetans. In Yunnan, the Pumi were given status as a separate ethnic group, whereas, across the border in Sichuan, the Premi (alternative spelling, Prmi) are classified as "Tibetans" (Ch: Zangzu). In both provinces, some of these people disagreed about the way in which they were classified as ethnic minorities.[43] In Sichuan, a number of so-called subgroups of Tibetans were recognized, such as the Ersu, Ergong, Duoxu, Zaba, Nameze, Se'er, Hu'ya, and Jiarong (T: *rgyal rong*). Among the groups in Sichuan previously known by the Chinese as *xifan* (western barbarians), only the Qiang were given separate minority status, while all the others were classified as Tibetans. Some insisted that all these subgroups are Tibetans, and even the separate identity of the Qiang was denied. In Gansu and Qinghai, the status of the Tu was also debated. At issue was the question of whether the Tu is a distinct ethnic group with its own identity or another subgroup of Tibetans or Mongolians. In a number of cases, Tu from particular villages argued that they were wrongly classified. For instance, near Rebkong (Tongren), we came across a village that was classified as Tu in the 1950s, although the villagers themselves claimed they were Tibetans. They declared that they speak Tibetan, dress Tibetan, eat Tibetan, are Buddhists, and are unable to understand the language spoken in other Tu villages in Qinghai.

Instead of trying to judge the correct way in which to classify people, it is interesting to note the kinds of arguments used in the debates and what seems to be at stake for those who participate. As one of the main criteria of ethnic minority defined by Stalin, languages have received a great deal of attention from Chinese scholars. Minority languages are classified in subgroups, branches, groups, and language families. The Pumi language, for instance, is classified as belonging to the Qiang subgroup of the Jiarong-Drung branch of the northern group of the Tibeto-Burman language family.[44]

Scholars disagree on a method of classifying Tibeto-Burman languages and especially on distinguishing languages from dialects. For instance, one source notes that many Tibetans in Sichuan speak languages other than Tibetan. Of a total of 308,467 Tibetans in Ngaba Prefecture in 1982, 153,000 reportedly use the Tibetan Amdo dialect, 91,000 use the Jiarong language, 41,000 use the Qiang language, 11,000 use the Ergong language, 4,000 use the Baima language, and 8,000 use Chinese.[45] The same source describes Ergong and Baima as recently confirmed languages. According to a Chinese government white paper, ten ethnic groups in China use thirteen written languages that have been "created or improved with the help of the government," including the Miao, Naxi, Lisu, Hani, Va, Dong, Jingpo, and Tu languages.[46] Both the Tu and Qiang languages have been developed into scripts using Roman letters.[47] Researchers from the Chinese Academy of Social Sciences created the Tu script as late as the 1980s. It was officially acknowledged in 1986 by the State Ethnic Affairs Commission and is reportedly used primarily in Gönlung (Huzhu) Tu Autonomous County, in Haidong Prefecture.[48] The problem of classifying languages is of more than academic interest. In fact, Chinese authorities are often guided by ideological considerations when defining a language, as opposed to a dialect, and choosing an alphabet for a previously unwritten language.[49] One such consideration may be the desire to obscure the resemblance between different dialects or languages, which would affect the classification of ethnic groups as either subgroups or separate ethnic groups.

Although dialect differences are sometimes exaggerated, they may create serious problems for the teaching of Tibetan and other minority languages in schools. We were told in several counties in Sichuan, for example, that the vast dialect differences created difficulties for bilingual education, since local Tibetan pupils had problems understanding the Central Tibetan they were taught by their teachers.[50] In both Kandze and Ngaba Prefectures, we were told that some Tibetan dialects were so different that they were mutually unintelligible.[51] Yet, we also encountered cases in which such language differences seemed to have little effect on the teaching of Tibetan. For instance, in Qinghai we paid a visit to a school at which Tibetan was the language of instruction and all the students were classified as Tu. Apparently, these students were satisfied with the use of Tibetan in their school. When we asked about the differences between the Tu and Tibetan languages, we were told, "Tu people have their own language, but it's like a dialect of Amdo Tibetan." Interestingly, other sources describe the Tu language as a Mongolian language. The Tu people we interviewed in this case may represent another example of "wrongly classified" people, which adds to the confusion. As suggested above, defining a particular spoken language as a dialect or a separate language is an extremely difficult task with obvious political consequences and is therefore very often controversial.

The claim that Baima is a separate language, for instance, is tied to a dispute over whether the Baima or "Dagpo" (T: *dwags po*) constitute their own ethnic group or are, as now classified, Tibetans. Janet Upton provides us with an illuminating description of this controversy in her presentation of the Tibetan scholar Muge Samten's writings on the Dagpo.[52] The case of the Dagpo was reopened in the late 1970s. A team of researchers from the Institute of Nationalities Studies of the Chinese Academy of Social Sciences, the Sichuan Province Ethnic Affairs Commission, Sichuan University, and Sichuan Provincial Museum conducted on-site investigations in Pingwu and Namphel (Nanping) Counties in 1978 and 1979 in order to determine whether the Dagpo constitute a unique ethnic group, perhaps as descendants of the Di, or are a subgroup of Tibetans, "Baima Tibetans" (Ch: Baima Zangzu or Baima Zangren). In their subsequent reports, the researchers suggested that the Dagpo are not Tibetans but are instead a unique ethnic group. However, Muge Samten later argued in several articles that the Dagpo are Tibetans, disagreeing with the researchers' claim that the language, customs, means of production, religious traditions, eating habits, dress, architecture, and social organization of the Dagpo differ from those of the Tibetans. In addition, he asserted that classical Tibetan annals and genealogies such as *The Great Tibetan Genealogy* (T: Bod kyi rus mdzod chen mo), *The Brocade Genealogy* (T: Rus mdzod za 'og ma), and *Assorted Genealogies* (T: Rus mdzod thor bu) describe the Dagpo and a number of other Tibetan subgroups as descendants of Tibetan armies sent to the border areas during the reigns of the eighth- and ninth-century Tibetan kings Songtsan Gampo (T: *srong btsan sgam po*), Tri Song (T: *khri srong*), and Tri Ral (T: *khri ral*). As for the name "Baima," Muge Samten stated that it is a local rendering of the Tibetan *bod dmag* (Tibetan soldier). He similarly called the Pumi *bod mi* (Tibetan people), arguing that there are even some who are "diligently planning to make Muli [County] a non-Tibetan [county]."[53]

What is interesting about these arguments is not only the way in which linguistics and classical Tibetan histories are employed as evidence but also the consequences implied—the loss of territory designated as Tibetan. At stake here is the definition of territories as well as peoples and the fear of losing autonomous status and its associated privileges. Whereas at least some members of the subgroups objected to being called Tibetans, others saw the reopening of cases in the late 1970s as yet another attack by the Chinese state on a Tibetan identity that had already been severely fractured in the preceding twenty years of social and political upheaval.[54] For these people, there is obviously much more to be gained from being recognized as members of one of China's largest ethnic groups than from achieving a separate, less significant minority identity.

There is nothing new about regional identities within the Tibetan areas. Dawa Norbu, a political scientist who grew up in Tibet, remarked on the prevalence of subnational identities in Tibet before 1950 and the growing consciousness of a pan-Tibetan identity:

> Regionally, Tibetans identified themselves as Khampa, Topa, Tsangpa and Amdo-wa of Kham, Toi, Tsang (Shigatse) and Amdo regions[54] But how do Tibetans differentiate themselves from non-Tibetans? Do Tibetans have an encompassing pan-Tibetan identity? Before the politicization of Tibetan ethnicity, "we" and "they," or Tibetan and non-Tibetan, was a Buddhist differentiation between believers and non-believers, *phyipa* and *nangpa*. However, since the Chinese takeover in 1959, there has been a growing consciousness, particularly among "urban" Tibetans, about a pan-Tibetan identity that sharply differentiates itself from *rgya-rigs* or *rgya-mi*—the Chinese/Han. The "in-group" is increasingly identified as *bodpa* or *bod-rigs*.[55]

Many scholars maintain that religion has been the main marker of Tibetan identity.[56] According to Dawa Norbu, the politicization of Tibetan ethnicity means that regional and other subnational identities have given way to the more encompassing Tibetan identity. He also argues that differences between Buddhist and Bönpo have increasingly been deemphasized. Religion certainly took on new meaning as an ethnic marker for Tibetans after the devastation of the Democratic Reforms campaign in the late 1950s and the Cultural Revolution in the 1960s. In addition, other criteria such as language, territory, and livelihood are understood by most Tibetans to be important ethnic markers.

Ethnic identities are multivalent and contingent. Several scholars have explained that minority identities in China are not merely passively accepted or denied by those who are classified but consciously employed in many ways and for different purposes.[57] Identities are being simultaneously negotiated and actively re-created.[58] Representation of minority ethnic groups is an important issue, considering the stereotypes found in official discourse on minorities.[59] However, the very practice of classifying ethnic minorities and the ideological premises, often referred to as scientific, on which the classification is based, seem to be exempt from negotiation. The connection between peoples and territories, and in this way between minority ethnic groups and autonomous administrative areas, is one such premise.

Contested or not, today every citizen of China is designated as belonging to a particular ethnic group. Population censuses provide detailed information on the demography of autonomous areas, and personal identity cards note each individual's ethnic affiliation.[60] In school, children learn about the special characteristics of their ethnic group while they are taught what it means to be a patriotic citizen of the motherland. The ideals of patriotism and the unity of the *minzu* are among the most explicit messages conveyed by the school curriculum. The implicit message is as powerful, in that it establishes a hegemonic view of both the categorization of people and the delimitation of territories in China.

The history of China-Tibet relations is complex, as is the question of the meaning of Tibetan identity. Needless to say, it is beyond the scope of this book to give a comprehensive account of either of these issues. Some important topics, such as the consequences for Tibetan identity of successive Chinese "civilizing projects," have received only very brief mention.[61] Nevertheless, it should be clear from the discussions above that Tibetan culture and Tibetan identities are not established entities that are available for us to find and document. Rather, they are undergoing a continuous process of negotiation and reconstruction. What is more, despite the fact that we question certain ways of categorizing persons in our discussions, these and the other categories we employ in our study were inevitably reinvented by the study itself. Tibetan culture is negotiated not only by Tibetans and Han but through the use of the categories Tibetan and Han, in the acceptance of certain definitions of culture, and by the definition of certain objects of study as relevant to an investigation of Tibetan cultural survival.

2 / Religious Sites and the Practice of Religion

Monasteries commonly are understood as the repositories of Tibetan culture, and Tibetan Buddhism has come to define a widely shared notion of Tibetan culture. This is not just a product of Western fascination with the otherworldliness of Tibet, or the Tibetan Diaspora's way of re-creating Tibetan culture in exile. It is an understanding that is often expressed by Tibetans and other inhabitants of the region, including members of the Chinese Communist Party (CCP) and the Chinese authorities. This notion of Tibetan culture has clearly dominated the thinking of Party leaders and cadres at least since the Cultural Revolution, when religious practice became the primary target of the Red Guard in the Tibetan areas.

In recent years, the CCP has attempted, for ideological purposes, to redefine Tibetan culture as non-Buddhist, declaring that Buddhism is foreign to Tibet and that its influence on Tibetans should be countered.[1] Official statements from the government also contend that monasticism had a negative impact on Tibetan society and culture before Tibetans were "liberated" by the People's Liberation Army (PLA). For instance, the Chinese government's white paper on Tibetan culture claims that theocracy was detrimental: "The long reign of feudal serfdom under theocracy not only severely fettered the growth of the productive forces in Tibet, but also resulted in a hermetically sealed and moribund traditional Tibetan culture, including cultural relics, historic sites, and sites for Buddhist worship."[2]

Contrary to these assertions, the Tibetan government-in-exile argues that Tibetan culture is in essence a spiritual culture that should be promoted not only for the sake of Tibetans but for the benefit of humanity at large:

"Our freedom struggle is not merely to serve the interests of Tibetans; it is to preserve the tradition of inner wisdom and unique Tibetan culture for the benefit of the whole world. Therefore, I do not see our movement as a political struggle; rather I see it as a spiritual practice."[3]

Before the establishment of the People's Republic of China, the larger Gelugpa monasteries functioned as political and administrative as well as religious centers. Monasteries were the corporate owners of a large number of agricultural estates and also held rights of taxation on communities of farmers and herders. In the 1950s and 1960s, Chinese authorities introduced far-reaching land reform in the Tibetan areas, and in this process the clergy and other influential landowners such as the landed gentry were regarded as "exploiters" and "enemies of the people." The monasteries and eventually religious practice in general thus came under attack.

This chapter describes the destruction of monasteries in Tibetan areas outside the Tibet Autonomous Region (TAR) and their subsequent reconstruction after 1978. It also discusses the conditions under which Tibetans have been allowed to revive their monasteries, religious sites, and religious practices in general and explores the current limitations to religious freedom in the areas under study.

DESTRUCTION OF MONASTERIES IN TIBETAN AREAS

Although Chinese authorities frequently blame the Cultural Revolution for the destruction of Tibetan monasteries, in fact the Red Army first inflicted damage on Tibetan monasteries as early as 1934–35 during the Long March through Ngaba (Aba) and Kandze (Ganzi) Prefectures.[4] We visited one monastery in Tashiling (Lixian) County, where local sources explained that evidence of these events was still visible. This monastery had not been fully restored and was in poor condition. According to an old monk, the monastery's wall frescoes were destroyed in the 1930s when the Red Army marched through the area. We were told that the monastery was uninhabited for several years and that the frescoes were damaged by rainwater because the building's roof was not maintained. Not until several years later did the monks return to the site to repair it.

CCP policy on religion in Tibetan areas has gone through several stages since the inception of the People's Republic of China. In the early 1950s, the CCP used religious leaders in an effort to influence Tibetans to accept the PLA intrusion. The strategy, according to Melvyn Goldstein, was to separate support for the Tibetan government from support for religion just before the PLA advanced into eastern Tibet.[5] PLA units under the leadership of the Southwest Military Command were therefore instructed to respect religious practice, and a proclamation was issued stating that the PLA would "protect religious freedom; respect local customs and practices; protect all monasteries and temples; the soldiers will not stay in monasteries without permission of the abbot, and the army will not destroy monastery buildings or destroy any religious items in the monasteries; it is not permitted to interfere or harm the monastic prayers of monks or religious achievements and if there are any violators of this they will be severely punished."[6]

After this initial attempt to appear as the new protectors of religion, the government abruptly changed its policies and announced the onset of "democratic reforms" in early 1956. Monastic properties were then confiscated, and religious leaders were persecuted. The campaign targeted monasteries as "feudal oppressors," and monastic estates were redistributed along with the estates of other "feudal lords." In the revolts that followed, monks often joined the lay population in armed resistance. Among the most famous resistance forces was Four Rivers Six Ranges. These forces first organized in Kham and Amdo, but the movement eventually spread into central Tibet as well. As a result of their activities, monasteries came under further attack and in a few cases were bombed by the Chinese air force.

By 1958, Democratic Reforms had been initiated in all Tibetan areas outside the borders of the present-day TAR as well as in areas of western Kham administered by the Chamdo Liberation Committee. It seems that monasteries in the remaining parts of the TAR were left undisturbed until 1959, but after the Lhasa Uprising in March of that year, monks and nuns could no longer stay in monasteries and nunneries, owing to persecution by Chinese authorities. Religious leaders received the same harsh treatment as had noble families and former government officials.

The Democratic Reforms campaign was the first massive land redistribution program implemented by the Communist regime in Tibetan areas outside the TAR and the first wave of destruction affecting monasteries in these areas.[7] According to one study, there were 722 Tibetan monasteries in Qinghai before 1958, with approximately 57,647 monks, 2,500 nuns, and 1,240 tulkus, but after the reforms campaign, only 11 monasteries were left intact. The same source states that of the 369 monasteries in Gansu, all but 8 were closed down in 1958; furthermore, of a total of 16,900 monks in Gansu before the campaign, only 571 remained afterward.[8] Most of the monks were forced to relinquish their status because of the persecution.

Further details on the effects of the Democratic Reforms campaign on

Tibetan monasteries are difficult to find in the Chinese literature; however, Tibetan refugees have provided firsthand accounts of what happened during the campaign. According to one such account, in 1958 the CCP issued a communiqué stating that "all monks and lamas are exploiters and enemies of the people," adding that the "clergy and the aristocracy (the Red and the Black enemies) must be exterminated." The account provides the following description of events at Dzogchen (Zokchen) and Shechen (Shichen) monasteries in Kandze: "[The Chinese] demanded that the monks of Zokchen and Shichen attend a special meeting. The Chinese then proceeded to occupy the best quarters in the monastery, which was the residence of the chief lama, Zokchen Rinpoche. They kept the Zokchen Rinpoche and all other prominent lamas as hostages with them. At the meeting, the Chinese informed the assembled monks that henceforth all monks were to defrock and marry."[9]

After this meeting, the monks of the two monasteries were forced to work and attend criticism sessions for about two months. Sacred images and scriptures were torn down, and the monks were forced at gunpoint to walk on them. Finally, it was announced that the monks would have to criticize their abbots and lamas in "struggle sessions." This led to a revolt against the Chinese forces in which all the Chinese and about fifty monks were killed. After the battle, the surviving monks fled, and many joined Khampa guerrilla forces.[10] Revolts such as this took place in many Tibetan areas, in both Amdo and Kham.

In 1962, the Chinese government reevaluated its policies toward the monasteries. Chinese sources associate these changes with the Northwest Nationality Work Meeting and state that the policy shift led to the reconstruction of a number of monasteries.[11] In Qinghai, 137 monasteries were reopened, about 107 monasteries were rebuilt in Gansu, and the number of monks in Tibetan areas of Qinghai and Gansu rose to about 4,000 in 1966.[12] Despite the more lenient policy in effect for a few years in the early 1960s, the Cultural Revolution soon brought further destruction of monasteries. Members of the clergy who were not already in prison or labor camps were in many cases subject to additional struggle sessions and public humiliation. A number of monks and nuns were forced to break their vows of celibacy by marrying.

During the height of the Cultural Revolution, official persecution in Tibetan areas extended to religious practices observed in the homes of ordinary Tibetans. People were forced to denounce the Dalai Lama during public struggle sessions. Religious scriptures and pictures of the Dalai Lama were burned in the streets. Prayer beads, prayer wheels, and amulets were confiscated. Private altars and prayer flags were destroyed. According to the former cadre Dhondub Choedon: "The Red Guards had the goal of destroying the Four Olds and establishing the Four News. The Four Olds: old thoughts, old culture, old habits, and old customs. The Four News: new thoughts, new culture, new habits, and new customs. The Four Olds are the things Tibetan and the Four News are whatever the Chinese say. . . . The Chinese and the Red Guards charged that all Tibetans keeping old objects were guilty of trying to resurrect the past, that they were the enemy within."[13] The Four Olds not only were the "things Tibetan" but also were closely related to religious beliefs and practices.

The worst destruction of religious sites occurred during this period, when Red Guards destroyed monasteries, temples, and shrines all over the Tibetan Plateau. According to estimates by Tibetan exiles, of the approximately 6,000 monasteries, temples, and shrines that they claim existed in Tibetan areas, only about a dozen were undamaged.[14] In interviews with Chinese government officials, we received confirmation of monasteries destroyed in all the areas under study. We were told that all monasteries were partially or completely destroyed in Dechen (Diqing) Tibetan Autonomous Prefecture (TAP) in Yunnan and in Kandze TAP in Sichuan. Although we were unable to get any such confirmation from Ngaba Tibetan and Qiang Autonomous Prefecture, we do not know of any undamaged monasteries there. Pu Wencheng claims that in Gansu and Qinghai, four Tibetan monasteries were left undamaged after the Cultural Revolution. The most well known of these are Labrang Tashikhyil and Kumbum, which were among the largest monasteries and constituted political and economic as well as religious centers in the region. Pu also states that Kanlho (Gannan) TAP in Gansu had one surviving monastery, Labrang Tashikhyil, and that Pari (Tianzhu) Tibetan Autonomous County (TAC) had another, Tethung Dorje Chang (Ch: Miaoyin).[15] In Qinghai, most monasteries were completely destroyed, and only Kumbum and Jotshang (Ch: Qutan) allegedly survived.[16] This is what Chinese sources say, but according to several other accounts, both Labrang and Kumbum were partially or largely destroyed during the Cultural Revolution.[17] Regarding the remaining two monasteries, we have no further information.

During the Cultural Revolution, many monastery buildings were torn down, others were simply abandoned and left to deteriorate, and some were put to other uses, for example, as schools, storehouses, or even living quarters. A county official described in detail the fate of one monastery in Malho

(Huangnan) TAP, the largest monastery in the county, with more than 500 monks before the onset of the Democratic Reforms campaign. In 1958, all the monks were forced to leave, and villagers moved in. The monastery was restored in 1963, but the monks did not return, although monks who had married lived in the monastery. Then came the Cultural Revolution, when all monasteries in the county were destroyed. The monastery had owned fields and grasslands, which the villagers started to use, and eventually the monastery became a commune. In 1981, the commune's land was redistributed to individual families, and a year later, the villagers moved out. Some monks returned to the monastery, but the married monks departed along with the villagers and did not resume the monastic life.[18]

RECONSTRUCTION OF MONASTERIES
AND RETURN OF THE TIBETAN CLERGY

The official attitude toward religion began to relax as early as 1972. Funds were set aside for repairing Potala Palace, Jokhang Temple, and Drepung Monastery in Lhasa.[19] In 1974, a group of forty Tibetans was allowed to attend a sermon given by the Dalai Lama in Bihar, in northern India.[20] The major policy shift occurred in 1978, after the Third Plenary Session of the Eleventh Party Congress. Beginning in the early 1980s, the CCP drew up new guidelines to reform its policy on religion, and religious freedom was officially restored in the 1982 revision of the constitution. Many Tibetans were eager to begin rebuilding their local shrines and monasteries, and an impressive amount of voluntary work and donations has since been devoted to monastic reconstruction.

As described in the introduction, we reviewed information from a variety of sources on the numbers of monasteries and monks before 1958 and since the religious reforms took hold in the early 1980s. Appendix 3 contains detailed information on certain areas and our methods of determining total figures for each province. Rebuilt monasteries have not necessarily been completely reconstructed.

Combined estimates for the four provinces under study are 1,886 monasteries and 177,583 monks prior to 1958. This includes all Tibetan-designated prefectures and counties in Gansu, Sichuan, and Yunnan and the entire province of Qinghai. Recent figures for the same areas are based primarily on interviews with provincial, prefectural, and county authorities, although we had to rely on literary sources for areas on which government authorities could provide no information. The literary sources date from the late

TABLE 1. Monasteries and Monks by Province

	Monasteries before 1958	Monasteries in the 1990s	Monasteries rebuilt (percent)	Monks before 1958	Monks in the 1990s	Pre-1958 figures (percent)
Sichuan	922	732	79	106,226	62,982	59
Qinghai*	722	666	92	57,647	28,128	49
Gansu	218	131	60	10,765	7,076	66
Yunnan	24	21	88	2,945	1,508	51
TOTAL	1,886	1,550	82	177,583	99,694	56

* Figures are for entire province.

1980s and early 1990s and therefore are not as recent as the information obtained from interviews. Figures for the same areas in the 1990s are 1,550 monasteries and 99,694 monks.[21] These totals are broken down by province in table 1.[22]

As table 1 shows, the rates of monastic reconstruction in the four provinces vary between 60 percent and 92 percent. Gansu, which has the lowest rate, is very similar to neighboring areas of Sichuan. For example, Ngaba Prefecture also has a reconstruction rate of about 60 percent, according to what we regard as our most reliable sources.

Comparing the share of monks in the 1990s in each province and the share of Tibetans by province as of the 1990 census, we find that Sichuan, which has the largest population of Tibetans outside the TAR, has by far the highest number of monks. Yunnan, with the smallest Tibetan population, has the smallest monk population.[23] Within Tibetan-designated prefectures in Sichuan and Qinghai, there seems to be a higher rate of monks in prefectures with higher percentages of Tibetans in the population. Thus, the areas where Tibetans are in the minority may have a disproportionately lower percentage of monks.

The sources we used are based entirely on available Chinese records. If we compare these with the records of the Department of Religion and Culture of the Tibetan government-in-exile, we find large discrepancies. Tibetan records indicate that there were as many as 5,542 monasteries on the Tibetan Plateau before 1958. Of these, 3,897 were located outside the present-day borders of the TAR.[24] The total monk population was 565,478 according to the same source, of which 449,596 were living outside the

TABLE 2. Tibetan Population and Monks by Province, 1990s

Provinces with Tibetan areas	Tibetan population in Tibetan areas	Percent of population	Monks in Tibetan areas	Percent of monks	Percent monks in Tibetan population
Sichuan	1,035,062	47.3	62,982	66.5	6.1
Qinghai	718,428	32.8	23,209	24.5	3.2
Gansu	332,461	15.2	7,076	7.5	2.1
Yunnan	104,422	4.8	1,508	1.6	1.4
TOTAL	2,190,373	100	94,775	100	4.3

present-day borders of the TAR. In comparison, for all areas outside the TAR (including areas that are not designated Tibetan), we found references to a total of 2,068 monasteries and 190,500 monks in the Chinese sources mentioned above. It is impossible to explain the discrepancies between these figures without more detailed information from Chinese and Tibetan records that were unavailable to us during our research, and for the time being we can only note the differences.

MONASTERIES AND FUNDING

During the Democratic Reforms campaign and the Cultural Revolution, the state confiscated monastic property and the personal property of monks. We have detailed information from one county in Ngaba Prefecture about the return of property during the implementation of new religious policies in the early 1980s. An unpublished document states that the local government conducted a thorough investigation of confiscated property and found twenty-three misjudged cases.[25] According to this document, the government subsequently paid ¥8,762 (US$1,070) to the people who had lost property worth a total of ¥988,303 (US$120,000). In other words, the compensation was merely symbolic. In addition to individual monetary compensation, the government returned landholdings to monastic communities. The same document claims that in Dzoge (Ruo'ergai) County, the government returned 1,630 *mu* of land (15 *mu* equal 1 hectare) to the monasteries, although monastic land totaled 1,856 *mu* prior to the Democratic Reforms. According to the document, this work ended in 1986.

The redistribution of land has been a complicated issue for a number of monasteries. It appears that the authorities may be reluctant to return the fields because they fear that monasteries will again become too powerful. At the same time, the monasteries must be self-sufficient, and in many cases it may be necessary to cultivate fields in order to generate income and provide for the monks. For example, Rabgya Monastery, located on the border between two TAPs—Golok and Tsolho (Hainan)—was one of the major Gelugpa monasteries in the Amdo region, with 50 tulkus and 2,700 monks before 1958. It was a rich monastery, with large agricultural estates, but all the fields were confiscated when Democratic Reforms were implemented in the area. Since it reopened in 1980, Rabgya has been a poor monastery. We were told that the government decided to return the monastic fields, but since the borders of two counties and prefectures now cut across the land, it has been impossible to reach an agreement on ownership. At the time of our visit, Rabgya Monastery was considered to be on the Machen (Maqin) County side of the border, in Golok TAP, although it traditionally belonged to Gepa Sumdo (Tongde) County, in Tsolho TAP. Caught in the middle of this dispute, the monastery is considering seeking a legal solution through the courts.

Chinese authorities claim that the government channeled financial support for rebuilding monasteries through county religious affairs departments during the 1980s and early 1990s; however, our interviews on-site indicate that local people and pilgrims provided the vast majority of funding. In most monasteries, the monks we interviewed, who were often senior monks or were working for management committees, denied receiving government funds for rebuilding. While it may of course be in the interests of monasteries to plead poverty to foreign visitors, we also suspect that government claims about its funding of monastic reconstruction are often exaggerated. We are therefore convinced that local people and pilgrims indeed provided the majority of reconstruction funds and the government contribution has been comparatively insignificant. For instance, according to the Kandze TAP Religious Affairs Department, 374 out of a total of 515 monasteries received financial support for repairs or reconstruction. This support appears to have been granted during the 1980s.[26] Nonetheless, during visits to several of the larger monasteries along the Northern Road in Kandze TAP, we asked about government support for restoration and in most cases were told that support had been nonexistent or only of symbolic amounts.

A study surveying eighteen monasteries (including Derge Sutra Printing Academy) was published in the United States in 1992 and gives exact

FIG. 2.1. The Assembly Hall of Dechenling Monastery in Dechen County was still under construction at the time of our visit in 1998. Adjacent to the monastery was a small boarding school where all subjects were taught in Tibetan.

amounts of government support.[27] The information differs from that obtained in our interviews, which states, in general, that the reconstruction and restoration of monasteries were financed by local volunteers as a form of "religious work" (Ch: *zongjiao yiwu*), for merit, at the monasteries. Lhagang Monastery (Ch: Tagong Si), a Sakyapa monastery in Dartsedo (Kangding) County, reportedly received ¥260,000 (US$33,000) altogether,[28] while our information indicates that it received no support for restoration work. Similarly, we were informed that Kandze Monastery, one of the important Gelugpa monasteries located in Kandze County, received only ¥10,000–20,000 (US$1,270–2,500), although the report claims it received ¥440,000 (US$55,000).[29] Dzogchen Monastery (Ch: Zhuqing Si), in Derge (Dege) County, is an important Nyingmapa mother monastery for approximately 300 Nyingmapa monasteries throughout the Tibetan areas and even in Nepal. The study reports that the monastery received ¥20,000 (US$2,500), which was "hardly enough," given the fact that it spent ¥300,000 (US$38,000) to make a gold-covered stupa (*chörten*),[30] but according to our information, the monastery received nothing. It was still in a rather dilapidated state in 2000. The cost of rebuilding these monasteries was covered mostly by the village population and pilgrims, especially in the forms of unpaid labor and

FIG. 2.2. A nunnery in Kandze. The nuns were working hard to build new living quarters.

donated building materials, funds for basic construction work, and wood-carving and interior decoration.

In Qinghai, we received numerous similar reports that the expense of rebuilding monasteries was borne almost entirely by local communities. In Malho TAP, for instance, government officials reported that local people did all construction work themselves. Funding and materials were provided by the local people, while the government supplied only trees for the beams. As in the other areas we visited, enormous amounts of voluntary work, donations of building materials, and local funding were necessary for rebuilding monasteries. When we consider the standard of living and average income levels in these areas, the resources spent on reconstructing monasteries are quite incredible. One county government in Tsochang (Haibei) TAP claimed that local people spent more than ¥10,000,000 (US$1,220,000) on rebuilding monasteries in that county alone. In addition to the funds, unpaid labor represents a very large contribution toward the rebuilding of monasteries and religious sites.

Although local people and pilgrims supplied the great majority of funds, in a few cases benefactors from outside the community also donated large sums of money to help rebuild monasteries and provide facilities for monks and nuns. Government funding accounts for a very small percentage of total costs, with the exception of a few select monasteries singled out as tourist attractions and cultural relic sites. Kumbum Monastery is one of these exceptions. Because it has been a high-profile tourist destination since the early 1980s, government agencies as well as private donors have supported its reconstruction. According to information from the Kumbum Monastery management and renovation committees, available at the monastery, the State Council in March 1962 listed Kumbum as one of China's foremost national, cultural, and historical sites. The committees further state that, in response to the proposal of the Qinghai provincial government, the State Council apportioned ¥37,000,000 (US$4,700,000) for the renovation of Kumbum for the period 1991–95. The provincial government reportedly allocated an additional ¥2,730,000 (US$340,000), while the Hong Kong businessman Shao Yifu (known outside China as Run Run Shaw) donated HK$3,000,000, equivalent to ¥3,180,000 (US$390,000). Renovation began in 1992 and continued until 1996. The management and renovation committees report that total expenditures on renovation work amounted to ¥43,000,000 (US$5,400,000). Nevertheless, daily maintenance of the monastery appears to be funded by contributions from visitors. According to our interviews, the most important sources of income in 1999 were ticket sales and parking fees.

In Tsolho and Jyekundo TAPs, we heard about several temples that had also received government funding: Jojo Lhakhang in Thriga (Guide) County, the Panchen Lama Memorial Stupa, and Wencheng Temple in Jyekundo County. We discovered that these three sites were somehow closely connected to the history of Chinese-Tibetan relations. None was classified as a monastery, and all had less than a handful of resident monks, who were living there as caretakers. All received pilgrims but were also considered tourist attractions. From the perspective of the authorities, we believe that these sites are considered significant because they exemplify the close historical ties between China and Tibet. Wencheng Temple, for instance, evokes the memory of the Chinese princess Wencheng, who married the Tibetan king Songtsan Gampo in the seventh century. Official Chinese histories often claim that this marriage marks the beginning of Chinese reign in Tibet.

We also found indications that monasteries with special connections to the lineage of the Panchen Lama may have had relatively easy access to government funding. Dzoge Monastery in Ngaba Prefecture is a good example. This is a branch monastery of Tashilhunpo Monastery in Shigatse, the seat of the Panchen Lama. According to the monks with whom we talked, the monastery had obtained ¥300,000 (US$38,000) for reconstruction from the prefectural government. We suspect that in the mid-1980s, before Chinese authorities started to fear the spread of separatism in Tibetan monasteries, the tenth Panchen Lama was able to generate financial support for certain monasteries. During this period, Chinese authorities were willing to aid in rebuilding a number of important monasteries and religious sites, and it was explicit government policy to gain the confidence of high-ranking religious figures as a means of promoting patriotism among the clergy and the Tibetan population at large. As the highest-ranking Gelugpa tulku who still lived in China, the tenth Panchen Lama played a very important role in this strategy.

By the late 1990s, authorities no longer sponsored the reconstruction of monasteries. During interviews, government officials stated that the current policy calls for monasteries to be self-sufficient. Government funding is granted only to repair damage caused by natural catastrophes such as earthquakes. According to the Sichuan Province Religious Affairs Department, monasteries were regarded by the authorities as "belonging to themselves, in charge of themselves, and responsible for their own repairs" (Ch: *shuyu ziji, fuze ziji, xiu ziji fu*).

The monks' needs are met through the monastery's common funds and contributions from their families. The monasteries have their own businesses and finances, and they also support each monk. We encountered various enterprises. One monastery had bought a small car for rental, others kept herds of yak and sold the butter by the *jin* (equivalent to a half-kilo), and several were operating small shops, where they sold everyday goods not related to religious life. One monastery we visited had its own clinic, which provided both income for the monastery and medical services for the community. Monks also earned money by conducting religious services at important events such as births, marriages, and deaths.[31]

Only a handful of the monasteries we visited or heard about charged entrance fees. Among these were Labrang Monastery, Kumbum Monastery, Gaden Songtseling Monastery in Gyelthang (Zhongdian) County, and Lhagang Monastery in Kandze TAP. The entrance fees were usually only

¥3–10 (US$0.35–1.25). Lhagang Monastery began charging entrance fees in March 2000, but the monks emphasized that the fee was for tourists, and pilgrims did not pay. Kumbum and Labrang Monasteries have charged fees for a number of years and were among the first monasteries to attract tourists, starting in the early 1980s. The fee introduced at Lhagang Monastery seems to be connected with recent plans to develop international tourism in Kandze TAP.

Another income source for monasteries is selling butter candles for pilgrims, who pay for the lighting of a prepared candle. In the monasteries we visited, the candles were generally ¥1 (US$0.12) each. At the Panchen Lama Memorial Stupa in Chabcha (Gonghe) County in Tsolho TAP, we were told that the sale of candles generated an income of ¥10–50 (US$1.25–6.35) per day. The butter candles were produced in Kumbum.

One interesting case is Jojo Lhakhang in Thriga County, also known as Little Jokhang. "Jo" in Tibetan refers to Sakyamuni Buddha, and Great Jokhang is the famous Jokhang Temple in Lhasa. The pilgrims, mainly from Amdo, come first to this site, stay for a while, and then continue on to Jokhang in Lhasa. They usually stay for three months and make a pilgrimage circuit every day. Jojo Lhakhang is administered by what locals consider its mother monastery, the nearby Gongba Monastery. Two or three monks from Gongba look after the temple and take care of the pilgrims. Every morning, the monks conduct a prayer ceremony and perform special recitations at the temple at the request of pilgrims or locals. Pilgrims paid ¥1 (US$0.12) per person per night for lodging. An average of 20–30 pilgrims stayed at the temple at any one time, and the monthly income is said to have been ¥700–800 (US$88–100). This money was spent on temple restoration work, new images, and butter for the lamps. We were informed that the total cost of the restoration was ¥1,000,000 (US$125,000), and that Qinghai Province had provided ¥11,000 (US$1,375) while villagers and pilgrims supplied the rest.

Monasteries are regarded as belonging to a particular village or group of villages, but nunneries do not have this kind of affiliation. The nunnery in Chentsa County, described as one of the largest in all the Tibetan areas, demonstrates one approach to funding. According to some of the nuns, they rebuilt the nunnery without help from the villagers or the government. The nuns' families helped, and the nuns went to the village to recite sutras or beg for food for the workers they hired. The nunnery had 50 *mu* of fields, which the women cultivated themselves. It was enough to ensure their sur-

vival, although they complained that they could not afford to invite outside scholars on such a limited budget.[32]

RELIGIOUS PRACTICE

The revival of monastic life in Tibetan areas is not just a question of how
many temples and prayer halls have been rebuilt and how many monks and
nuns have been admitted. The qualitative aspects of religious revival are more
important than these quantifiable conditions. What are the conditions for
the revival of ceremonies and rituals, arts and crafts, medical practice, printing, the transmission of teachings, and study programs within the various
branches of Buddhism and Bön, the Tibetan religion that predates Buddhism?

During our visits to Tibetan areas, we witnessed a variety of aspects of
religious practice that are connected to monastic life as well as to the popular beliefs of lay Tibetans. On numerous occasions, we observed lay
Tibetans making offerings at sites inside and outside of temples and monasteries. These included offerings of barley wine, *khata* (scarves), fruit, grain,
and money; lighting butter lamps; and burning juniper and incense sticks.
We saw Tibetans on pilgrimage and visiting the temples of the *yul lha* (territorial deities) to pray for a good harvest, burn incense, and offer grain and
barley wine.[33] As we drove over mountain passes, we saw pilgrims and trav-
elers throw *lungta,* small pieces of cloth or paper printed with "wind horse"
symbols, onto the roadside as prayers for good luck along the way. Prayer
flags and piles of *mani* stones, inscribed with mantras or prayers, placed at
mountain passes or sacred sites, were seen along the roads. In several places
in Qinghai, we saw large inscriptions (one of them reading "Om bodhisatva")
nicely spelled out in white stones on the mountainside. Tibetan dwellings,
including the brown, woven yak-wool tents of the nomads on the open grasslands, also regularly have prayer flags on the roofs. We observed a large number of stupas along the roads and visited some of them. In almost every area
we visited, we saw *labtse,* special sites, usually on a mountain pass, marked
by branches with prayer flags and set on a foundation of stones. In many
places, we also found offering sites for *tsa-tsa* (religious images made of clay).
In a village in Dartsedo County, Kandze TAP, we were able to observe the
production of *tsa-tsa* figures, with young and old, men and women, all participating in the work.

There are close ties between the monasteries and local villages. For
instance, we were told in several places that monks from local monasteries
go to neighboring villages to read scriptures at funerals and weddings and

FIG. 2.3. Tibetans from Dartsedo making *tsa-tsa* figures for offerings. The figures are made of molded clay, which is sun-dried and painted.

perform divination for people in their homes. During fieldwork, we also heard about public religious teachings held by tulkus or famous lamas. In Tawu (Daofu) County, Kandze, we saw a throne that had been newly built in an open space for public religious teachings near the town center. Workers at the site had just finished the cement platform and were decorating the throne in bright colors. We were told that the construction was sponsored by local Buddhists.

We also observed the use of religious sites by lay practitioners. Most of these worshipers were Tibetans, but some were members of other minorities or were Han. On a hillside above Gyelthang (Zhongdian) Town, in Dechen TAP, for example, we visited a temple that was being used as a place of worship by both Tibetans and other local Buddhists, although it was dedicated to the local mountain god.[34] Inside the temple, images and wall paintings in Chinese Buddhist style shared space with Tibetan-style frescoes. We arrived in the middle of an offering ceremony conducted by a Han family. Lit cigarettes and small bowls of food had been placed in a square formation on the porch of the temple, and one of the worshipers was performing recitations. At the end of the ceremony, everybody sat down to eat the dishes they had prepared and invited us to join them.

Nechung Dorjeling Monastery (Ch: Anjue Si) in Dartsedo, a Tibetan Buddhist monastery that belongs to the Gelugpa school, was undergoing heavy reconstruction during our visit in May 2000 and appeared to be popular among both Tibetans and Han. We saw elderly women spinning the large prayer wheel near its entrance. Inside, in a side chapel, an ancestral altar with black-and-white photos and offerings had been arranged according to Han ancestral worship practice. In another part of Dartsedo, across the street from the Khampa university, we found a small Chinese Guanyin temple with a local Han caretaker.[35] We were told that this temple had to close down during exam periods because too many students from across the street ran over to the temple to pray for good luck.

As we have seen, the monasteries and temples in these cultural border areas—such as in Gyelthang County in Dechen TAP, Dartsedo County in Kandze TAP, and Chabcha and Thriga Counties in Tsolho TAP—are places of worship for more than one local ethnic group. For example, Jojo Lhakhang, in Thriga County, is called Zhenzhu Si (Pure Pearl Temple) in Chinese. The names of the temple are connected to the different mythologies linked to the site. The "pure pearl" in its Chinese name relates to its construction, when ground pearl powder is said to have been mixed with clay to make its first images.[36] The Tibetan name Jojo links the temple with the Jokhang Temple in Lhasa, the most holy of the Gelugpa sites. Jojo Lhakhang is also classified as a Gelugpa site by local authorities. Nevertheless, during our visit in August 1999, plans for its altar, which was still under construction, called for representations from the four main branches of Tibetan Buddhism: Nyingmapa (represented by the Indian guru Padmasambhava), Kagyupa (represented by Atisha), Sakyapa (represented by Saban), and Gelugpa (represented by its founder Tsongkhapa).

"Sky burial" (Ch: *tianzang*)[37] still takes place at many locations, and Chinese burial customs are also practiced by Tibetans in some areas. For instance, in Tawu County, Kandze, we visited a graveyard known locally as the Tibetan graveyard, which is next to the Chinese martyrs' memorial site. Several of the Tibetan tombs had no inscriptions on the stones except for bilingual inscriptions of Chinese and Tibetan names. We saw the tomb of a Tibetan woman, buried in 1992, who had probably been married to a Han man. The Chinese inscription on her grave contained both her Chinese and her Tibetan name, the latter in brackets. The tombstone had been sponsored by her five children one year after her death, and their Chinese names were also inscribed on the stone.

We visited local villages at the feet of two important sacred mountains during our fieldtrips: Amnye Machen (Ch: Animaqing Shan or Maji Xueshan; T: a mye rma chen) in Qinghai and Kawa Kharpo (Ch: Meili Xueshan) in Yunnan. Every year, many pilgrims circumambulate these mountains. We were told by locals that 5,000–6,000 pilgrims from all over Tibet visit Kawa Kharpo every year. Amnye Machen, which stretches across central Golok, receives 1,000–2,000 pilgrims annually. It was officially reopened as a pilgrimage site in 1979. In an interview with the local tourist agency, we were told that about 100 foreign tourists also make the circuit every year.[38] The nine-day circumambulation of the mountain may be conducted clockwise (Tibetan Buddhist) or counterclockwise (Bön). The pilgrimage is especially important in a year of the horse, which occurs every twelve years, because, according to legend, the mountain first appeared in a horse year.

In a small village near the Amnye Machen pilgrimage trail, we visited an old man in his seventies, living in a simple house with his wife and their grandchildren. From this house, they had a view to the snow-capped ridge of Amnye Machen. He was the oldest man in the village. He could not write and knew no Chinese words, but he knew the local names of the mountain peaks and all the local myths. He told us that he had made several pilgrimages around the mountain before 1949, "perhaps twenty to thirty times," according to his own estimate. During the "closed" years before its reopening in 1978, nobody dared to go around the mountain. After 1978, he considered himself too old to make the pilgrimage again. In 1999, there were many pilgrims, and he thought the reason might have been that two local tulkus had recently passed away and their incarnations had not yet been found, so the locals did the pilgrimage to secure blessings for this process.

In addition to pilgrimage, traditional festivals have also been revived. We attended five such festivals during the summer of 1999, and three of them had a religious foundation. The most popular festival in Tsolho TAP is the Sixth Month Festival (Ch: Liuyuehui), which lasts for a week and takes place every summer during the sixth month of the traditional lunar calendar. Originally, people offered sacrifices to the local mountain gods and *yul lha*, seeking blessings for the harvest. Images of *yul lha* were made and brought (and thereby invited) to each home to give blessings. During the festival, the throne of the *yul lha* was brought out of the shrine to receive offerings and respect. This is still being done in the *yul lha* temple in Thriga, where we participated in the festival. Local Tibetans and Han gathered in the temple to give offerings and receive divinations.

In the past, the Sixth Month Festival in Thriga included horse races, song contests, and picnics as well as a trade fair. Song and dance contests are still part of the Thriga festival. Two singing spots were popular at the festival we visited. One was equipped with a stage and a microphone, as for karaoke, and all songs were in Chinese. The other, on the outskirts of the festival grounds, was obviously more popular among the young local Tibetans, who were dressed in their best outfits. Singers sat on the ground, surrounded by onlookers. Pepsi-Cola and local beer had replaced the traditional barley wine, and a bottle of each was passed from one singer to the next, alternating between men and women. Traditionally, this was a popular way for young Tibetan farmers to flirt and perhaps meet someone to marry, and the songs are both romantic and humorous.

Athough the *yul lha* tradition persists and singing contests are still held, the Thriga festival is now mainly a weeklong trade fair. In neighboring Malho, however, a Sixth Month Festival, the Lurol (T: *klu rol*)[39] Festival, is celebrated in a traditional manner in all the villages in the Rebkong (Tongren) area.[40] As in the Thriga festival, the *yul lha* is brought out to receive offerings, and all the young men and women of the village perform elaborate dances. Lurol ceremonies in Rebkong take place in special community houses called *lu khang* (T: *klu khang*), which are managed by the elder men in the village. We were told that opinions on whether the ceremonies are for the mountain (i.e., the mountain god), the dragon (T: *klu*),[41] or the army differ from village to village.

According to participants at the festival in Sagyel village, the ceremonies are Bön because they used to include blood (i.e., animal) sacrifices. Nowadays, no animals are sacrificed, but young men still participate in traditional body piercing during dancing sessions. They pierce themselves with small spears: twelve on each shoulder, one through both cheeks, and one on top of the head. A medium, who is believed to be possessed by the *yul lha,* plays a central part in the ceremonies. The role of medium is hereditary. During the three-day ceremonies, the medium goes into a trance several times a day, directing the dancers and making offerings of liquor, grain, milk, flowers, and fire. The medium in Sagyel was a young man in his twenties.

In addition to such popular religious festivals, often associated with ter-

FIG. 2.4. The Lurol Festival in Rebkong, Malho. The senior men of the village gather at the offering place for the final stage of the three-day ceremony. The village medium makes the offerings in a state of trance. In the courtyard below, the young men and women of the village perform their dances.

ritorial deities, a number of religious festivals also take place within the monasteries. In several of the monasteries we visited, we received lists in Tibetan of the religious festivals celebrated during the year according to the traditional lunar calendar. We attended one such festival in Kumbum Monastery, where we saw a giant *thanka*—an embroidered or painted silk image of a deity—at the *gyegu* (ceremonial display of *thanka* on a slope or a hillside) and *'cham* (masked ritual dances performed by monks).

Most monasteries appeared to keep a strict yearly schedule of festivals, although several mentioned that they did not have enough monks to conduct the ceremonies in the correct manner. Still, we observed and received information about a number of revived monastic traditions, including the

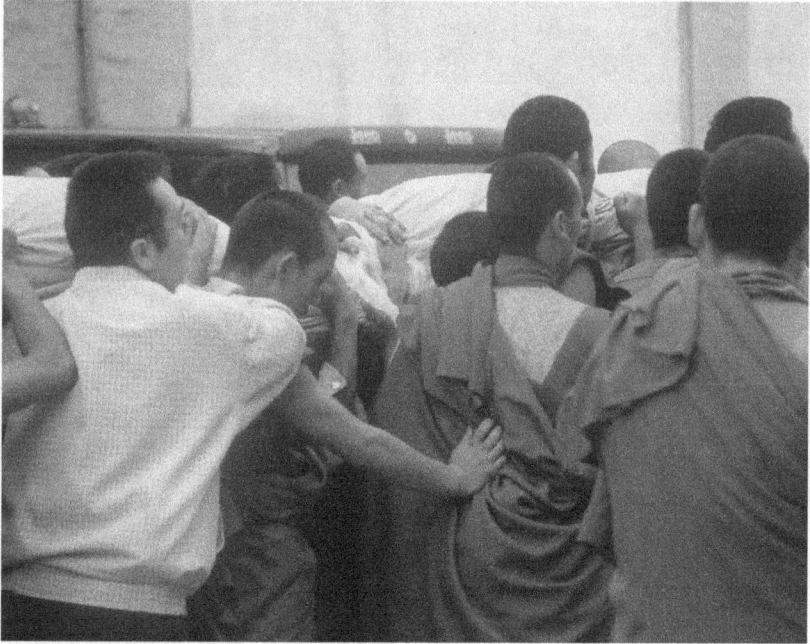

FIG. 2.5. A procession of monks and pilgrims carrying the giant *thanka* at Kumbum Monastery.

making of butter sculpture, *torma* (small barley-flour figures for religious rituals), and mandalas. We even observed a senior monk performing divination in one monastery.

Monasteries play a significant role in the preservation of ancient texts. For instance, Kumbum Monastery in Qinghai has a large collection of Tibetan religious texts, one of the most comprehensive in the Tibetan areas.[42] Another large collection of ancient texts can be found in Labrang Tashikhyil Monastery. In 1982, the State Council declared Labrang Tashikhyil a national center for the preservation of antiquities. According to a Xinhua news report, since 1984 the government has spent more than ¥1,000,000 (US$125,000) building a new storehouse for Buddhist scriptures in Labrang. Xinhua also stated that a researcher with the Kanlho Prefecture archives bureau reported a total of 65,000 scriptures at Labrang, the largest collection of its kind in China.[43] The collection includes Buddhist teachings and books on medicine, craftsmanship, history, biography, astrology, and numerics.

Woodblock printing has been revived in a number of monasteries. We observed monks printing sutras and other Buddhist texts, and traditional

FIG. 2.6. Displaying the giant *thanka* at Kumbum Monastery. The audience includes Western Buddhists as special guests, Tibetan pilgrims, overseas Chinese, local Hui and Han, and a few Western tourists. Kumbum is located in an area inhabited largely by Hui Muslims.

scroll texts were being sold in bookstores and markets. There are large printing academies for religious texts in Lhasa, Labrang, and Derge. The Derge Sutra Printing Academy in Derge County, Kandze TAP, is the largest. Derge also has the largest collection of traditional printing blocks (270,000) and more than 1,000 woodblocks of Buddhist images and mandalas.[44] We visited the academy in May 2000 and were informed that 70 percent of traditional Tibetan literature was available there. The printing academy survived the Cultural Revolution, but a large number of woodblocks were lost or destroyed. Since the mid-1990s, however, large private donations have funded the recarving of several of the missing blocks.

The complete Kangyur and Tengyur have been printed in recent versions

FIG. 2.7. Derge Sutra Printing Academy, Kandze. Handmade paper is soaked in water to prepare for the printing process.

in China, yet some monasteries had received their version of the texts as donations from overseas Buddhist societies. In Golok TAP, we visited a monastery where the monks did not dare to use the precious gift, a gold-edged Nyingmapa version in 118 volumes (produced in the United States and printed in 1980), and kept the texts wrapped in red silk and in their original boxes on the shelves of the main assembly hall. Instead, they used a cheaper factory-produced edition for their ceremonies.[45]

Several of the monasteries we visited displayed mainly new *thanka* paintings in their assembly halls, since most of their old ones had been destroyed. In other monasteries, old *thanka* had been hidden away during the persecutions and were being returned to their original sites. For instance, in Taling, also known as Tashi Chodanling (Ch: Chalang), Monastery in Dari County, Golok TAP, we counted ninety old *thanka* in the main assembly hall as well as an interesting collection of old gilded deities and Buddhas inlaid with precious stones. Rebkong-area artists had created all the new frescoes and *thanka* paintings. At the time of our visit, a group of monks was preparing scriptures to be inserted and sealed in newly produced images, to consecrate them. The images had not been made in the monastery.

When we visited monasteries, we tried to find out who was responsible for the decorations and carpentry work. We learned that skilled artists and workers were concentrated in a few areas and that some areas did not have local workers who could reconstruct monasteries. For example, all the monasteries we visited in Kandze TAP were rebuilt by local carpenters and decorated by local artists. Kandze is rich in timber resources, so wooden construction appears to be a common craft in the area, and it was unusual to import workers from outside the prefecture. Derge County was considered a cultural center in Kham.[46] Artists from Derge were sometimes hired by villagers in other areas to create decorations for monasteries. In Nechung Dorjeling, located in the center of Dartsedo Town, we talked with one such artist from Derge. He had been hired to make clay models, later to be carved in wood, for the heads of new pillars.

Other areas imported skilled labor. In Ngaba Prefecture, artists were brought in from Rebkong in Malho TAP, Qinghai. Most of the Qinghai monasteries we visited had invited artists from Rebkong or from Labrang in Gansu. In general, most monasteries reported that artists from one of these two places, and in particular from Rebkong, had done the artwork, although local villagers usually took care of construction. Interestingly, we were told in several places that Han craftsmen from neighboring provinces such as Gansu and Shaanxi had supplied the woodcarving.

One village we visited in Golok had hired a Rebkong-educated artist to supervise the construction work.[47] This artist told us that it would take less than two months to construct and decorate the small temple. The artist masterminded the decoration and selected the images for the temple, and workers would then make the building and do the woodcarving. When we visited the site, artist and villagers were in the process of deciding which religious images to place in the temple. The villagers said that if they used clay figures, they could produce them locally, but if they wanted images in bronze or other materials, they would have to import them from Derge County.

Golok and Jyekundo TAPs in Qinghai have close connections with Ngaba and Kandze Prefectures in Sichuan. Printed Buddhist texts and gilded metal images were often imported to this region of Qinghai from Derge County. Gilded images apparently were difficult to make in many areas and were often transported for long distances. Along the main road near Matö (Maduo) County in Golok, we saw a whole truckload of brass gilded images, enough to decorate several altars, that had overturned, and all the images and roof decorations were spread out on the ground.

MONASTIC EDUCATION

Monasteries were the academies of the former Tibetan world, and monastic education was the traditional type of education available in Tibetan areas. The first Buddhist monastery in Tibet, Samye (T: *bsam yas*), was established in 779. With the development of the Gelugpa school in the fifteenth century, monastic education was formalized and scholasticism was revitalized within the older traditions as well as in Bön monasteries.

Before the 1950s, monks made up an estimated 25 percent of the male population.[48] A young boy usually entered the monastery under the guidance of a senior monk, often a relative. At first, he was a *genyen* (T: *dge bsnyen*), or candidate monk, but after a period of instruction in reading, writing, and recitation, he could advance to the level of *getsul* (T: *dge tshul*), or novice. At this stage, the monk took a vow of celibacy and commitment to a religious life. Further training, usually at one of the larger monasteries, led to the level of *gelong* (T: *dge slong*), or fully ordained monk. Within the Gelugpa tradition, monks could undertake higher studies leading to the degree associated with the title of *geshe,* or master.

Nunneries (T: *ani dgonpa*) were organized in much the same way as monasteries (T: *dgonpa*), but they were often subordinate branches of a head monastery led by a *khenpo* (abbot). Nuns could engage in studies, but they could not become fully ordained, and the higher stages of religious training were inaccessible to them.

Although monastic education was in theory accessible to most monks, not every monk chose to become a "reader" (*pechawa*)[49] and follow a study program. In the three great Gelugpa monasteries of Lhasa (Sera, Drepung, and Ganden), approximately 25 percent of the monks were formerly engaged in the philosophical study program, a curriculum that usually took about twenty years.[50] In Sera Me (T: *sera med*) College, 29 percent of the monks were readers.[51] These great centers of learning attracted monks from the entire Tibetan Plateau as well as other areas influenced by Tibetan Buddhism, including Ladakh, Nepal, Mongolia, and the Mongolian areas of the Soviet Union such as Buryat and Kalmuck. Outside of Ü-Tsang, only Kumbum and Labrang Tashikhyil Monasteries were comparable in size and importance as scholarly centers within the Gelugpa tradition. Nevertheless, many of the smaller monasteries also offered study programs in philosophy and logic and served as centers for the study of literature, grammar, handwriting, and traditions such as painting, sculpture, ritual music, 'cham, chanting, astronomy, calendar calculation, and medicine.

Tibetan language is still taught as a basic subject in the monasteries, and all further studies are conducted in Tibetan. At present, some parents prefer to send their children, particularly sons, to study in a monastery rather than in a school, for several reasons. For many devout believers, sending a son to the monastery is a form of offering that will bring merit to the entire family. People also value the traditional knowledge upheld by monasteries. In addition, a student's future is economically secure due to common monastic funds, although most monks rely on financial support from their families as well. Compared with monastic schooling, public education represents a heavy financial burden, and the returns in terms of employment opportunity are often questionable.

Reports from nongovernmental organizations (NGOs) on religious repression in Tibet suggest that there have been restrictions on the reestablishment of "monastic colleges" (T: dratsang), the study centers of larger monasteries.[52] During interviews, we received general comments about problems with the authorities and specific information about limitations on the number of students in monastic colleges. Still, according to monks and monastic leaders we interviewed, many traditional colleges have been reestablished in major monasteries over the past twenty years.

In Dechen TAP, for instance, at least two Gelugpa monasteries—Gaden Songtseling,[53] the largest in the prefecture, and Dhondrupling, the largest in Dechen County—provided some kind of monastic education. We were informed that both these monasteries taught logic, debate, and writing. We visited Gaden Songtseling, which, according to the information we received there, has eight monastic colleges, with three of the teachers holding geshe degrees.

The largest monastery in Malho TAP, Qinghai, is Rogwo Gönba Dechen Chökorling (T: rong bo dgon chen bde chen chos 'khor gling), situated in the county seat of Rebkong County.[54] At the time of our visit, it had about 430 monks and 10 tulkus.[55] Grammar, Buddhist logic, philosophy, and medicine were taught in three monastic colleges: Thösam Nampar Gyalbeling[56] (350 monks), Sangnga Dargyeling[57] (60 monks), and Eba Chökhorling[58] (20 monks).

At the time of our visit, Kumbum Monastery had four monastic colleges, for the study of philosophy, kalachakra (wheel of time), medicine, and tantra. We were informed that 30 geshe stayed in the monastery, teaching about

200 monks. Arts taught in Kumbum included *'cham* performance and butter sculpture. In Rabgya Monastery, another large Gelugpa monastery in Qinghai, we were informed that six monastic colleges had been reopened.

Labrang Tashikhyil in Kanlho TAP also offers monastic studies leading to a *geshe* degree. According to Li An-che's study, from 1938 to 1941 there were six monastic colleges in Labrang.[59] The largest was the college of Exoteric Buddhism, Thösamling (T: *thos bsam gling*), with 3,000 monks. At the time of our visit, approximately 1,000 monks attended this college, while in the other five colleges, there were no great changes in the numbers of monks compared to Li An-che's study.[60] In 1999, Labrang had about 1,200 monks and 28 tulkus. In addition, 48 tulkus from other monasteries in Kanlho were staying at Labrang to study. Studies currently available include the five main doctrines within the sutra[61] and the four tantric scriptures, on action, behavior, meditation, and supreme meditation. There were 20 monks in Labrang who held the title of *geshe,* and about two new monks obtained a *geshe* degree annually. According to local sources, about 120 monks in Labrang were studying for a degree in 1999.

The monasteries mentioned so far are all Gelugpa monasteries. We have less data on the other branches of Tibetan Buddhism and Bön religion. In Golok, however, we received some interesting information about the Jonangpa tradition, a rare branch of Buddhism that originally had its seat in the Jonang Monastery in central Tibet. Golok is the only place in Qinghai where one can find Jonangpa monasteries. According to written sources, there were seven Jonangpa monasteries and 549 Jonangpa monks in the prefecture in 1994.[62] The Qinghai Ethnic Affairs Commission reported that as of 1996 the province had nine Jonangpa monasteries and 872 monks. In an interview with Jonangpa monks in 1999, we were told that there were a total of forty-four Jonangpa monasteries, including monasteries in all the Tibetan areas and even some abroad.[63] One of the monasteries in Gade runs a Buddhist school for Jonangpa religious practice. We were told that as of 1999, this monastery had given sixteen three-year courses. Between 30 and 108 monks participated in each course, and the monastery had trained about 1,000 monks so far. Some monks stay on for additional courses, while some continue their practice as hermits in the mountains. The students may attend up to five courses (fifteen years of study).

In Malho TAP, we visited a Bön monastery and were told that the monks regularly practice debate and also have a printing house where they keep woodblocks for the Dzogchen text. Four of the monks had studied at a major Bön monastery in Ngaba Prefecture and returned to act as teachers. Another two monks from this monastery were studying at a private school in a neighboring prefecture, where the students had access to computers. The two monks were planning to use the school's scanner to scan all the monastery's ancient texts, which could then be printed by computer.

In Kandze TAP, we were given surprisingly detailed information on the number of educated monks in the prefecture. In the prefecture's 515 monasteries, the religious affairs department had registered 7,663 lamas who had studied for at least six years in one of the three big Lhasa monasteries and another 35 *geshe* or *khenpo* who had studied for nine years or more. If this information is reliable, Kandze has quite a few educated teachers.

In Kandze we were also informed about a number of newly established Buddhist institutes. The Kandze Prefecture Religious Affairs Department provided details about nine such institutes, mainly established by local tulkus or *khenpo*. The list of names and locations indicates that these institutes are often located next to monasteries. Through interviews, we learned that they accept as students monks from all Buddhist branches, even Bönpo monks, as long as they are at least eighteen years old. We visited two of the institutes, which were located apart from monasteries and were referred to locally as Nyingmapa institutes. We were told, however, that these institutes taught basic Buddhism without sectarian biases, which meant that monks from all traditions were accepted as students. Classifying an institute by a particular Buddhist order identifies the order of the founder. The two institutes were both sponsored by Nyingmapa religious leaders and therefore were classified as Nyingmapa. We confirmed through interviews that those who adhered to other traditions also studied there—one of the institutes even reported 10 percent Bön students—but in both monasteries, 60–70 percent of the students were Nyingmapa. Students came from all over the Tibetan areas, including the TAR and a few from Hong Kong. Study and lodging were usually free, but students supplied their own clothes and food. The subjects taught included Tibetan language and grammar, poetry, Buddhist logic, Sanskrit, astrology, and Tibetan medicine. One of the institutes we visited also taught Chinese language on a voluntary basis. None of the schools we visited reported that they taught politics, as do provincial Buddhist colleges (described later in this chapter).

It is difficult to say why Buddhist institutes such as these are becoming so popular, but we assume that it is probably much more difficult to obtain permission to establish a monastery than an institute. It may be impossible to set up a new monastery where none existed before the Democratic Reforms campaign.

Although a great effort has been made to revive religious traditions, many monasteries today suffer from the lack of competent teachers. Monks and nuns mentioned this problem in many of our interviews. We were informed that there was a shortage of teachers, especially in tantric studies, even in larger Gelugpa monasteries, while elderly monks in smaller monasteries complained that they were not sufficiently knowledgeable to act as teachers for the young monks. We were frequently told that teachers had to be invited from other monasteries, or that the monks engaged only in self-study.[64] We encountered cases in which the reconstruction of buildings and monuments was impressive but debating yards were locked up and reportedly used only on special occasions, when a *geshe* visited the monastery. Students did not have the opportunity to practice debate on a regular basis.

During the late 1950s and 1960s, the educated monastic elites experienced serious persecution that often led to imprisonment in labor camps and penitentiaries. The death toll was high. Among those who were not imprisoned, a large number escaped to India and Nepal. During the years from about 1957 to the early 1980s, monastic education was unavailable, and in the meantime, a generation of teachers died of old age. The combination of all these factors has led to a serious lack of teachers in Tibetan monastic institutions. The less populated branches of Buddhism and Bön may have experienced particular difficulty in keeping religious traditions alive and transmitting oral teachings that were known only by a few masters in each generation.

Tibetan refugees in India reestablished some of the more important monasteries in India, such as the three great monasteries Sera, Drepung, and Ganden; Nechung, the seat of the state oracle; and Namgyal, formerly located at the Potala Palace. Prominent lamas and religious leaders within the Kagyupa, Nyingmapa, and Sakyapa traditions also established monasteries in India.[65] These have become centers of learning attracting Tibetans in India, Buddhists in general, and, to an even greater extent, monks and nuns from the Tibetan side of the border. These Tibetans have been crossing the Himalayas in substantial numbers, not only because of political persecution but because they believe their chances to study and gain access to qualified teachers are much better in India than in their native Tibetan areas. In fact, during the 1990s, the majority of monks in Tibetan monasteries in India were recent arrivals from Tibet.[66]

It is difficult, if not impossible, to make a valid comparison of the quality of monastic education in Tibetan monasteries prior to 1958 and during the 1980s and 1990s. The best we can do is to discuss the available information about the differences between monastic education in monasteries in

Tibetan areas and in Tibetan settlements in India, where monasticism has had a chance to flourish. According to a study of Tibetan monasteries in India conducted in the early 1990s, many of the monks who escaped from Tibet stated that their main motivation for studying at a monastery in India was to return to Tibet in order to teach in their local monasteries after graduation.[67] These monks further expressed the need to restore or develop their monasteries in Tibet and heighten the level of education. Many also explained that the monasteries and their traditions were in danger of being eradicated in Tibet in the present situation and that they wished to contribute toward maintaining and strengthening these traditions.[68] This information indicates that the monastic education available in Tibetan monasteries in India is of a higher quality than the education available in Tibetan monasteries in China. Other reports make the same point, claiming that the new arrivals from Tibet have a much lower level of knowledge compared to the monks who have grown up in exile and received their monastic education in Tibetan monasteries in India.[69]

As noted above, during the 1990s, new arrivals from Tibet constituted the majority of monks in Tibetan monasteries in India. However, there are indications that in major Nyingmapa monasteries in India such as Namdrölling, compared to Sakyapa and Gelugpa monasteries, newcomers from Tibet are far fewer in number. The explanation offered is that large numbers of Nyingmapa monks were being recruited into the Serthar Buddhist Institute (Ch: Wuming Foxueyuan) in Kandze.[70] The crackdown on this institution in 2001 presumably changed this situation.

CONTROLLING THE TULKUS

Tulkus play a key role in Tibetan society as informal leaders, not only in the monasteries but in society at large. As in earlier times, many Tibetans have great respect for tulkus, which is why they are often called upon to settle disputes in the community. People generally follow the advice of tulkus and look up to them with reverence as spiritual and secular guides and masters.

In the late 1950s, the recognition of tulkus was prohibited, but in the 1980s, tulkus who had been recognized before the Cultural Revolution were again acknowledged and new tulkus eventually were recognized. Chinese authorities also started to give tulkus official titles and positions in the People's Congresses and Chinese People's Political Consultative Committees (CPPCC) at all administrative levels, as leaders of the local Buddhist Associations, and sometimes even as government officials. It appears that these positions have been granted in a very controlled manner. For instance, in Dzoge County in Ngaba, a number of local religious figures were appointed to various official posts, apparently all in 1987.[71] Many tulkus now earn government salaries through their various official positions. As a result, a number of tulkus no longer stay in their monasteries but live in townships in order to fulfill their political obligations.

In 1992, the seventeenth Karmapa, Ugyen Trinley, in exile in India since January 2000, became the first tulku to be officially approved by both the Chinese central government and the Dalai Lama. The Karmapa is the highest-ranking tulku of the Karma Kagyupa, a separate order of Tibetan Buddhism. The Kagyupas have always settled the matter of finding new tulkus themselves, and the Dalai Lama or other leaders of the Gelugpa apparently were never involved in discovering a new Karmapa. The Dalai Lama's acceptance of Ugyen Trinley therefore was not a requirement for the Kagyupas. Recognition of a new Panchen Lama is different, however, as he is considered the second most important tulku of the Gelugpa order. Traditionally, the Dalai Lama is responsible for confirming each reincarnation of the Panchen Lama and vice versa. The current Panchen Lama will thus presumably play an important role in the recognition of the next Dalai Lama. Since the eighteenth century, the Chinese have promoted the Panchen Lama as a rival of the Dalai Lama and used him to advance Chinese interests in Tibet.

Since the Dalai Lama went into exile in 1959, no tulku in Tibet has been more important than the tenth Panchen Lama. After spending more than a decade under house arrest, the tenth Panchen Lama reappeared in the 1980s as an advocate of religious revival and a great source of inspiration for those who sought to rebuild monasteries and religious sites. The importance of the Panchen Lama became clear to us during fieldwork when we were told repeatedly that local monasteries were rebuilt after being visited in 1986 by the tenth Panchen Lama or on his advice. After the death of the tenth Panchen Lama in 1989, recognition of his successor became a major conflict between the Dalai Lama and his government-in-exile and the Chinese leadership. The search for a new Panchen Lama was conducted by a party from his monastery, Tashilhunpo, in Shigatse, according to tradition. However, the State Council soon announced the following criteria: "First, the principle of patriotism; second, the principle that the Tashilhunpo Monastery is in charge; third, the principle that the search must be carried out in China; fourth, the principle of approval by the central authorities; and fifth, the principle that the installation ceremony and training take place in Tashil-hunpo Monastery."[72]

In the initial stages, Chinese authorities agreed that the search party could communicate with the Dalai Lama. However, when the Dalai Lama announced in May 1995 the recognition of Gedhun Chökyi Nyima as the eleventh Panchen Lama, Chinese authorities rejected the candidate and arrested a number of those involved in the search, including the leader of the party, the high-ranking tulku Chadrel Rinpoche. Six-year-old Gedhun Chökyi Nyima and his parents were also taken into custody and kept under house arrest at an unidentified location. Amnesty International and Tibet support groups have described the boy as the youngest political prisoner in the world. His fate has been brought up in bilateral discussions by a number of foreign delegations to China. Despite this, nobody has been allowed to meet the boy or his parents, and there have even been rumors that he may have died in a prison in Lanzhou, the capital of Gansu.[73]

In November 1995, a golden urn ceremony was conducted at Jokhang Temple in Lhasa, recognizing another candidate, Gyaltsen Norbu, as the Chinese-sanctioned eleventh Panchen Lama. According to Chinese authorities, the golden urn ceremony was supervised in the past by the *amban,* the representative of imperial China in Lhasa, for the purpose of selecting the new reincarnations of the Dalai Lama and the Panchen Lama. The Chinese cite this "historical fact," which is denied by Tibetan historians, as the most important evidence of imperial Chinese sovereignty in Tibet. The political intent of using the golden urn ceremony to identify the eleventh Panchen Lama is thus clear: to reaffirm Chinese authority in Tibet.

The search for a new tulku in present-day Tibetan areas is similarly conducted by a team of monks from the monastery where the tulku originated. However, all new tulkus must be approved by government authorities, usually at the provincial level. After the tulku is identified, the county religious affairs department applies to the prefectural government, provincial Ethnic Affairs Commission, and provincial government. The provincial government then confirms that the tulku is in accordance with tradition and that the determination conforms to the government's reincarnation policy, which includes detailed regulations on the methods of finding tulkus. We were informed in Qinghai that the Buddhist Association has agreed to these methods of approving tulkus.

Policy guidelines issued by the central government in 1991 state that "there can be reincarnates, but not all can reincarnate; these issues must be handled strictly."[74] According to one source, the provincial government in Qinghai has a committee that provides recommendations to the government on the approval of new tulkus and whether a particular tulku lineage is traditional. This committee consists of scholars and experts on Tibetan Buddhism, including several tulkus. This type of committee exists in several Tibetan areas. In some cases, the committee is administered directly by the provincial government or supervised by the Ethnic Affairs Commission, and in other cases, it is managed by the United Front (Ch: Tongzhanbu) department of the CCP. After the committee makes its recommendation, the government eventually grants its "approval" (Ch: *pizhun*) of the new tulku. This process may take several years.

A report from Ngaba Prefecture confirms the existence of explicit policies that aim to limit the number of tulkus. It states that during the 1990s, Sichuan Province authorities instructed the prefectural governments to decide on quotas for tulkus. Detailed information was collected on the number of monasteries that historically had tulkus. This source also states that the government policy to restrict the number of tulkus was implemented locally. In Ngaba Prefecture, authorities decided to allow only 149 tulkus in total: 3 for large monasteries, 2 for medium-size monasteries, and 1 for small monasteries.[75] During our interviews with prefecture-level religious affairs departments, we were never informed of monasteries with more than 3 tulkus in any area. As described by the prefectural officials we interviewed, the number of tulkus always ranged from 1 to 3. Only in a very few interviews, and always at the county level, did we receive information about more than 3 tulkus at any single monastery. Yet, in several cases, monks and other local sources we interviewed told us about larger numbers of tulkus, including tulkus living secular lives and holding political positions or even residing abroad.

The number of officially approved tulkus in Qinghai today appears to be less than half the number of the early 1950s. The Qinghai Province Ethnic Affairs Commission claims that there were 497 tulkus in the province as of 1996, whereas Pu Wencheng reports that there were 1,240 prior to 1958.[76] Local interviews indicated that many applications for approval of new tulkus were awaiting decisions from higher authorities. There is therefore reason to believe that the number of tulkus in both Qinghai and Sichuan is being tightly controlled. During our interviews, several local officials spoke of the need to control the recognition of new tulkus and the problem of having too many tulkus. According to government officials in one county in Qinghai, too many tulkus negatively affects economic development: "In the past there were too many tulkus. Religion has obstructed the development of Tibetan areas because the monasteries have no role to play in the development of the communities; they just use the resources of the local people. In addition large numbers of celibate monks impede population growth." This last statement is interesting, since it contradicts the idea that population growth needs to be limited, even in the minority areas.

In another interview, we were told that the quality of tulkus is more important than the quantity. According to yet another account, owing to the disorder of the Cultural Revolution, some people were incorrectly claimed as tulkus after their deaths. After 1980, the tenth Panchen Lama became aware of this problem, and one reason for the establishment of the Beijing Buddhist college, formally known as the High-Level Tibetan Buddhist Institute of China (Ch: Zhongguo Zangyuxi Gaoji Foxueyuan),[77] was to set up a clear rule of tulku lineages. The college was founded in 1987 and was headed by the tenth Panchen Lama until his death.

Government approval is not extended to all recognized tulkus. In Golok, for example, we learned that 9 tulkus were accepted, 18 awaited approval, and 101 were denied. We do not know anything about the fate of these so-called self-appointed tulkus,[78] but many are probably living in their monasteries and are recognized by their local communities.

The most important policy guideline on religion is Document 19, *The Basic Viewpoint and Policy on the Religious Question during Our Country's Socialist Period*, issued in March 1982, which states that CCP policy is to "foster a large number of fervent patriots in every religion who accept the leadership of the Party and government, firmly support the Socialist path, and safeguard national and ethnic unity." The document calls for establishing schools or seminaries to educate a new generation of clergy that "fervently love their homeland and support the Party's leadership and the Socialist system." These young patriotic religious professionals are meant to become the "mainstay ensuring that religious institutions follow the correct direction in their activities."[79]

In Tibetan areas, this policy has led to the establishment of one central and five province-level Buddhist colleges for the education of future monastic leaders, in particular the education of tulkus. Three colleges were established in 1985, at Nechung Monastery, in Lhasa (TAR); Labrang Tashikyil Monastery, in Sangchu County, Gansu; and Kumbum Monastery, in Huangzhong County, Qinghai. Since 1985, similar institutions have also been established in Kandze County, Sichuan, and at Gaden Songtseling Monastery, in Gyelthang County, Yunnan, although Sichuan Province Buddhist College has been without students since 1998. These institutions are all funded and managed by provincial and state-level religious affairs departments, which also regulate their "study method" (Ch: *xuexi fangshi*) and "teaching method" (Ch: *jiaoshi fangwei*).

The political education of tulkus and other monastic leaders in Buddhist colleges is a very important tool for controlling religious life in the Tibetan areas. This became clear to us after interviewing administrators and former staff of Gansu Province Buddhist College, Qinghai Province Buddhist College, and the High-Level Buddhist Institute of China, in Beijing. The scope of this program is quite ambitious. For instance, at the time of our visit to Gansu, 30–40 students were graduating from the Gansu Buddhist college each year to become leaders of their home monasteries. In comparison, only 2 students per year were obtaining the *geshe* degree at Labrang Monastery. Whereas the Gansu Buddhist college had 134 students, only about 120 monks were studying toward a degree at Labrang Monastery. In Qinghai, we learned that graduates from the Qinghai Buddhist college are now in most of the monasteries in the province and play an important role in the development of their monasteries. Qinghai Province Buddhist College previously had two types of classes, one for monks who were to become monastic administrators in their local monasteries and one for tulkus. Since 1999, the college has had only a tulku class. According to our sources, this is because government policy since 1998 has been to educate all new tulkus in these schools, which teach only basic Buddhism, regardless of the branch of Tibetan Buddhism to which they belong. However, in interviews with experts from the different branches, we were told that Jonangpa, Kagyupa, and Sakyapa monks and tulkus prefer to be educated within the monasteries of their own tradition rather than sent to a Gelugpa monastery for basic education. The Beijing Buddhist college also aspires to educate tulkus from all branches. As of 1999, nearly 300 tulkus had graduated from this institution, and we were told that the long-term goal was to educate all 1,700 tulkus in China here.

Curriculum is another important aspect of this educational program. In several cases, we were told explicitly that the purpose of the Buddhist college is to teach the monks to love their country and religion. In another interview, we heard that the colleges were set up according to the guidelines of Document 19. The curriculum includes Buddhist sutras and Tibetan language but also Chinese language and history, politics, and science. In the Qinghai Buddhist college, we were told that sutras and traditional culture constitute 70 percent of the curriculum; modernization and science, 15 percent; and politics, 15 percent. A new 1999 policy calls for the creation of a common curriculum in politics for all five province-level Buddhist colleges.

The Beijing Buddhist college provided the following description of its objectives in an introductory booklet: to safeguard the unity of the motherland, to strengthen national unity, and to advance Tibetan Buddhism. Politics reportedly makes up 10 percent of the curriculum. According to the staff, the students have realized that the activities of the Dalai Lama contradict the traditions of their religion, which gives a clear indication of the political purpose of educating tulkus in this institution. The Beijing Buddhist college plays a key role in the education of tulkus, publishing a number of textbooks that are used in province-level institutions and, as stated in one report, deciding which subjects are to be taught at province-level colleges. As mentioned above, the college appears to be involved in establishing clear rules determining which tulku lineages are eligible to receive government approval.

At the Sichuan Province Religious Affairs Department, we received information that Sichuan Province Buddhist College was currently not active due to lack of students. Although it was not considered closed, it had not functioned since 1998. The authorities were looking for a way to change this and suggested during our interview that perhaps the location—in Kandze County, Tuoba Township, Si'e Village—was not right.[80] We were also told that the Buddhist college might have been closed because "historical traditions" (Ch: *lishi xiguan*) place monastic colleges within monasteries rather than in separate institutes. Independent sources provided yet another explanation, that the Buddhist college was closed under pressure from the large Buddhist community in Serthar (Seda) County. With no province-level Buddhist college in Sichuan, students were permitted to attend a college in another province, such as Qinghai or Gansu.

During interviews in 1998, government officials in the Dechen Prefecture Religious Affairs Department reported that the central government had given permission to set up a Buddhist college at Gaden Songtseling Monastery near the prefecture seat of Dechen and that the Yunnan provincial government had allocated funds for the building. Information from interviews we conducted in August 1999 indicates that the Yunnan Province Buddhist College was then in the process of being set up at the monastery. Interestingly, Gaden Songtseling previously ran its own private school for monks in the prefecture. Monks from all Tibetan Buddhist traditions could join the school, which taught history, poetry, grammar, *uchen* and *ume* (printed and calligraphic Tibetan scripts), and *lamrim,* the study method introduced by Tsongkhapa, founder of the Gelugpa tradition. We were told that the school was open for three to four years only and received about ¥10,000 (US$1,250) annually from the government, but eventually it had to close because of insufficient funding.

The Buddhist college in Beijing admits tulkus from all the Tibetan areas and Inner Mongolia to two-year courses. Students receive financial support from the government. The staff reported that the standard of living is high, since this school is also a place for demonstrating a favorable policy toward tulkus. It was emphasized, however, that the tulkus must develop a new view of themselves as ordinary students and are expected to manage their own food and clothing rather than rely on caretakers. Visitors were also restricted. The headmaster explained that many villagers used to travel on pilgrimage to Beijing while the tulku from their local monastery attended the school. This could be quite problematic for school administrators, since the pilgrims expected to stay near their tulkus and the school did not have the facilities to house them. Consequently, they issued a regulation prohibiting villagers from following their local tulkus to Beijing.

MONASTIC CONTROL

While the late 1970s and early 1980s were marked by a sharp break in CCP religious policies and a relatively high degree of official tolerance for religious expressions, by 1987 this situation was changing. The year 1987 was in many respects a momentous one for the revival of religion in Tibetan areas. It may well characterize the peak of the tenth Panchen Lama's efforts to promote the reconstruction of monasteries and the revival of monastic education, as well as the teaching of Tibetan in schools, throughout the Tibetan areas. During 1986, he undertook extensive visits throughout the entire Tibetan Plateau, and in 1987, as his experiences were being evaluated, he was elected head of the newly opened Buddhist college in Beijing.

Meanwhile, in September 1987, the Dalai Lama made his first official visit to the United States, where he addressed the Congressional Human Rights Caucus and proposed a five-point peace plan for Tibet. The Dalai Lama's aim was to set the stage for negotiations with the Chinese government on the future status of Tibet. In response to Chinese authorities' angry denunciation of the Dalai Lama's proposal, twenty-one monks from Drepung Monastery near Lhasa initiated a demonstration in the Barkhor area of Lhasa. Police mistreatment of the monks during and after their arrest led to two large-scale demonstrations that became violent when authorities shot at the demonstrators and caused a number of casualties.

Under the conditions of Communist rule, religion has increasingly provided the symbols of a Tibetan collective identity.[81] Since the initial pro-independence demonstration in Barkhor, there have been a large number of protests. Although most occurred in Lhasa, other parts of the Tibetan Plateau were also affected, and monks and nuns were often actively involved in these events.[82] The authorities reacted by inaugurating a series of anti-splittist campaigns and imposed a one-year period of martial law in the TAR in March 1989.[83]

CCP leaders were alarmed by the large numbers of young monks and nuns entering monastic communities and the political protests in which some of them were involved. At the Third Work Forum on Tibet in 1994, leaders drew up a strategy to combat what was perceived as growing "splittism" (Ch: *fen lie zhuyi*). Since 1996, a campaign known as Patriotic Education has sought to extinguish all forms of political activism in the monasteries throughout the Tibetan areas. According to Tibetan exile sources, by the end of 1999, about twenty monasteries and nunneries had been closed down and 11,400 monks and nuns expelled as a result of this campaign, which focuses on condemning the Dalai Lama and educating monks and nuns in political ideology and patriotism. A number of monks and nuns were also arrested and imprisoned.

The Patriotic Education campaign has decreased the level of religious freedom in monasteries and nunneries. Of particular concern are reports that monks and nuns have been detained when they refuse to follow the Patriotic Education program, remove pictures of the Dalai Lama, or sign papers denouncing the Dalai Lama as a religious and political leader. The Chinese constitution protects freedom of belief but stipulates that religious practice must not lead to the splitting of ethnic minorities. Interpretation of this stipulation, however, is controlled completely by the CCP.

Because it is a politically sensitive issue, we did not explicitly study political education in monasteries and nunneries. However, government officials confirmed that political education was still taking place in Qinghai during the summer of 1999 as part of the Patriotic Education campaign. The content of the campaign in Qinghai was described as primarily the study of laws and regulations on religious practice and minority policy, but, as in the TAR, it also included denouncing the Dalai Lama.[84] During such campaigns, the enforcement of age limits seems to constitute a major source of dissension, and monks and nuns under eighteen years of age were ordered to leave the monasteries and nunneries. This has particularly affected the largest monasteries, such as Labrang and Kumbum. In April 1998, the campaign was initiated at Labrang, leading to the confinement of Gungthang Rinpoche, Labrang's second most senior lama.[85] At Kumbum, the campaign was one of the factors that led Agya Rinpoche, the former leader of Kumbum, to go into exile in 1998.[86]

It is difficult to know how many of those who were expelled during these campaigns have actually left their monasteries or nunneries, whether some have been able to return at a later date or join another monastery or nunnery, and what has happened to those who are unable to return. We do know, however, that being expelled is a traumatic experience. As one of our sources described it: "Once they have cut their hair it is very difficult, maybe impossible, to return to secular life." Many of those expelled find their situation so difficult that they choose to cross the Himalayas and join one of the monasteries or nunneries in the Tibetan refugee communities in India.

The authorities have sought to control the reconstruction of monasteries and the return of the clergy through various regulations. Document 19 states that religious sites in cities and famous historical sites should be restored, but indiscriminate building and repair of temples in rural villages must be guarded against, "lest we consume large sums of money, materials and manpower and thus obstruct the building up of material and spiritual Socialist civilization." Specific regulations on the management of religious sites were issued in 1994 (no. 145 Decree of the State Council). These declare that registration is necessary in order to establish a religious site, and those who plan to renovate buildings and set up enterprises must obtain permits. The regulations also state that every religious site should establish a management committee that will maintain the property and oversee its income.

In principle, all former monasteries and temples may reopen after applying for permission. Sometimes, prefectural and provincial authorities take years to process applications from county religious affairs departments. In the meantime, many sites are rebuilt without permission. Many officials we interviewed acknowledged this situation and informed us of unofficially reopened monasteries. For instance, in Jyekundo we were told that 30 out of a total of 169 monasteries had reopened illegally. Local officials appeared to have accepted the situation, and we did not hear of any cases in which they had taken action against these monasteries; however, the illegal reopenings could become problematic if there is a future campaign.

We likewise did not hear of any cases in which people were forced to stop rebuilding monasteries, or of regulations forbidding reconstruction, but we were informed in one county of a regulation that forbids the construction of two mosques in the same village. This prohibition was meant to prevent conflict between Muslims of different sects. Nevertheless, we saw several villages in the area with at least two mosques, and local authorities admitted that they were unable to enforce the regulation.

Every monastery that once existed may apply for permission to reopen. We were told of only a few places where the local people did not want to reopen a monastery, such as in Derge County, Kandze TAP, and in Gepa Sumdo County, Tsolho TAP. We also heard about monasteries that had been rebuilt in new locations. For example, several monasteries in Dechen County were rebuilt closer to the town and the main road between Dechen and Gyelthang Counties. The famous Sakyapa monastery Gönchen Gompa (Ch: Genqing Si)[87] in Derge County, Kandze TAP, has been completely rebuilt in the same area, a few hundred meters away from its original site near the Derge Sutra Printing Academy.

Other monasteries were rebuilt some distance away from their original sites, closer to the towns. We visited Drango Monastery (Ch: Shouling Si), in Drango (Luhuo) County, Kandze TAP, which is now located near the county seat, overlooking the town. A local Tibetan government official told us that the former location was outside the town. The new monastery was built closer to the town for two reasons: it was more accessible for the city people and, more important, the old location was considered inauspicious and to have bad *fengshui*.[88] In support of the latter reason, we were told that the old monastery had been leveled. It is interesting to note that a local Tibetan cadre explained the unfortunate destiny of this monastery in terms of *fengshui*.

In other places, the local population wanted to construct religious sites in completely new locations, a complicated proposition. We talked with locals who complained about the very slow process of obtaining permission, and if the site could not be related to a pre-destruction-period religious site, chances of being granted permission were considered small. Some communities had given up waiting for permission and started construction. For example, in one village with a view to the magnificent Amnye Machen range, the villagers wanted to erect their own temple. They had applied repeatedly to the local religious affairs department and received no reply. After years of what they called "bureaucratic waiting," they decided to construct a temple without permission.

A report from Dzoge County gives a detailed description of the current regulations concerning monastic revival.[89] It states that any reconstruction

FIG. 2.8. A new stupa under construction at Machu Monastery, Kanlho. The work was performed by Tibetans and Han migrant workers from Qinghai.

must follow the government guidelines and rules regulating everything from construction to farmland cultivation. Most important, any building or rebuilding of monasteries has to be approved by the local Buddhist Association and religious affairs department.

In Ngaba Prefecture, the authorities decided in 1986 that any monastery seeking permission to rebuild must have sufficient resources and provide a yearly plan for the proposed reconstruction, including a schedule and a list of personnel. The plan must first be thoroughly discussed by a "monastic control team" (Ch: *siyuan guanli jiegou*) made up of religious experts, lay believers, and district government representatives.[90] The team's responsibilities are to review the plan, survey the monastery's original location, investigate the monastery's history, and consider the number of monks it should accept and the resources required for reconstruction. The plan must then

FIG. 2.9. Villagers in Drango County, Kandze, working on a new stupa.

be approved by the district government before it is submitted to the county religious affairs department and then to authorities at higher levels for approval before any construction begins.

The Dzoge County report also mentions several requirements for monks and nuns joining religious institutions: they must be more than eighteen years old as documented by official ID, must be law-abiding and love the nation and religion, must have parental consent, must be healthy, and must be sufficiently educated (equivalent to the sixth grade of primary school). The state set the minimum age for monks and nuns at eighteen years in the 1982 revision of the constitution.

Since the mid-1990s, the authorities have also regulated the number of monks and nuns allowed in each monastery and nunnery. County religious affairs departments were asked to prepare quotas for monks and nuns in each monastery. Several sources told us that this took place in 1996. The quotas were to be fixed on the basis of such conditions as the number of monks in a monastery in the 1950s and, after the reopening of monasteries in the 1980s, the number of monks there at present, the size of the monastery, and how many people it could house. Another factor was the number of Buddhists in the county compared to the total population. According to a government official we interviewed in 1999, prefectural officials were conducting an investigation that year in order to establish new quotas for monks based on the needs of the population and conditions in the monasteries.

Today, the local religious affairs departments keep detailed lists of monks. An official in Kandze informed us that these records are checked by local officials as often as every third year. There are at least two sets of records, one listing the officially accepted quota for each monastery and another indicating the actual number of monks believed to be residing permanently in each monastery at the time of the latest visit by local officials. When we were given access to both sets of lists, we found that in general the quotas were smaller than the true numbers of monks, although there were exceptional cases in which quotas were larger than the actual numbers. In one county, the records that were shown to us indicated fewer monks than were allowed by quota in all but one of the county's monasteries.

In Golok TAP, county officials produced a document containing a detailed list of monasteries, actual numbers and official quotas of monks, and the numbers of tulkus, retired or deceased monks, monks residing outside of the monasteries, and monks who had "returned to secular life" (Ch: *zixing huansu*). The list included 12 tulkus between the ages of nineteen and sixty. This document offers a good example of the different categories used in registering monks. The religious affairs department emphasized that the number of monks in the county was lower than the allowed quota. The quota for monks was 200, but in 1998 there were only 148, whereas there were 178 in 1996. On closer inspection, however, it became clear that the number of monks was almost unchanged from 1996 to 1998. When a monk retired but continued to live in the monastery, he was reclassified, hence lowering the figure.

County religious affairs departments also keep detailed accounts of tulkus and their lineages. Tulkus living abroad are not included in the statistics, although officials in the religious affairs departments often have a comprehensive knowledge about how many tulkus originally belonged to the different monasteries and the countries in which they are currently residing. We received a complete list of details of more than 100 monasteries and nunneries within three counties in Kandze TAP and a list of the most important monasteries in a fourth county. The information includes their exact location by village, Buddhist order, 1999 numbers of monks and nuns, the accepted quota (often lower than the actual figures), numbers of tulkus, and sometimes more detailed information about the tulkus. We found that figures at the local departments sometimes corresponded with figures acquired at the monasteries and nunneries, but in several cases the numbers of monks or nuns given in on-site reports were substantially higher.

It is interesting to note the comparatively sparse information available on nuns and nunneries. When we requested statistics on nuns, we often received rather vague replies about the insignificance of nuns, and in several prefectures we were told that there were no nuns at all or that there were a few nuns but no nunneries.[91] Many officials appeared to know little about nuns and nunneries, and we have the impression that some may have felt there was little reason to keep records on nuns. In fact, in 1999, we learned that even the province-level Ethnic Affairs Commission had not been collecting statistical information on nuns and nunneries. One interview elicited the rather remarkable comment that the state does not want nuns. Several of the officials we interviewed revealed quite unsympathetic attitudes toward nuns. For instance, officials gave us the following information about the nuns in their prefecture: "They are all quite old, over fifty years old. They become nuns because their husbands are dead and all their children have grown up and left home. To become a nun is just a way to make a living, and this is one way of feeding themselves."

Except during the implementation of a political campaign, restrictions on the numbers of monks and nuns did not seem to be strictly enforced at the local level. Quotas were usually exceeded, but we also found that some monasteries and nunneries had more monks and nuns than reported by authorities. It is unlikely that local officials were unaware of the actual number of monks and nuns. We suspect that monks and nuns under eighteen and those who have retired are sometimes left out of the statistics so as to comply with quotas. If this is true, the real number of monks and nuns may sometimes be higher than that reported by the authorities.

We were told by one monastery's management committee that the monastery had 100 monks more than the quota allowed. The extra 100 monks were described as either retired or below the age of eighteen and hence were not included in the count. In another case, a local official seemed almost to apologize that the age limit was not enforced in his county. The official reported that there were 72 monks under the age of eighteen in his county, explaining that the underage monks were there to care for the old monks who needed help and to learn a handicraft.

Local religious affairs departments have detailed knowledge of the monasteries under their jurisdiction. They not only keep track of the number of monks but also register their income and all their ritual activities. During one interview in Qinghai, the county official opened a large brown envelope and revealed that his office registered the name of every monk in the county.

Monks who attend a Buddhist institute are registered at their home monasteries, although the authorities certainly keep records of the monks attending such institutes, particularly the large ones. At the time of our fieldwork, one of the largest communities of Tibetan Buddhist monks and nuns in all the areas under study was the Serthar Buddhist Institute, established in the early 1980s by the Nyingmapa spiritual master Khenpo Jigme Phuntsok. As of 1999, there were 7,716 monks and nuns registered at the site, and the associated nunnery was probably the largest nunnery in all the Tibetan areas, with about 4,000 nuns.[92] Because this community of monks and nuns was defined as an institute rather than a monastery, it did not have to comply with all the regulations pertaining to monasteries. Nevertheless, it did have admittance quotas, and in the late 1990s, these quotas were being seriously violated. In 2000, people who had visited the site over the previous few years told us that during important religious ceremonies the number of participants sometimes reached 100,000. According to the prefectural religious affairs department, monks were permitted to come for religious ceremonies but could not stay for a longer period or permanently. The site was allowed to have 1,000 monks and 400 nuns as permanent residents, while another 400 monks were permitted to live permanently in a nearby monastery. In an interview, local government officials informed us that "it is a problem for the local community in the village that thousands of people go to stay there, because there is not enough food or water. It is too big now. Most monks live there permanently, and some are also over sixty years old. They pray all the time to go to heaven!"

We were told during the interview that the authorities had no immediate plan to drive away people who had already settled there, although they were working on finding a "means to make it more difficult to enter." However, in June 2001, only about a year after our interview was conducted, CCP officials from the United Front in Beijing and Sichuan, troops of armed police, and work teams descended on the institute. According to reports, they tore down living quarters, set up roadblocks manned by the PLA, and removed Khenpo Jigme Phuntsok from the complex against his will. As of August 2001, he was supposedly being held in a military hospital, although he was not formally detained. At the time of the crackdown, the institute was believed to have between 7,000 and 8,000 monks and nuns, of whom nearly 1,000 were Han and the majority were nuns.[93]

All monasteries are now governed by a "management committee" (Ch: *guanli weiyuanhui*), which is supervised by the religious affairs department. The management committee is responsible for the finances and most of the activities of the monastery, including study programs and religious ceremonies. In the larger monasteries, management committees may be divided into several departments responsible for finances, cultural relic preservation, study, and internal propaganda work. For instance, the management committee of Labrang Monastery has several departments, including a bureau for the protection of cultural relics, a bureau of study and propaganda, and a production department. In addition to the management committee, an assembly of monks with its own elected leader takes care of monastic affairs. Management committees in the smaller monasteries are made up of ordinary monks and nuns, elected for a three- to five-year period, who are responsible primarily for running the monastery or nunnery on a day-to-day basis. They are also sometimes forced to implement government regulations, however, and in such cases they function as extensions of government or party organs within their institutions.

Before conducting religious ceremonies or other activities, a monastery must obtain permission from the religious affairs department.[94] However, the numerous guidelines and directives that regulate the activities of monasteries are not consistently applied. In some remote rural areas, there is little or no interference in the affairs of monasteries, while officials exercise very tight control in the larger, more prominent monastic institutions. For instance, reports indicate that in the larger monasteries there may be regulations on the number of monks allowed to pursue studies and the regimens of examination. Restrictions seem to be taken more seriously in the larger Gelugpa monasteries, but it is difficult to say whether this is solely because of their size or because the branch is the largest and politically most important.

The study of Bön is a priority area in research on Tibetan religion. Although Bön is often regarded as a branch of Tibetan Buddhism, it is frequently discussed in Chinese publications in more positive terms than is Buddhism.[95] While Tibetan Buddhism has become closely associated with Tibetan national identity, and the Gelugpas in particular held secular authority in Tibet in recent history, the Bön clergy has not been politically powerful in Tibet and represents less of a threat to Chinese authority today.

This may explain why officials impose fewer restrictions on Bön monas-teries. At the same time, whereas religion is permitted, superstition is often under attack, and some local officials may treat Bön and Nyingmapa monas-teries and religious sites as centers of superstitious rather than religious activities.

Mechanisms of control are in place in almost all monasteries and nun-neries, but the degree of control that is actually exercised fluctuates accord-ing to the political climate and campaigns directed by higher-level authorities. Permits that are processed quickly may become difficult or even impossible to obtain.[96] Local authorities may also enforce policies differently. Therefore it is difficult to predict the consequences of a policy guideline in any par-ticular area. Our impression is that some local authorities simply do not have the will or the power to enforce regulations unless a campaign makes it necessary to take some kind of action. County government officials informed us on several occasions that they "don't enforce that regulation here" or that "there is a regulation, but we are incapable of enforcing it." At the county level, the religious affairs departments usually lack the authority to issue permits for the rebuilding of monasteries or to set quo-tas for monks and nuns. Such permits and quotas are generally issued by prefecture—or province—level departments, especially for important issues such as the recognition of new tulkus.

As with Patriotic Education, most campaigns are clearly conducted according to directives from the central authorities. One such case is a cam-paign implemented in all Tibetan areas in 1996 involving the removal of pho-tos of the Dalai Lama from religious sites. In 1998 and 1999, such photos could be found in only a few sites, although prior to 1996, they could be seen almost everywhere. A less publicized campaign to register all religious sites was also conducted in the mid-1990s.[97] A document from Dechen TAP describes the local implementation of this campaign. All religious sites were registered in detail, including monasteries, churches, mosques, temples (T: lha khang), tulku residences (T: bla brang), sacred mountains and holy places, Buddhist stupas, and incense-offering sites. Although the religious affairs department was directly responsible for registering the sites, work teams included members from the CPPCC, the CCP propaganda office, the police department, the land distribution department, the urban development department, and the forestry department.

Internal government documents we have obtained expose practices that can only be characterized as repressive. One such document reveals that work teams were sent to monasteries to conduct propaganda work, even during religious events. The document states that in 1982, the police department, CCP propaganda office, religious affairs department, CPPCC, and armed forces organized a work team to establish monastic control in the area. According to an official document, this team entered villages and monasteries three times to conduct investigations under the guiding principles of "efficient control of religion, unity of all ethnic minorities, and stability in frontier regions." The document further states that the aim of such investigations was to demonstrate the policies, laws, and rules for establishing monasteries and temples.

Monastic leaders in particular were under pressure to attend meetings and conferences, where they might be confronted with problems that had occurred in the process of reconstructing monasteries. According to our sources, some tulkus were further accused of forging their identities (maybe because they had been denied official recognition as tulkus) and collecting money under false pretenses. Monks and nuns were also subjected to various methods of propaganda education aimed at "raising their level of thinking and consciousness, improving patriotic feeling and discipline, protecting socialism, and safeguarding the unity of all ethnic minorities within one motherland." On religious occasions, government representatives reportedly held talks and directed propaganda at monks and nuns.

At the lower administrative levels, religious affairs departments are staffed mainly by Tibetans, usually supervised by a Han Party cadre. Leading members of Buddhist associations and staff of provincial and national Buddhist colleges are also Tibetans, and some are monks or tulkus. These cadres and officials have the difficult job of serving as mediators between local Tibetan communities and representatives of the CCP, who sometimes ask them to carry out policies that offend the sensibilities of Tibetan believers. Regardless of their personal opinions, they are required to support every Party policy or campaign, whether they think it is sensible or not. Some of the dilemmas these Tibetans face became evident in our interviews and discussions with them and made us rethink the notion of government authorities as belonging to a unitary and faceless entity. It also brought to our attention the need to distinguish clearly between policy and implementation and the importance of focusing future research on the complexities of implementation as well as on campaigns and policies as such.

The implementation of religious policies is unpredictable, and religious leaders identify as a major problem the lack of laws protecting the religious freedom provided by the constitution. As described by the former leader of Kumbum Monastery, Agya Rinpoche, this creates a climate of uncertainty among religious leaders: "Since there is no law, the policy makers can dictate whatever they like, and when religious freedoms are crushed there is no avenue for appeal. . . . Sometimes certain practices would be permitted, and then there would be a change of policy which made the same practices prohibited and punishable with no recourse at all."[98]

The many sporadic changes in policies and the differences in implementation over time and from one area to the next make it difficult to summarize conditions for religion in Tibetan areas today. This irregularity also creates a climate of doubt and suspicion that is a significant problem for Tibetans. It is evident, however, that there has been an ongoing process of tightening government control over religious practice, particularly after 1987 and again after 1996. State intervention in religious affairs represents an enormous obstacle to local forces that are trying to protect and promote religion.

Although Tibetans have been able to revive a great number of monasteries and religious sites in the areas under study, we found that monks and nuns, and especially tulkus and religious leaders, were under great pressure from the authorities. Their situation was made particularly difficult by inconsistent and often contradictory indications from the authorities on what is permitted and by a system that forces individual monks and nuns to take responsibility for the actions of others. The tightening of political control over monasteries and members of the clergy clearly represents a serious impediment to religious practice and causes considerable tension within monasteries and nunneries. With the crackdown in June 2001 on the Serthar Buddhist Institute, one of the major centers of Buddhist teaching in all the Tibetan areas, the situation appears to have deteriorated further.

CCP policy makers evidently see religious practice as an obstacle to the development of Tibetan society and culture and regard the revival of monasteries with considerable suspicion. They fear monasteries not only because they suspect the religious sites may harbor separatists. More important, since the devastation of the Cultural Revolution, monasteries have become the focal points for Tibetans' efforts to preserve and maintain what they consider to be the core of Tibetan culture. As such, monasteries have become the primary symbols of the determination of Tibetans to reinforce their national identity and resist Chinese domination. The methods by which the authorities have tried to control Tibetan monasteries have only made religion more significant as a marker of Tibetan identity and toughened resistance.

3 / The Dilemmas of Education
in Tibetan Areas

Tibetan-language education plays an important role in the reconstruction of Tibetan culture, especially in the sense that teaching Tibetan in schools provides a venue for the expression of a common Tibetan identity.[1] Yet, one of the primary goals of education in Tibetan and other minority areas is to consolidate "ethnic minorities" (Ch: *shaoshu minzu*) and persuade their children to become patriotic members of the all-inclusive family of China.[2] Education is directed toward disseminating Chinese Communist Party (CCP) ideology, and officials of the educational system still state that the goal of minority education is to maintain socialism. More important, the educational system aims to subordinate local ethnic identities to national unity and at the same time convey the message that the minorities are "backward" (Ch: *luohou*) compared to the Han.

Concerns have even been raised that the Chinese educational system is assimilating Tibetans into the Chinese mainstream and wiping out a separate Tibetan identity altogether. The authorities evidently do not share these concerns but rather see it as their duty to help raise the "cultural level" (Ch: *wenhua chengdu*) of Tibetans. For instance, when asked by a foreign journalist whether Chinese schools were "killing Tibetan culture," the headmaster of the Beijing Tibetan Middle School stated that their intention instead was to "help Tibet develop with talented people."[3] According to the Tibetan Centre for Human Rights and Development, a Tibetan exile nongovernmental organization (NGO), the problem lies in the Chinese belief that modernization equals sinicization: "Education is for them a tool through which cultural differences are suppressed under a hegemonic doctrine of Chinese supremacy. Where Tibetan history is taught at all, it is expressed in terms of a backward and barbaric land liberated by China, and Tibetan students are made to feel ashamed of both their background and identity."[4]

The standard curriculum in Chinese schools emphasizes patriotism and nationalistic sentiments. Chinese authorities have even promulgated guidelines for the implementation of patriotic education, directed particularly at young people, which were issued in September 1994. The guidelines call for highlighting patriotic education at various historical and scenic sites and creating an atmosphere of patriotism in different social sectors by emphasizing the importance of respecting the national flag, anthem, and emblem. Chinese schools thus start the week with a flag-raising ceremony, and patriotic education in one form or another constitutes a significant part of the curriculum in Chinese, "ideology and politics" (Ch: *sixiang zhengzui*), "ideology and morals" (Ch: *sixiang pinde*), and other subjects. While actively promoting patriotism, textbooks also disseminate the notion that minorities are inferior and backward compared to the Han. Moreover, most non-Han students feel that their language, history, religion, and customs are considered useless or insignificant in the Chinese school system.[5]

Although these problems should be recognized, there is another side to the story. First, the educational system may not have the ability to make minorities identify with the state and assimilate them into Chinese society. The implementation of this policy today may in fact produce the opposite effect: an increased emphasis on ethnic identity and cultural differences.[6] Second, the Tibetan curriculum teaches Tibetan students to value their own traditions and offers Tibetans an opportunity to create their own version of Tibetanness. This is one of the reasons why many officials regard Tibetan-language education as a potential cause of local nationalism and a threat to stability.[7] As noted by Janet Upton, the trans-provincial scope of the new Tibetan curriculum and its emphasis on the unity of Plateau culture also provide ways of breaching the provincial political boundaries that currently separate the Tibetan population into different administrative units.[8] The curriculum thus creates a space for the construction of a Tibetan identity that encompasses all Tibetan areas. Finally, if the Tibetan written language is to survive today, it clearly needs to be taught in schools and used in official and everyday communications. The success of education in promoting or undermining a Tibetan identity thus depends largely on whether students are given the opportunity to learn the Tibetan language at school and whether they can overcome the problems presented by the educational system.

DEVELOPMENT OF BILINGUAL EDUCATION
IN TIBETAN AREAS

In Amdo and Kham, public education was introduced on the margins of the Tibetan Plateau. In Qinghai, schools were first established in the Muslim communities around Xining, and by 1922 there were seven primary schools in the area. Not until 1934 was the first school in a Tibetan area set up in Jyekundo (Yushu), with only a few students. Another primary school was established in Golok (Guoluo) in 1942.[9] In the following years, two more schools for Mongolian and Tibetan children were established in Jyekundo.[10] The first public school opened in Mili (Muli) in about 1946.[11] By that time, a number of schools were already operating in other Tibetan areas of Sichuan. Public schools were opened as early as the 1930s in Yunnan, in Gyelthang (Zhongdian) Town, and by 1950, Dechen (Deqin) County also had at least one public school.

Soon after the founding of the People's Republic of China, public education spread into many of the minority areas. The emphasis on educational facilities was originally connected with the CCP's strategy to solidify control of the border areas and "civilize" the people who inhabited the frontiers of China. During the 1950s, schools were thus set up throughout the Tibetan areas, and after 1952, young Tibetans were sent away to schools such as the Nationalities Institutes in Beijing and Chengdu. In 1955, the central government of China launched a school program for Tibet, and within a year, one middle school and sixty primary schools were open in the Tibet Autonomous Region (TAR). During the early years, many Tibetans welcomed these educational opportunities. Some monks with *geshe* degrees even sought employment in institutions such as the Central Nationalities Institute (Ch: Zhongyang Minzu Xueyuan) in Beijing.[12]

In the mid-1950s, newly established education departments in Tibetan areas issued their first guidelines on bilingual education. A number of primary school classes were set up as bilingual during the period 1956–58, but this process was soon interrupted by the Democratic Reforms campaign. During the Cultural Revolution, many schools closed down, and communes were instructed to establish their own schools. Commune schools taught only the Chinese language. The goals of the policy were mass education and at least basic literacy for all, but in practice many of the commune schools were oriented toward work rather than studies. Higher education in particular suffered a serious setback, and the Tibetan language was removed from the curriculum. Bilingual education and Tibetan-language instruction disappeared for a period of approximately twenty years, until about 1978, when *minzu* education was again promoted.

During the 1980s, officials in the education and ethnic affairs departments again emphasized the importance of developing programs suited to the special characteristics of the *minzu* and began discussing the best teaching methods for *minzu* primary and middle schools. Minority-language education was the main focus of these discussions, and the initial trend was to promote the use of minority languages in schools so that pupils could be educated in their native languages. China's Law on Regional Autonomy, passed in 1984, gave autonomous areas the right to train and employ cadres belonging to ethnic minorities, develop education and ethnic culture, and use local spoken and written languages. Regarding education in particular, the autonomous areas had the right to set up their own local educational programs—which included establishing schools, length of study, course contents, language of instruction, and procedures of enrollment—and to develop a type of education based on their ethnic minority characteristics.[13]

After the policy shift of the late 1970s, the teaching of Tibetan was gradually expanded during the 1980s, in the TAR as well as in neighboring provinces. In 1987, the TAR Congress passed a resolution stipulating that all junior middle schools were to use Tibetan as the medium of instruction by 1993 and that most subjects in senior middle schools were also to be taught in Tibetan by 1997.[14] This policy was never implemented, however, and during the 1990s, bilingual education seems to have met with increasing disapproval, at least within the TAR. For instance, in 1997, Deputy Secretary Tenzin, of the TAR Communist Party, announced that authorities in Tibet were to begin introducing Chinese-language studies from the first year of primary school.[15] According to the Tibet Information Network, citing Xinhua News Agency, the deputy secretary further explained that the regional government had reversed its 1987 decision on the expansion of Tibetan-language teaching. He described the 1987 policy as impractical and not in conformity with the reality of Tibet.

In Tibetan areas outside the TAR, policy shifts on bilingual education have not necessarily followed those in the TAR. Rather, each province had its own policies and guidelines, which were implemented differently from place to place. As a result, there are large variations among provinces, prefectures, and even counties, which means it is not easy to describe the situation in general terms. Nevertheless, in spite of great variation, some common features are discernible, particularly in methods of organizing bilingual education. One such feature is the system of having two parallel classes in schools for Tibetans: one taught in Chinese and the other in Tibetan.

In Kanlho (Gannan) Tibetan Autonomous Prefecture (TAP), in Gansu, and in Ngaba (Aba) Prefecture and Kandze (Ganzi) TAP, in Sichuan, we found that bilingual schools at the county level and above normally had two parallel "tracks" (Ch: *ban*), one in Tibetan and one in Chinese.[16] According to this system of bilingual teaching, students in both primary and middle school are taught in separate classes in their principal language, although they follow the same curriculum in all subjects except language. Language instruction depends on the track in which the student is enrolled, either the "Chinese track" (Ch: *Hanwen ban*), with Chinese as the main language, or the "Tibetan track" (Ch: *Zangwen ban*), with Tibetan as the principal language. Chinese and Tibetan are usually taught in both tracks, but the curricula are different, as we will explain.

In Ngaba, we were told that the principal language (whether Chinese or Tibetan), which is the language of instruction, is also taught as a subject for the entire six years of schooling, while the second language is taught as a subject only up to about the fourth grade. In the Chinese track, primary school students are required to reach the third-grade level of Tibetan for admission to middle school, and students in the Tibetan track are required to reach the same level in Chinese.[17] In addition, students in both tracks must attain the same level as ordinary students in all other subjects. In the schools we visited, the number of students in both tracks was usually about the same.

In 1982, the Ngaba Prefecture Education Department's teaching plan included a discussion of bilingual education.[18] According to this plan, in pastoral areas inhabited by nomadic herders, children do not have the chance to practice Chinese language, and people in these areas prefer Tibetan as the language of instruction. Students in such areas should therefore receive their education in Tibetan, with Chinese language taught as a subject beginning in the fourth grade.[19] The duration of primary school at this time was seven years. Upon completion of primary school, the students' level of Chinese was supposed to be equivalent to that of the fourth grade of primary school. The plan further stated that people in settled farming areas usually have a relatively good knowledge of Chinese. In such areas, Chinese should be the language of instruction, and pupils should start to learn Tibetan in the fourth grade.[20] When pupils complete primary school, their Tibetan should be at the fourth-grade level and their Chinese should be equivalent to the first- or second-grade level of middle school.

Kakhok (Hongyuan) County, in Ngaba, provides a good example of how this system is put into practice.[21] According to local officials in Kakhok, nineteen of the twenty-three primary schools in their county were bilingual, with 2,594 out of 3,074 pupils in bilingual primary schools (84 percent). Of the 2,594 pupils in bilingual schools, 1,543 were in the Tibetan track (59.5 percent), while 1,051 were in the Chinese (40.5 percent). In the Tibetan track, Chinese was taught from the first grade, and in the Chinese track, Tibetan was taught from the third grade. In the Tibetan track, Chinese was taught four to six hours per week and Tibetan was taught six to eight hours per week. In the Chinese track, students had four to six hours of Tibetan per week and six to eight hours of Chinese per week. When Tibetan-track pupils finished primary school, they were expected to have reached the fourth-grade level of Chinese, and Chinese-track pupils should have attained the fourth-grade level of Tibetan. Students usually continued in the same track in middle school. In the Chinese track, they had six hours of Tibetan and eight hours of Chinese per week. Tibetan-track pupils had six to eight hours of Chinese per week and eight hours of Tibetan.

In a bilingual primary school we visited in neighboring Dzoge (Ruo'ergai) County, the situation was described in similar terms.[22] The school was a typical, county town boarding school in a predominantly herding area. There were six classes in the Chinese track, from first to sixth grade. Chinese was the language of instruction, with Chinese language taught twelve hours per week and Tibetan seven hours per week. The Tibetan track, however, had only three classes, from fourth to sixth grade, because the school boarded students from all county districts, and these students entered in the fourth grade. Tibetan-track classes used Tibetan as the language of instruction, with Tibetan language taught twelve hours per week and Chinese seven hours per week. We were told that although district schools did offer six years of education, students took an examination after the third grade, and the best ones went on to the boarding school.

Several educators told us that in schools with both tracks, students are free to choose which one they would like to enter, although there are restrictions on changing tracks after junior middle school. In practice, however, many students would find it difficult to change tracks, since pupils from village schools do not have a choice of tracks during their first years of schooling and others have been taught only one language.

The two-track system has enabled students to continue their education in Tibetan from the primary to the university level. In Gansu and Sichuan in particular, senior middle school graduates on the Tibetan track have several options. Students from Kanlho, for instance, have the opportunity to study at the Tibetan language department of the Hezuo Nationalities Teachers Training School.[23] These students could pursue additional studies taught in Tibetan at the Tibetan Department of the Northwest Minzu Institute in Lanzhou.

In Ngaba, Tibetan-track students have the options of attending a *minzu* teachers training school or studying at the Tibetan department of the Southwest Nationalities Institute (Ch: Xinan Minzu Xueyuan), in Chengdu.[24] The department had 240 students in 1999–2000, all Tibetans. Within the department, there were two tracks, one taught in Tibetan and one in Chinese, with about 100 students in each.[25] The main subjects were Tibetan, Chinese, and English languages, but the department offered twenty to thirty subjects, including history, literary history, grammar, literature, tourism management, and computer science. We were informed that the central government in Beijing decides every year which subjects should be taught, when courses should be available, and for how many students.

In Kandze, Tibetan-track students could attend the Ganzi Tibetan School (Ch: Ganzi Zangwen Xuexiao), which is administered and funded by the Sichuan Province Ethnic Affairs Commission. At the time of our visit in spring 2000, the school had 597 students, all Tibetan.[26] It had four departments: Tibetan-Chinese translation (four years); Tibetan art (three years); Tibetan language for teachers (four years), for Tibetan teachers from outside the TAPs; and Tibetan language (four years), which included classes in Tibetology, Sanskrit, and Buddhist logic.[27] Tibetan astrology was also taught at the school. All courses were taught in Tibetan except for three subjects, which were taught in Chinese: Chinese language, translation, and ideology and politics. The school had thirty-six teachers in 2000, of which thirty-four were Tibetan.

After completing senior middle school, Tibetan students from Kandze may take university-level courses conducted in Tibetan at the local Kangding University, popularly known as the Khampa university (Ch: Kangba daxue), administered by the Sichuan Province Education Department.[28] At the time of our visit, enrollment was about 2,000 students in seven departments: economics, Chinese, art, English, mathematics, administration, and Tibetan. The Tibetan students were said to comprise only about 10 percent of the students and were studying mainly in the Tibetan department. We were told that only 20 percent of the classes in the Tibetan department were actually taught in Tibetan.[29] The Tibetan department had two main courses of study, one for teachers and the other for Tibetan-Chinese translators.

ACCESS TO EDUCATION IN TIBETAN AREAS

China has adopted a nationwide policy of compulsory nine-year education, but local governments in Tibetan areas, especially in rural regions, have serious problems implementing this policy. Education is poorly developed in these areas, resources are scarce, and, in may cases, teachers themselves are virtually uneducated. In herding areas in particular, many schools are described merely as teaching stations, known as point schools. Many point schools have only one teacher, who may not be qualified for teaching, and usually offer no more than a very basic level of primary education with extremely low-grade teaching, equipment, and books. Facilities are poor and may lack desks, benches, and sometimes even a schoolhouse. Pupils at all levels often are taught together in one class, and many of these schools offer only three to four years of basic education. Under such conditions, many parents prefer to keep their children at home and put them to work on the farm or in the household. Others are so determined to give their children an education that they send them to India to attend the schools for Tibetan refugees set up by the Tibetan government-in-exile in Dharamsala. Every year, an average of 3,000 Tibetans trek for weeks to cross the borders into Nepal and India, risking their lives on the high passes of the Himalayas. Nearly one third of them are children.[30]

In some of the Tibetan areas we visited, local authorities were struggling to make even a basic three-year education available to all children. In Tsochang (Haibei) TAP, in Qinghai, we were told that Dola (Qilian), Semnyi (Menyuan), and Dashi (Haiyan) Counties were able to provide a six-year education by the time of our visit in 1999. Kangtsa (Gangcha) County, however, had made only three or four years of education available to all. Kandze TAP, in Sichuan, is another area that has problems with the compulsory nine-year education policy. In 1984, the prefecture was divided into four areas, and each area was given a time limit for implementing "compulsory primary education" (Ch: *puji chudeng jiaoyu*). Chaksam (Luding) County was supposed to reach the six-year level by 1987; Dartsedo (Kangding), Gyesur (Jiulong), Rongdrak (Danba), Nyakchuka (Yajiang), and Tawu (Daofu) Counties were assigned the target date of 1995; and the deadline for Bathang (Batang), Chathreng (Xiangcheng), Dabpa (Daocheng), Drango (Luhuo), Kandze, Derge (Dege), and Nyarong (Xinlong) Counties was 2000. The remaining counties—Sershül (Shiqu), Pelyül (Baiyu), Serthar (Seda), Lithang (Litang), and Derong—were given until 2010 to provide six years of compulsory education.[31] In 1987, these plans were revised and the dates postponed. By 1992, only three counties—Chaksam, Rongdrak, and Gyesur—were able to provide six years of education to all. According to contemporary statistics, this represented 37.8 percent of the pupils in the prefecture. In our interview with the prefecture educational authorities, we were informed that their expectations concerning compulsory education had been lowered even further. They were involved in plans to make a basic four-year education available for everyone by 2005 and hoped to extend it to six years a few years later. A document issued by the Tawu County Education Department in March 2000 states that the county was still only 72.7 percent of the way toward providing education covering the "first four years in primary school" (Ch: *puchu*).[32] Other counties in Kandze are in a similar situation.

Not only is there the problem of local authorities being unable to provide educational facilities for all school-age children, but there is also a problem with parents neglecting to send their children to school. We received reports in some areas of the use of economic sanctions to force parents to send children to school. Either the parents had to pay a small fee for each day of absence or those who failed to enroll their children were threatened with a very large fine. In a village school in Drango County, Kandze TAP, parents were fined ¥0.5 (US$0.06) per day of absence from school. Apparently these penalties were responsible for increased attendance. In Matö (Maduo) County, Golok TAP, in Qinghai, we were told that the parents of children who failed to show up were fined ¥7,000 (US$885) and that "everybody sends their children to school." According to the principal of a school in a herding area, very few children did not attend school. He explained that the fine for nonattendance was so high that it "clearly states the importance of learning," and up to the time of the interview in July 1999, no family had refused to comply, since all want their children to "have some knowledge."[33]

After the introduction of new educational policies in the mid-1980s, the cost of education increased dramatically, while income levels remained relatively low, especially in rural areas. By the late 1990s, an increasing number of parents could not afford to send their children to school. Although we were told that tuition fees were to be levied only in middle school and above, primary schools in many places charged parents for textbooks and "miscellaneous fees" (Ch: *zafei*). For rural Tibetans at least, schooling became a heavy economic burden. The rising cost of education was a particular problem for boarding school students and those above primary level, where high tuition fees were common.[34] In Ngaba Prefecture, for instance, miscellaneous fees amounted to about ¥100 (US$12) per year in primary schools in towns, excluding the cost of boarding. In middle schools, we found tuition costs as high as ¥1,300 (US$160) per year, with an additional ¥400 (US$50) per year for boarding. Tuition alone was commonly about ¥400–750 (US$50–95) per year, and boarding expenses as much as ¥90 (US$11) per month. In comparison, as of 1996, the average annual income of herders and farmers in Ngaba was ¥882 (US$108).[35] In the neighboring prefecture of Kandze, annual fees in township primary schools were ¥150–300 (US$19–38), including books and miscellaneous fees. Middle school tuition was generally higher, often as much as ¥500–600 (US$60–75), excluding boarding expenses.

Primary point schools in herding areas and farming villages were reported to be free of charge, and local governments claimed they sometimes even provided grants for clothing and food. However, in schools we visited along the highways, in agricultural areas and in towns, even primary school pupils had to pay for textbooks and miscellaneous fees. In addition, the overall quality of point schools and their level of teaching were described by many as substandard.

Primary school enrollment rates reported by the local education departments indicate low school attendance in rural areas, especially herding areas. In Kandze TAP, the entrance rates reported to us were slightly more than 84 percent in town areas and only about 50 percent in herding areas.[36] In Ngaba, the school enrollment rate for the prefecture as a whole was reported to be 90 percent, but in counties where herding is predominant, such as Kakhok and Ngaba, enrollment was considerably lower. In Kakhok County, local officials reported an enrollment rate in 1999 of only 69.4 percent.

Statistics also reveal that as of 1982, less than 27 percent of Tibetan school-age children (at the primary and middle school levels) in Qinghai were enrolled in schools.[37] According to our own information from 1999, in Jyekundo TAP, Qinghai, enrollment rates in primary schools were still as low as 28.3 percent in two counties, Dritö (Zhiduo) and Dzatö (Zaduo). The primary school enrollment rate for Jyekundo TAP as a whole was reported by local officials to be 41.2 percent, with 81.6 percent in Jyekundo County, where the prefecture seat is located. In Malho (Huangnan) TAP, also in Qinghai, the primary school enrollment rate for 1998 was reported as 73.8 percent. Unpublished government documents from 1998 give the following enrollment rates by county: Rebkong (Tongren), 90.4 percent; Chentsa (Jianza), 95.6 percent; Tsekhok (Zeku), 43.4 percent; and Yülgennyin (Henan), 48 percent. The latter two counties are predominantly herding areas. In Golok TAP, we visited two counties where nomadic herding is predominant, Darlak (Dari) and Matö, and interviewed the local education departments. In Darlak County, we were told that only 40 percent of the nomadic children entered school, while the county average was 48.7 percent. In Matö County, the situation was similar, although the entrance rate was supposedly higher, at 64.1 percent.

It is often difficult to obtain accurate information on school enrollment from local officials. For instance, government officials in Kanlho TAP reported to us in 1999 that 90.1 percent of school-age children in their prefecture entered primary school, while 95–98 percent completed sixth grade. However, official statistics from 1997 state that only 84.5 percent of school-age children in Kanlho were enrolled in primary school.[38] Interviews with school staff also indicated that the figures provided by the prefectural government were not accurate for the areas we visited. As noted by one local cadre, the high overall figures in some prefectures can be explained by the fact that almost 100 percent of school-age children in the densely populated towns attend school. However, the conditions are very different in rural areas where most Tibetans live, especially in herding and poorer agricultural areas. The enrollment rates for girls in herding areas were particularly low. One education specialist in Machu (Maqu) County, a herding area in Kanlho, estimated a 50 percent attendance rate for girls in his county. We found a similar situation in some of the schools we visited in Qinghai, where less than a third of the pupils were girls.

Dropping out is a major problem in most Tibetan areas. For instance, according to official sources from Dechen TAP, Yunnan, the yearly dropout rate in 1995 was 13.3 percent of primary school pupils and 12.2 percent of junior middle school students. In 1997, the yearly dropout rate was 9.5 percent of primary school pupils and 7.6 percent of junior middle school students. While 92 percent of school-age children entered school, only 54.8 percent completed sixth grade. Of those who finished primary school, 73.6 percent went on to middle schools, but only 56.4 percent completed junior middle school.[39] The numbers were similar in Tibetan areas of Qinghai. According to a source in the Qinghai provincial government, during the late 1990s, approximately 30–50 percent of the pupils in Qinghai's bilingual schools failed to complete a six-year education. Our source noted that this was evidenced by a corresponding drop in the circulation of Tibetan-subject textbooks between the first and sixth grades of primary school. There are two likely reasons for such a decrease. Some pupils drop out of school, and others are unable to continue because their schools offer only three or four years of education.

In some areas, people live far apart in tiny settlements or still lead nomadic lives. Children have to walk for many hours to get to school, and roads may not be considered safe for young children. As a solution, the current trend seems to be to establish more boarding schools, especially in herding areas. However, the cost of boarding makes education particularly expensive for herding families. In the herding areas we visited in Kanlho TAP, boarding and textbooks in a county-level school cost about ¥500 (US$60) per year. In comparison, the average annual income of farmers and herders in Kanlho was ¥901 (US$110) in 1997.[40] In these circumstances, it is very difficult for most Tibetans to send their children to boarding school.[41]

Boarding school students usually spend most of the year away from their families. In order to give the children more time with their families, some boarding schools organize the school year according to their own schedules. We visited one boarding school for nomadic children in Matö County, Golok TAP, where students stayed at school from March through December (including the summer holidays) and returned to their families between December and March. The headmaster, who had himself been raised in a local family of nomadic herders, told us that this particular school emphasized preserving the area's traditional lifestyle. He knew that several families passed the school at least twice a year and invited them to put up their tents on the wide grasslands near the school. In this way, the children could attend school and help shear the animals during the summer. In autumn, the families came once more to pay a nomad tax at an office near the school.[42]

Despite school schedules that accommodate the seasonal migration patterns of nomadic herders, the children still must spend long periods away from home. Many parents are reluctant to send their children to boarding school until they are old enough to take care of themselves, which is understandable in view of the poor living conditions at many schools. Furthermore, as we were told by a nomadic family in Golok, the education provided by schools is largely irrelevant for life in the Tibetan countryside. In addition, since the children must leave home to attend the boarding schools, it is difficult for their parents to pass on important knowledge and teach the children the skills necessary for a life of farming and herding.

Many parents in rural areas simply fail to see the need for education, since very few local jobs require schooling. Educators have also argued that the cultural bias in the curriculum creates problems. According to one Tibetan education specialist, since the curriculum is based on conditions in central China, the educational content has no connection to the real-life experience or knowledge of Tibetan students.[43] This was confirmed by our interviewees. One man commented that as a child in school, he was perplexed when reading about traffic lights in his textbook, since he had never seen such a thing. In Chinese primary and middle schools, students spend a large part of their school day learning Chinese language, history, ideology and politics, and ideology and morals. The curriculum includes lessons on Marxist-Leninist ideology, patriotism, the thoughts of Mao, respect for the Revolutionary Heroes, and love of the CCP. This type of education has very little to offer rural Tibetan children.

Authorities have recognized that language represents one of the main problems in minority education. Minority children have difficulties competing with Han children for admission to institutions of higher education. The national entrance exam for universities has thus been made available in several minority languages, including Tibetan. A number of vocational schools, colleges, and universities also offer one- or two-year preparatory courses for minority students. Preferential policies give minority students increased access to higher education through a system of quotas and adjustments in admission requirements.

These policies, however, do not address the problems experienced by minority children in primary and middle school, when they are introduced to new subjects in an unfamiliar language. Students who receive a bilingual education also have difficulties. Their schedule, textbooks, and curriculum are the same as those of an ordinary school, except for the addition of a second language to their list of subjects. The heavier workload makes it more difficult for Tibetan students to compete in the educational system, whether they receive bilingual teaching or not. Many fail their exams and are unable to go on to senior middle school, college, or university. These problems are reflected in statistics on the ethnicity of middle school students. For instance, as of 1990, less than half the middle school students in Kandze TAP were minority students, while, according to the 1990 census, about 78 percent of the registered population were minorities, 75 percent of whom were Tibetans.[44]

According to Chinese sources, before 1954, about 90–95 percent of the Tibetan population was illiterate. The small literate population consisted of monks educated in the monasteries or people who belonged to the upper class, many of whom received their education in private schools. Although it is difficult to check the accuracy of such claims, if we were to use this data as a basis for comparison, we would find that in some Tibetan areas the situation today is not much better than it was before the People's Republic of China was established. When we visited Tsolho (Hainan) TAP, in Qinghai, in 1999, the prefectural government was involved in a project to combat illiteracy. Prefecture documents attested that 70 percent of young and middle-aged Tibetans were illiterate.[45] The educational attainment of Tibetans is still among the lowest in China. According to the 1990 national census, 19.4 percent of all Tibetans had completed only primary school, 4.6 percent had graduated from junior middle school, 2.1 percent from senior middle school, and only 0.4 percent from colleges and universities. In comparison, 19.9 percent of Han living in the TAR had completed only primary school, 38.8 percent had graduated from junior middle school, 24.6 percent from senior middle school, and 7.6 percent from colleges and universities. Thus, less than 10 percent of Han living in the TAR had failed to complete primary school, while the figure for Tibetans (in all of China) was 73.5 percent. The illiteracy rate for the TAR in 1990 was 73.8 percent, the highest of all China's provinces.[46]

FUNDING EDUCATION

Chinese authorities explicitly acknowledge the importance of educating ethnic minorities as a means of speeding up economic development in minority areas and have allocated special funds for that purpose.[47] In addition, both NGOs and local governments in the rich coastal areas are encouraged to contribute to the funding of education in minority areas. However, educational policies introduced in 1985 gave local governments final responsibility for funding their own primary and secondary education. Since the poorer counties are unable to provide adequate funds, these policies have created a disparity in quality of education between poor and wealthy regions. Many minority areas are among the poorest in China and are now experiencing serious problems, such as inability to pay teacher salaries, insufficient or poorly qualified teachers, and difficulties in providing education to all school-age children.[48]

County officials informed us that a local government typically would spend at least 30 percent of its income on education. In addition, the counties rely on financial support from the prefecture, province, and central government. For example, Tashiling (Lixian) County, in Ngaba, spent about half its income, ¥4,800,000 (US$600,000) in 1998, on education, mainly on salaries for its 700 teachers. The county had a total expenditure of ¥18,000,000 (US$2,200,000) and an income of only ¥10,000,000 (US$1,220,000). The balance was paid by the higher-level governments. In Haidong Prefecture, officials in Bayen (Hualong) County reported that they had more than 1,500 teachers and spent a total of ¥20,000,000 (US$2,500,000) annually on education; county income was only ¥15,000,000 (US$1,900,000). Educational expenditures accounted for 30–40 percent of county expenditures, or about ¥5,000,000 (US$630,000), while outside support was needed to cover the remaining ¥15,000,000 (US$1,900,000). Special funds from the central government are available for the construction of new schools in minority regions and poor areas; however, sources such as the Poor Areas Fund normally require the local government to provide 50 percent of the funding. Thus, it is difficult for the poorest local governments to utilize such funding.

Since the 1985 educational reforms, local education departments have been allowed to levy fees and taxes to provide funds for education. Funding strategies introduced in some Tibetan areas also include providing free grasslands and herds as income sources for individual schools. Fees collected from the parents of primary school children typically cover heating, cleaning, and wall decorations for the classroom. Students must often pay for their own textbooks and writing materials. Since these expenses have been increasing, some parents are unable to meet the costs. Officials in one county in Qinghai reported that more than 300 students in the county (4 percent of the students) were already unable to afford textbooks. Therefore, they initiated a system in which "one helps one," meaning that one government official subsidizes one student.

In several prefectures (including Golok and Kandze), we received information about an ongoing centralization process in which village-level schools were transformed into "key schools" (Ch: *zhongxin xuexiao*). Several village-level schools were merged to create larger boarding schools. The main reason for this type of restructuring was to provide better teachers and facilities. Local educators argued that the quality of education in these key schools is better than in the smaller, village-level schools. In addition, centralization of schools is cost-effective. As already mentioned, however, boarding schools tend to be more expensive for parents.

During our visit to Sichuan in the spring of 2000, the new policy Develop the Western Region, officially launched during the National People's Congress in February 2000, had stirred a new optimism among some officials in the education sector. Although infrastructure and telecommunications were among the main targets of the development plan, these officials hoped that funds would also be allocated to education. In Tawu County, Kandze TAP, we received a copy of a document produced by the education department, stating its strategy for taking advantage of the new policies on development. The article was titled "The Policy to Develop the Western Region.

FIG. 3.1. A newly rebuilt village district school in Drango County, Kandze.

What Will Happen to Tawu? Seize the Opportunity, Promote Development, and Foster High-Quality Talents."[49] This strategy contains eight steps for development and strongly emphasizes that education must be the first issue addressed. The plan suggests importing more qualified teachers from "developed" areas and establishing special classes in "developed" areas as ways of improving the standard of education.[50] The document's authors contend that development cannot succeed without a well-educated and skilled population. Minority-language education, however, is not included in these eight steps for development, which mention only the need for a general strengthening of *minzu* education. This statement may be interpreted as the intention to educate more students of minority background rather than to provide a better education in the Tibetan language and culture. Education authorities also stressed that investments from the rich coastal

FIG. 3.2. Tibetan girls in a Drango County primary school preparing for a math exam in Chinese.

areas of China are business, not development aid, and that investors expect returns on their investments.

Bilingual education in several areas is partially or fully sponsored by national or, in some cases, international NGOs. In certain areas, local governments seem to rely almost entirely on NGO funding to provide Tibetan students with the opportunity to learn Tibetan. In Dechen TAP, for instance, we found that NGO funding played a very important part in the teaching of the Tibetan language in schools, while education in Tibetan was available only because of private initiative. During our stay in the prefecture in 1998, we visited three bilingual schools that received funding from NGOs. Two were sponsored by the Rokpa Foundation, a charitable organization based in Britain, and run by the Tibetan tulku Akong Rinpoche.[51]

NGOs such as the Rokpa Foundation help fund a number of Tibetan schools, for example, the Tibetan middle school in Gyelthang (Zhongdian) County, Dechen TAP, and in Kakhok County, Ngaba Prefecture, and the Kangding Tibetan Middle School (Ch: Kangding Zangwen Zhongxue) in Kandze TAP. When the Tibetan middle school in Gyelthang was established in 1994, the Rokpa Foundation funded half the construction costs. At the time of our visit in 1998, this school offered the only courses in Tibetan language above the primary level for Tibetan students in Yunnan.[52] Since 1997,

FIG. 3.3. A *minzu* boarding school in Kangtsa County, Tsochang. This school was sponsored by several nongovernmental sources, including the Hong Kong magnate Shao Yifu and the China Women's Association.

the Rokpa Foundation had also provided annual scholarships for 60 poor students at Kangding Tibetan Middle School. When we visited this school in May 2000, it had 317 students, 200 of whom were boarding.[53] The students paid ¥200 (US$25) per term for tuition alone. We were told that 85 percent of the students came from farming or herding areas and were considered poor. The 60 sponsored students received ¥40 (US$5) per month from the Rokpa Foundation. In 2000, the Trace Foundation initiated a trial year of cooperation and sponsored another 60 poor students. Students were selected for scholarships on the basis of academic results and their families' economic situations. The school had a high reputation, and apart from languages, the students also studied Tibetan calligraphy.[54]

While most Tibetan schools we visited taught the general middle school

FIG. 3.4. Gyalten Rinpoche's private school in Kandze County. It opened in 1994 and is sponsored by a local tulku.

curriculum, some also provided vocational training. For example, the Hong-yuan County Tibetan Middle School in Kakhok had several vocational departments such as veterinary medicine and animal husbandry.[55] We found that vocational subjects were taught in Tibetan, although the textbooks were in Chinese. The Rokpa Foundation supported the school and covered expenses for 180 senior students per year, mainly in the vocational departments.

Private schools have in many cases been particularly successful in obtaining funding from foreign NGOs. In Tsolho TAP, we found that several private schools had opened during the 1990s and attracted foreign teachers to teach English. A few of these schools also received financial support from abroad. An educator in one of the private schools explained that the current attitude was that "Tibetan culture is worth protecting." Nevertheless, the curriculum at his school was the same as that of other schools, and the language of instruction was Chinese, with Chinese textbooks, except in the additional Tibetan-language class, which had textbooks in Tibetan. Even when a private school received funding from abroad, the curriculum was controlled by the local education department at the prefectural, county, and village district level.

MONASTERY-RUN SCHOOLS

Monasteries often play an important role as sponsors of private schools and particularly of schools that use Tibetan as the language of instruction. For instance, in Kandze TAP, we heard of a number of private primary schools (at least eight) that had been initiated and were sponsored by local tulkus. The classes in these schools were usually taught in Tibetan and focused on cultural education, including the Tibetan language. Some schools also offered classes in Tibetan art and medicine. The great majority of students in such schools were boys.

It appears that education authorities not only approved the establishment of private Tibetan schools but actually relied on these private initiatives to provide education in Tibetan. However, this did not mean that the establishment of private schools was unregulated. For example, according to information received from the Kandze Prefecture Education Department, the opening of private schools was subject to the following conditions: They must not be inside monasteries, they may use only recent and approved study materials, they must be administered by the local education department, their teachers must be assigned by the local education department, and teachers' wages must be no higher than the national level.

Despite the stipulation requiring approved study materials, one private school we visited was using traditional Buddhist texts to teach the Tibetan alphabet, reading and writing, and Tibetan grammar. These books were produced in the printing house of the monastery in charge of the school. The students ranged in age from six to thirty and were divided into four classes according to their knowledge rather than by age. According to the elderly monk who was their teacher, the pupils at this school did not learn Buddhism because they were "too young for that." The primary schools run by monasteries are usually considered standard primary schools. However, one source claimed that the majority of children sent to monasteries for basic education stayed on and became ordained monks later, when they reached the minimum age of eighteen.

Local charitable organizations also run schools that teach Tibetan. In Dechen County, for instance, we visited such a school adjacent to Dechenling Monastery. Its low cost was said to be one of the reasons parents preferred to send their children there, rather than to the nearby Dechen County Nationalities Primary School, which also taught Tibetan. The school had two teachers and about forty regular pupils between seven and nineteen years of age. Subjects taught in the school were Tibetan language, mathematics, drawing, and music. The textbooks were all in Tibetan and had been published in the TAR. The school received some funding from the Yunnan Province Religious Affairs Department and the Dechen County Education Department, but reconstruction work on the buildings had been performed entirely by volunteer labor.

Some of the monasteries we visited in Qinghai ran their own primary schools for village children. Most of these schools followed the national standard curriculum and taught Tibetan as well. We visited one such school where the advanced students even studied Sanskrit texts.

Several schools run by monasteries did not charge for tuition. Some private schools, such as the Jigme Gyaltsen Private School (Ch: Jimei Jianzan Sili Xuexiao), emphasized the preservation of the Tibetan language and culture while providing free education for poor children.[56] We were told that this school was especially concerned with taking care of orphans. It was established in 1994 and is named after its founder, Jigme Gyaltsen, a highly educated monk and the abbot of the nearby Radya Monastery. In 1999, the school had 140 students between the ages of nine and twenty-eight. Most of the students were Tibetan and came from Qinghai, but that year a few were also from Gansu. A small number of students were Mongolian. The students undertook a five-year course of study with traditional Tibetan culture, which included Buddhist logic and Tibetan language and grammar, as the main subject. All classes, even English, were taught in Tibetan with the exception of Chinese language.[57] The students also took a "labor class" (Ch: *laodong ke*), and at the time of our visit they were all participating in construction work by carrying stones for a new building. The school had both monk and lay students, all of them boys. Some of the monk students had studied in monasteries before joining the school and were planning to return for further monastic studies, while some of the lay students expected to go on to middle school after graduation. All students needed permission from their local governments before they could be admitted. Although the principal was the abbot of a Gelugpa monastery, there was reportedly no distinction made among the different Buddhist traditions. In 1999, the school had a staff of twelve teachers, five monks, and seven laymen.

TEXTBOOKS IN TIBETAN

With the exception of private schools, the bilingual primary and middle schools we visited used a series of textbooks known as the Five Provinces textbooks. These Tibetan textbooks are published cooperatively by the five regions and provinces that comprise Tibetan administrative areas: the TAR, Gansu, Qinghai, Sichuan, and Yunnan. The cooperative is managed by the Five Provinces and Regions Tibetan Textbook Coordinating Group,[58] which was governed by the Qinghai Province Education Department at the time of our visit in 1999.[59]

The editing of primary school textbooks began in the early 1980s and was completed by the end of the decade. Junior middle school textbooks in all subjects were edited by 1995, and by 1999, the series included textbooks in all subjects for primary and middle school, although reference and exercise books for many subjects were not yet done. However, Tibetan-language teaching materials for vocational schools, colleges, and universities were not included in the series. Schools had to produce such materials for themselves, either individually or in partnership with other schools.[60] In Qinghai, several projects were under way to edit new textbooks in Tibetan for courses above the middle school level. During our visit in 1999, the Qinghai Province Law School had just produced its own textbooks for courses in the Tibetan language and modern law, while the Nationalities Department of the Qinghai Province Teachers College had finished editing textbooks in Tibetan for most subjects, including mathematics, geography, physics, and chemistry. A great deal of effort was also being spent on producing dictionaries of Tibetan terminology for natural science subjects such as physics and chemistry.

The Five Provinces and Regions textbooks are translations of the standard Chinese (Mandarin) textbooks used all over China, except for textbooks used to teach Tibetan language, which are written specifically for Tibetan students and cover Tibetan subject matter. In addition to teaching basic writing skills and grammar, these textbooks are important as a means of conveying an understanding of Tibetan culture and a sense of Tibetan identity to Tibetan children. They present Tibetan literary heritage but also include a number of texts devoted to Chinese Communist ideology and daily life in Chinese towns.

The American anthropologist Janet Upton has concentrated her research on the content and use of Tibetan textbooks in bilingual schools in Ngaba Prefecture's Sungchu (Songpan) County. She notes of junior middle school textbooks that 24 percent of the texts are translations from Chinese, 47 percent are modern Tibetan, and 29 percent are what she terms "traditional" Tibetan.[61] Of the latter, 5 percent are classical texts and 13 percent are aphoristic sayings. The remaining traditional texts are on calligraphy and grammar. According to Upton, the translated texts are somewhat more likely to be weighted with political messages.

The ideological content of Tibetan textbooks clearly reflects the particular aims of *minzu* education, which is focused on promoting the idea of China as the "great Motherland" of all the different *minzu*. In fact, only a few selections in textbooks for Tibetan language deal with Tibetan history and religious life. The third-, fourth-, and fifth-grade textbooks we collected in 1999–2000 make references to the Potala Palace and the Norbulingka (Summer Palace) in Lhasa and to Kumbum Monastery. The text about the Norbulingka mainly describes the beauty of the parks and gardens, while the text about the Potala Palace mentions two famous figures in Tibetan history who were responsible for the construction of the main buildings of the Potala: King Songtsan Gampo, the first religious king of the Tibetan Empire, and the Great Fifth Dalai Lama. As far as we know, the text about Kumbum Monastery contains the only mention of the plight of Tibetan monasteries before the Liberalization period. This passage tells the story of a boy whose mother tells him about the remarkable "flower offering ceremony" (T: *me tog mchod 'bul*) that takes place during the Mönlam Chenmo festival at Kumbum, when elaborate butter sculptures are displayed to the pilgrims. The boy grows up and eventually visits Kumbum, but the monastery is closed down, and he is very disappointed. However, all his expectations are fulfilled on his next visit, when the monastery is open and he is able to witness the flower offering.

In addition to texts written originally in Tibetan and texts translated from Chinese, one can also find texts translated from Russian, primarily modern Russian literature, and other European languages. Upton notes that a number of classical Tibetan texts have been altered, with references to religion removed or replaced by secular alternatives, and that this creative editing has "radically secularized the Tibetan past." She concludes that translated texts are not used to the same extent by teachers, or in exams, as are texts written originally in Tibetan and that modern Tibetan literature is in many ways the most important for students, both as a model of good writing and because contemporary authors "speak directly to Tibetan concerns."[62]

Until 1998, the central government subsidized Tibetan-language textbooks in the Five Provinces series. According to our 1999 interviews, however, those who edited the textbooks were no longer receiving payment for their work, and the central government had cut its printing subsidies for Tibetan textbooks. According to our sources, students in areas that were not subsidizing textbooks through local taxation would have to start paying the market price for textbooks. Although Tibetan-language textbooks have been subsidized by regional authorities in the TAR, this has not been the practice in Tibetan areas outside the TAR. The reduction in funding from the central government would thus make the situation particularly difficult in these areas, where Tibetan-language textbooks were already more expensive than standard Chinese textbooks.

BILINGUAL EDUCATION IN TIBETAN AREAS OUTSIDE THE TAR

By comparing the percentage of Tibetans in the population with the percentage of students in bilingual schools, we get a very rough impression of the extent of education in Tibetan in the four provinces under study, as reported by the local governments. The following table presents the available figures from all Tibetan-designated prefectures by province:

As table 3.1 shows, there are great variations among provinces and seemingly very little correspondence between the percentage of Tibetans in the population and the percentage of students in bilingual schools. However, the situation in Yunnan does seem to indicate that where Tibetans constitute a relatively smaller minority, bilingual education may be given even less priority than one would expect considering demography alone.

Sichuan

Sichuan has three Tibetan autonomous administrative units: Kandze TAP, Ngaba Tibetan and Qiang Autonomous Prefecture, and Mili Tibetan Autonomous County (TAC). Of the three Tibetan-designated areas, Tibetans constitute the largest majority, 76 percent according to the 1990 national census, in Kandze. Ngaba had a registered population of 48 percent Tibetans, while Mili had only 30 percent according to the same census.[63] We visited Ngaba and Kandze in 1999 and 2000, and although they are neighbors in the same province, we found that the availability of bilingual education differed considerably. The percentage of Tibetans in the registered population is higher in Kandze than in Ngaba, and as we shall see, there are similar differences in the availability of bilingual schools in the two prefectures.

We interviewed officials in Ngaba Prefecture in 1999 and were informed that the prefecture had a total of 1,418 primary schools with 113,000 pupils.[64]

TABLE 3. Tibetans in Bilingual Schools

Province	Percent Tibetans in population	Students in primary and middle schools	Students in bilingual primary and middle schools	Percent students in bilingual schools	Percent Tibetan students in bilingual schools
Sichuan	62.6	237,492	75,698	31.9	51.0
Qinghai	49.2	201,104	82,599	41.1	83.5
Gansu	47.8	80,886	20,782	25.7	53.8
Yunnan	33.1	48,425	1,140	2.4	7.3

SOURCES: 1990 census and interviews with prefectural governments.

Of these, 233 schools (16.4 percent) were described as bilingual, located mainly in Ngaba, Kakhok, Dzoge, and Dzamthang (Rangtang) Counties and primarily in herding areas. The prefecture had 70 middle schools, with 29,400 students. Of these, 6 (8.6 percent) were said to use Tibetan as the language of instruction, and about 20 schools (28.6 percent) had Tibetan as a subject.[65] Five counties lacked bilingual middle school education: Trochu (Heishui), Tsenlha (Xiaojin), Tashiling, Maowün (Maoxian), and Wenchuan (Lunggu). The number of students in middle schools teaching in Tibetan was 2,900. The total number of students in bilingual schools (primary and middle schools) was reported to be about 20,000 (14 percent of all primary and middle school students).

According to statistics from the education department in Kandze TAP, which we visited in 2000, the prefecture had 1,216 primary schools at the end of 1999, including small, local point schools. Of these, 821 were classified as bilingual (67.5 percent), but only 211 were classified as teaching in Tibetan (17.4 percent). The prefecture had 81,336 pupils in primary school, 50,386 of them in bilingual schools (61.9 percent). Of these, only 11,999 were reported to receive their primary education in Tibetan (14.8 percent).[66] Kandze TAP had 40 middle schools according to 1999 statistics, including 18 junior middle schools, 19 senior middle schools, and 3 mid-level vocational schools. The Kandze Prefecture Education Department reported that 28 of these were classified as bilingual; 24 were taught in Chinese, while only 4 were taught in Tibetan. Of these, 3 were junior middle schools, located in Drango County, Kandze County, and Sershül County, and the other, the Kangding Tibetan Middle School, was a complete middle school (both junior and senior levels).[67] The prefecture had a total of 8 mid- and higher-level vocational schools with 4,423 students altogether in 2000. One of these was the Ganzi Tibetan School, administered and funded by the Sichuan Province Ethnic Affairs Commission. There were then 13,756 middle school students, and 5,412 of these were said to be attending a bilingual school (39 percent). Of these, 842 (6 percent) were being educated in Tibetan, while the other 4,570 students (33 percent) were learning in Chinese with the opportunity to take Tibetan as an additional subject. However, we were told that "bilingual" could also refer to schools where English is taught as a second language, which means that Tibetan is not necessarily the second language in a bilingual school in Kandze. Study of English is an entrance requirement at Chinese universities, and we were told that Tibetan classes are increasingly being replaced by English classes.[68]

Although the two Tibetan prefectures in Sichuan, Kandze and Ngaba, operate the same two-track system of bilingual education and thus appear to be following the same guidelines for the teaching of Tibetan, we found a remarkable difference in the availability of bilingual education. According to our interviews with government officials, only 14 percent of students in Ngaba Prefecture attended a bilingual school, whereas nearly 59 percent in Kandze did so. If we take into consideration the share of Tibetans in the population, we may assume that approximately 30 percent of Tibetan students in Ngaba and 77 percent in Kandze received an education in bilingual primary and middle schools at the end of the 1990s.[69] Again, we see that bilingual education was disproportionately less available in areas with a smaller percentage of Tibetans in the population.

Gansu

Gansu has one Tibetan prefecture, Kanlho TAP, and one Tibetan county, Pari (Tianzhu) TAC, in Wuwei Prefecture. According to the 1990 national census, Tibetans constituted 48 percent of the population of Kanlho and 26 percent in Pari.[70]

When we visited Kanlho TAP in 1999, the education department officials we interviewed provided us with the following information. They reported that the prefecture had a total of 680 primary schools, with 67,812 pupils. Of these, 211 were bilingual primary schools, with 16,720 pupils (25 percent of the total). The prefecture had 27 middle schools, with 13,074 students.[71] There were 10 bilingual middle schools, and 14 bilingual nine-year schools that included junior middle school students.[72] Altogether, there were 4,062 students in bilingual middle schools in the prefecture (31 percent of the total). There were 4 mid-level vocational schools in Kanlho, and only 1 was described as bilingual.[73] Bilingual schools in Kanlho were concentrated in three counties: Machu, Luchu (Luqu), and Sangchu (Xiahe). In these three counties, 126 out of 139 primary schools (90 percent) were described as bilingual. In the remaining four counties in the prefecture, only a small percentage of primary schools were bilingual. Of these, Batse (Lintan) County had the fewest, with only 3 bilingual primary schools out of 140 (2 percent).[74]

According to a study published in 1996, only 34 percent of schools for Tibetans in Kanlho taught in Tibetan.[75] Education departments in both Sangchu County and Kanlho TAP reported that Tibetan was the language of instruction in primary schools in herding areas, whereas in "ethnically mixed areas" (Ch: *zaju qu*), the language of instruction was Chinese. Government officials further reported that in Batse and Drukchu (Zhouqu), Tibetan middle schools taught mainly in Chinese, and the remaining five counties all had classes in both Tibetan and Chinese in their Tibetan middle schools. This indicates that Tibetan students had the option of choosing a middle school education in Tibetan in most county towns in Kanlho. As might be expected, the counties where bilingual education and teaching in Tibetan were least available were those with the smallest share of Tibetans in their populations. Batse's registered Tibetan population was only 11 percent, while Drukchu registered 31 percent Tibetans in the 1990 national census. The remaining five counties in Kanlho had Tibetan majorities of between 61 percent and 90 percent.

Yunnan

Within Yunnan, Dechen is the only Tibetan Autonomous Prefecture. Although the population of Dechen consists largely of ethnic minorities, bilingual education has not been promoted.[76] At the time of our visit in 1998, only two minority languages were taught in schools: Lisu and Tibetan. The prefecture education department reported that there were primary schools teaching Tibetan in all three counties in the prefecture.[77] Two middle schools were also described as bilingual (Tibetan and Chinese): the Tibetan middle school and the medical school.[78] The number of pupils in bilingual (Tibetan-Chinese) schools was 1,140, only 2.4 percent of the pupils in the prefecture.[79] Compared to other Tibetan-designated prefectures, Dechen thus had the lowest rate of bilingual education. Moreover, education in Tibetan was close to nonexistent in the prefecture.

Qinghai

Qinghai has six Tibetan-designated prefectures, which we visited during 1999: Tsonub (Haixi) Mongolian and Tibetan Autonomous Prefecture, Tsochang TAP, Tsolho TAP, Malho TAP, Golok TAP, and Jyekundo TAP. Six of the seven prefectures in Qinghai are Tibetan autonomous, covering approximately 97 percent of the province. In comparison, Tibetan-designated areas cover only 44 percent of the total area of Sichuan, and even less in Gansu and Yunnan. Qinghai thus has the largest Tibetan-designated area of the four provinces in this study as well as the largest share of Tibetans in the population.[80] We also found that of the four provinces, Qinghai had the highest rate of students in bilingual schools. However, due to major variations among the different prefectures, it is difficult to evaluate the conditions for bilingual education and teaching in Tibetan in Qinghai as a whole. In particular, we found significant differences in the availability of bilingual education in prefectures where Tibetans are in the minority as compared to those where Tibetans are a registered majority.

Table 3.2 compares the relative size of the Tibetan population in each prefecture with the availability of bilingual education, based on information from local interviews.[81] The table suggests that the percentage of students in bilingual schools rises with an increase in the percentage of Tibetans in the population. It is important to keep in mind, however, that this kind of quantitative presentation of the availability of bilingual schooling says nothing about the quality of the schools.

As shown in table 3.2, four prefectures in Qinghai have registered Tibetan majorities: Tsolho, Malho, Golok, and Jyekundo. Tibetans in these prefectures composed between 58.5 percent and 96.5 percent of the total population, according to the 1990 national census. In these prefectures, the government reported rates that suggest at least 90 percent of Tibetan students attended bilingual schools. In two prefectures, Golok and Jyekundo, the percentage of students in bilingual schools was actually reported to be higher than the percentage of Tibetans in the population. In the other two prefectures, Malho and Tsolho, the reported share of students in bilingual schools was 90–97 percent of the Tibetans in the registered population. It appears that in these four prefectures, a very large percentage of Tibetan children attending school had the opportunity to learn Tibetan.

However, in the two prefectures with the smallest share of Tibetans, Tsonub and Tsochang, bilingual education was available only to an estimated 36 percent and 57 percent, respectively, of Tibetan students. We found a sim-

TABLE 4. Tibetans in Population and in Bilingual Schools, Qinghai

Prefecture	Percent Tibetans in population	Students in primary and middle schools	Students in bilingual primary and middle schools	Percent students in bilingual schools
Tsochang	20.2	35,462	2,575	7.3
Tsonub	9.9	52,671	2,966	5.6
Tsolho	58.5	54,704	28,802	52.6
Malho	63.6	24,857	15,318	61.6
Golok	88.0	10,068	9,596	95.3
Jyekundo	96.5	23,342	23,342	100
TOTAL	49.2	201,104	82,599	41

SOURCES: 1990 census and local interviews conducted in 1999.

ilar situation in Bayen County in Haidong, which is not designated as Tibetan but has about the same percentage of Tibetans in the registered population as does Tsochang (20.2 percent). Bayen reported a slightly higher percentage of students attending bilingual schools (10.3 percent) compared to Tsochang (7.3 percent). It is also worth noting that areas within Tsonub and Tsochang where Tibetans compose a particularly small share of the population did not appear to have bilingual Chinese-Tibetan schools at all.[82]

Education conducted in Tibetan appeared to be less comprehensively developed in Qinghai than in Tibetan areas of neighboring Sichuan and Gansu. As far as we know, the system of parallel classes taught in Chinese and Tibetan that has been implemented in Sichuan and Gansu is not used in Qinghai, and some parts of Qinghai do not teach in Tibetan at all. Furthermore, in most areas, we found that Tibetan was used as the language of instruction only in primary schools, whereas the great majority of bilingual middle schools were taught in Chinese. At the middle school level and above, Tibetan was usually just an extra subject in *minzu* schools.

With the exception of Golok, it is difficult to find middle schools that teach in Tibetan in Qinghai. Primary school pupils who have been taught in Tibetan therefore experience a shift in the language of instruction if they continue to middle school. Furthermore, we found that higher-level education in Tibetan was limited to teacher training and Tibetan medicine. Although it is difficult to know the effects of this situation, there is evidence that Tibetan children fail to complete primary school more frequently than do Han children. In addition, statistics from both Jyekundo and Golok confirm that Tibetan students tend to continue to junior and senior middle school less frequently than do non-Tibetan students.

Tsochang. The Tsochang TAP Education Department reported that most Tsochang schools used Chinese as the language of instruction, while *minzu* schools used Chinese and Tibetan or Chinese and Mongolian.[83] A school was defined as a *minzu* school if more than 65 percent of the students were from minority *minzu*. We were informed that at the time of our visit, every village had a primary school, every district had a boarding school, every county had a *minzu* middle school, and the prefecture had a *minzu* teachers training school, a *minzu* vocational school, and a medical school with a Tibetan medicine department.[84] By 1999, the prefecture had 257 primary and middle schools with 35,462 students.[85] According to the prefecture government, Tsochang had altogether 23 bilingual primary schools and 3 bilingual middle schools (10 percent of the schools).[86] Of these schools, 3 taught in Chinese and Mongolian and 20 in Chinese and Tibetan. The total number of students in bilingual schools (including Chinese-Mongolian schools) was 2,575 (7.3 percent of the students), of which 2,346 were in primary school and 229 in middle school.[87]

Tsonub: The education department of Tsonub Mongolian and Tibetan Prefecture reported a total of 159 primary schools with 36,236 pupils and 50 middle schools with 16,435 students at the time of our visit. Tsonub's 43 bilingual primary schools, both Chinese-Mongolian and Chinese-Tibetan, had 4,348 pupils. Of these, 1,736 were in Chinese-Mongolian schools and 2,612 were in Chinese-Tibetan schools (7 percent of primary school students). Tsonub had 5 bilingual middle schools with 1,192 students. These included 4 Chinese-Mongolian schools, with 838 students, and 1 Chinese-Tibetan school, with 354 students (2 percent of middle school students).[88] Tsonub's registered Tibetan population was 10 percent of the total according to the 1990 census, which indicates that roughly 72 percent of Tibetan primary school students attended a bilingual school in the prefecture. The equivalent figure for middle school would be 22 percent. Most of the bilingual schools in Tsonub were classified as minority *minzu* schools.[89] Within Tsonub, only Themchen (Tianjun) County had a Tibetan majority (nearly 80 percent, per the 1990 census). In all other counties and districts, Tibetans composed less than 20 percent of the population. Themchen County also had 13 of the 18 *minzu* primary schools that were described as bilingual (Tibetan-Chinese) and the only Tibetan-Chinese bilingual *minzu* middle school in the prefecture. When we visited Themchen, the education department confirmed that the county had 13 primary schools, which all used Tibetan language for instruction and were described as minority *minzu* schools, and 1 "standard" (Ch: *putong*) primary school, which was located in the county seat. Officials also informed us that there were 2 middle schools in the county: a standard middle school and a *minzu* middle school where Tibetan was taught although the language of instruction was Chinese.[90]

Tsolho. The education department in Tsolho TAP informed us that the prefecture had a total of 446 schools with 54,704 students.[91] Of these, 283 schools (63.4 percent) were described as bilingual and had a total of 28,802 students (52.6 percent). Officials explained that the prefecture leader provides guidelines for the use of Tibetan language in the prefecture. We were told that since 1996, all minority *minzu* students have been able to learn Tibetan, based on guidelines issued by the former prefecture leader. It was uncertain, however, whether the new prefecture leader, appointed in 1999, would continue this policy.[92] The prefecture education department further reported that in *minzu* schools, all subjects in the first two years of primary school were taught in Tibetan. From the third grade onward, classes were taught in Chinese. The *minzu* middle schools were said to be the same as standard middle schools except for the addition of Tibetan-language classes.

Malho. Bilingual schools also appeared to be available to most Tibetan students in Malho TAP. According to the prefecture education department, Malho had 221 schools in 1999: 205 primary schools (110 of them bilingual), 14 middle schools (8 bilingual), and 2 mid-level vocational schools (both bilingual).[93] These schools had a total of 25,583 students,[94] whereas the bilingual schools had 15,318 students (61.6 percent of primary and middle school students in the prefecture). The education department was unable to provide precise information on the language of instruction in bilingual schools but stated that in primary schools, education was "mostly Tibetan," whereas in middle schools it was "mostly Chinese."

Golok. According to our information, middle schools that teach in Tibetan were regularly available only in Golok TAP, where every county was reported to have one Tibetan middle school with Tibetan as the language of instruction and one Chinese *minzu* middle school with classes in Tibetan language available. In addition, the prefecture had one standard middle school where Tibetan was not on the curriculum. The Golok TAP Education Department further reported that there were 89 schools in the prefecture in 1999: 13 middle schools[95] and 74 primary schools with a total of 8,728 primary school pupils. Of the primary schools, 43 were "village district" (Ch: *xiang*) boarding schools and 31 were "village" (Ch: *cun*) schools. Although all the primary schools were officially classified as bilingual, the district-level schools used Chinese as the language of instruction, while the village-level schools taught in Tibetan. We were told that village-level schools generally used Tibetan as the language of instruction at least for the first three or four years of primary school.

Jyekundo. At the time of our visit to Jyekundo TAP, the prefecture had 142 schools: 129 primary schools, 10 middle schools, 2 vocational schools, and 1 province-level college.[96] According to the Jyekundo Prefecture Education Department, all the schools were *minzu* schools and all schools in the prefecture were bilingual. The medium of instruction was said to be Chinese, although Tibetan-language classes were taught in Tibetan. According to this information, it appears that Jyekundo TAP is actually not using Tibetan as the language of instruction at the primary school level, which makes it an exception among other Tibetan areas of Qinghai.[97] The total number of primary school pupils in the prefecture was 19,224, of which 18,560 were Tibetan (96.5 percent). The total number of middle school students was 4,118, of which 3,278 were Tibetan (79.6 percent). Jyekundo's registered population was 96 percent Tibetan according to the 1990 census, which makes the information that all schools were using Chinese as the language of instruction even more difficult to believe.

TEACHERS AND TEACHER TRAINING

A shortage of qualified teachers is a common problem in Tibetan areas. In Kandze County, we visited one of the prefecture's five "first-rate" primary schools and were surprised to discover that only two teachers had a senior middle school background. One, a Mongolian, taught physical education, and the other, a Tibetan, taught Tibetan language.[98] The other teachers were even less educated. From two different county-level education departments in Golok TAP, we received detailed information about the educational background of teachers in the two counties. In Matö County, 60 of 103 teachers had graduated from junior middle school and taken an additional teaching course, 12 had completed senior middle school, 27 were educated as teachers, and 4 had completed only junior middle school. In Darlak County, 78 of 103 teachers had completed junior middle school, while only 18 were educated as teachers and 7 had other educational backgrounds. The last category was not defined.

In addition to a lack of professional teachers among the teaching staff, even those educated at the prefecture's teachers training school may not be well qualified. All graduates of such schools must take a national standard test in order to obtain their teaching certificates. According to the staff of the Guoluo Minzu Teachers Training School (Ch: Guoluo Minzu Shifan Xuexiao), the graduates achieved extremely low scores on this test. The average score was reportedly 0 percent, which meant that the new teachers were qualified to teach in Golok only. The average results by subject were math, 0 percent; Chinese, 6 percent; and Tibetan, 68 percent.[99] Like many other *minzu* teachers training schools, the school in Golok offered a preparatory year during which students could improve their junior middle school qualifications, including their Chinese-language skills. The students had to pass an entrance exam. We were informed that passing scores were different for different types of students. The average minimum was 300, but the children of cadres could enter with slightly lower scores, and the children of herders could enter with a score as low as 188.[100]

In almost all the areas we visited, educators and officials in the education departments remarked on the need to raise the educational level of teachers, and departments in some areas had formulated specific plans for this purpose. The education department in Kandze TAP, for example, had established the goal that by 2005, all primary school teachers below the age of forty-five should have completed twelve years of school or the equivalent of senior middle school in order to teach.[101] English is becoming a popular subject even in primary and middle schools, and in Tsolho TAP, the Gepa Sumdo (Tongde) County government supported a project, initiated in 1997, in which English teachers from Australia and the United States were invited to teach English to local teachers. We were told that, beginning in autumn 1999, all primary schools in the county were to teach English from the fourth grade onward.[102]

Tsochang is another prefecture that has made significant efforts to promote the education of teachers. One of the high-profile projects undertaken in 1999 was the construction of new buildings for the Haibei Minzu Teachers Training School. The impressive new buildings covered 5,800 square meters, including a conference hall of 1,100 square meters, the largest in the prefecture. The school was described locally as the "best prefecture-level *minzu* teachers training school in Qinghai." We were told that ¥8,000,000 (US$980,000) from the central government and ¥3,000,000 (US$370,000) from the prefecture government were being spent on the construction of buildings alone. The prefecture was spending an additional ¥2,800,000 (US$345,000) on equipment, including ¥200,000 (US$25,000) on forty computers. We were given a tour of the still unfinished classrooms and science labs, a linguistics lab, computer and music rehearsal rooms, a 230–chair lecture hall, a dance practice room, and a TV studio for broadcast classes. According to the headmaster, the school's classes would be taught in both Chinese and Tibetan.[103]

As in Tsochang, some teachers training schools offer parallel courses taught in Tibetan and Chinese. This provides an opportunity for students from the Tibetan track to continue their education in Tibetan and eventually become teachers at schools that teach in Tibetan. However, relatively few of the students in teachers training schools appeared to be receiving their training in Tibetan. For instance, at Ma'erkang Minzu Teachers Training School, one of two teachers training schools in Ngaba Prefecture, we were told that of a total of 644 students, only 118 were taking the Tibetan track. The school had three departments—Tibetan, Chinese, and athletics—and instruction in Tibetan was provided only in the Tibetan track of the Tibetan department.

In some cases, a particular effort has been made to train more teachers for bilingual schools. In the Tibetan school in Dartsedo, one of the few Tibetan-language vocational schools in Sichuan, a special class has been established to improve the language skills of Tibetan teachers, especially teachers from Tibetan areas outside of Kandze and Ngaba. In Qinghai, the province-level teachers college established an adult education department aimed at primary and middle school teachers from herding areas in the TAR, Gansu, Sichuan, and Qinghai. At the time of our visit, this department had more than 300 students and was offering three-year courses in Tibetan, physics, math, and chemistry, all taught in Tibetan. The Nationlities Department of the Qinghai Province Teachers College was also teaching natural science subjects such as math, geography, physics, and chemistry in Tibetan to ordinary students, the future teachers of bilingual schools in Qinghai. This was one of the few colleges that taught courses in the natural sciences in Tibetan.

The teaching of Tibetan was completely discontinued during the Cultural Revolution, which has resulted in a serious shortage of teachers trained to teach Tibetan in bilingual schools. Several of the young Tibetan students with whom we talked explained that teachers are perceived by Tibetans as highly valuable and that much of their motivation for becoming teachers was to keep the Tibetan written language alive. Their ambition was to teach in Tibetan, and after graduation, they planned to go back to their home villages and work in the local schools. These young students were well aware of the desperate need for qualified teachers. We also encountered a large number of enthusiastic teachers in Tibetan areas who told us that they were willing to accept low salaries in order to help preserve the Tibetan language and culture and saw it as their duty to teach in Tibetan.

CONTEMPORARY CHALLENGES
FOR BILINGUAL EDUCATION

During the 1980s, the Chinese state adopted a number of policies allowing for bilingual education, which made it possible for many Tibetan children to learn to read and write their own language. Since the mid-1990s, however, the development of bilingual education has met with growing difficulties. When it is necessary to choose between a standard Chinese system and a bilingual method of education, the standard Chinese system is increasingly favored. There are simply not enough funds to provide extra teachers and subsidize more expensive textbooks.

Balancing the teaching of Chinese and Tibetan as subjects and as languages of instruction in bilingual schools represents another major challenge. During the 1980s and 1990s, a number of trial projects were carried out to test the benefits of teaching in Tibetan in schools for Tibetans.[104] These projects generally received glowing reports, and as a result many educators acknowledged that Tibetan students are better off being taught in their native language, at least during their first years of schooling. In many Tibetan areas, however, primary school classes may be taught in Tibetan but middle school classes are taught in Chinese. Since most high-level education is offered in Chinese only, Tibetan students in these areas must learn Chinese if they want to continue their education beyond primary school. The inevitable shift from Tibetan to Chinese as the language of instruction creates difficulties for Tibetan students that Chinese-speaking students do not experience. Nor is it easy for Tibetan students in bilingual schools to master two very different languages, using two different scripts. Although Tibetan students usually know how to speak Tibetan, in bilingual schools they also learn written Tibetan, which often varies greatly from their native spoken dialect.[105]

Schools that instruct in Tibetan are located mainly in rural areas with no Chinese inhabitants. Teaching in Tibetan under such conditions is not necessarily an explicit educational strategy but may be a consequence of local teachers' lack of competence with Chinese, insufficient resources, and a general inattention to education. Although Chinese is one of the main subjects in the Chinese primary school curriculum, Tibetan children in many of the point schools in Tibetan areas may not be able to learn Chinese at all. When this is the case, Tibetan children are seriously disadvantaged and will in most cases be unable to continue to middle school. The unavailability of middle schools that teach in Tibetan thus represents a serious barrier for Tibetan students and causes many to end their education upon completing primary school.

The introduction of bilingual schools with parallel classes has remedied many of the problems faced by Tibetan students and represents an evident improvement. The two-track system has enabled many Tibetan students to learn both Chinese and Tibetan and to choose which should be their main language. Yet, despite the obvious advantages of this system, there are also difficulties. A major disadvantage for Tibetan-track students is the limited range of higher-level courses available in Tibetan. Apart from Tibetan medicine, which is taught in all Tibetan autonomous areas in mid- or higher-level schools, courses taught in Tibetan are mainly in the subjects of the arts, mathematics, and language training for teachers in bilingual schools.[106] In comparison, a wide range of courses is available in Chinese, including such subjects as natural science, economics, law, and business management. Forestry, engineering, and agricultural and veterinary studies, for example, are taught in Chinese only.

Not only are Tibetan-track classes limited in number but the number of students admitted to these courses has been decreasing, indicating that higher-level education is available to fewer students in the Tibetan track.[107] Educators in Kanlho, for instance, described the situation for teaching in Tibetan as increasingly difficult. Decreased admission quotas for Tibetan-track students at colleges and universities mean that fewer of these students are able to continue their education after senior middle school.

Another problem is that choosing Tibetan as a second language precludes Tibetan-track students from taking English classes where these have been available. English is becoming more important for university studies and in tourism and is also critical for contact with foreign countries. Entrance exams for universities demand a basic knowledge of English. While many middle schools that use Chinese as the language of instruction now include the English language in their curriculum, the Tibetan-track students often must choose between Tibetan- and English-language classes. Although we were told that the entrance exams took this into account, the lack of English skills will affect career opportunities for graduates from the Tibetan track.

Formerly, under the "job assignment system" (Ch: *fenpei zhidu*), middle school graduates were assured a stable income and social security benefits in a "work unit" (Ch: *danwei*) that provided for their basic needs. In 1998, new regulations ended this system, leaving graduates from middle schools and colleges to compete on the open market. During our visit to Sichuan in 2000, we were told that immediately after this system ended, dropout rates increased in schools at all levels in the Tibetan areas of Sichuan. Tibetan students and parents were forced to reconsider their choice of education, including the choice of language, as an investment in future employment. Many realized that in an open job market, employment opportunities for Tibetan-track graduates are especially limited. Tibetans compete with Han for jobs, and desirable jobs often require a good command of the Chinese language. At the same time, there is much less need for people qualified in Tibetan. We interviewed an education expert in Kandze TAP, who said, "There is a limit to how many Tibetan translators are needed."

During our fieldwork, we found that the importance of learning Chinese was emphasized even in bilingual schools, where the use of Tibetan was regarded as a means by which Tibetan students could eventually gain an adequate command of Chinese. There was also a tendency to increase the use of Chinese in primary and middle schools, since fluency in Chinese was thought to increase students' chances of passing the entrance exams for middle school or institutions of higher learning. For instance, in Derge County, Kandze TAP, we visited a boarding school where all classes were taught in Tibetan. In an interview, the head of the school informed us that, starting in fall 2000, math would be taught in Chinese because increased instruction in Chinese would better prepare pupils for middle school. This view acknowledges the fact that Tibetan students must use the Chinese language to compete with Han students in most higher-level studies.

According to a report by local education specialists in Tibetan areas of Sichuan, bilingual education fails to fulfill "the needs of the people" in both nomadic and agricultural areas.[108] Furthermore, the report notes that the teaching of science lags far behind instruction in the arts and humanities in minority education. It describes the quality of education in Tibetan areas of Sichuan as poor. Among the reasons given are a backward economy, a remote and difficult environment, limited resources, incompetent educational management, poorly qualified teachers, and inappropriate teaching methods. The report concludes that *minzu* education in Tibetan areas of Sichuan is also inadequate to meet the needs of society. A large number of graduate-level students cannot pass their final exams. For instance, in the junior middle school final exams in 1994, less than 20 percent of students in Kandze passed in the subject of Tibetan language, whereas about 45 percent passed in the subject of Chinese.[109]

A number of Chinese and Tibetan educational experts have openly expressed their views on bilingual education, recognizing that language training is one of the main problems in minority education.[110] Their speeches and writings reflect a grave concern among Tibetan educators about the future role of the Tibetan language, in schools as well as in society at large. They note that an alarming number of Tibetans are incapable of reading and even speaking their own language.

Economic reforms, including those related to the funding of education, have weakened the role of Tibetan-language education. Since the beginning of market reforms in the 1980s, knowledge of Chinese has become increasingly necessary for people in minority areas, both for doing business and for obtaining government employment. The end of the job assignment system made market forces even more important. Even where Tibetans have a choice among standard Chinese education, schools that teach in Chinese with Tibetan classes, and education in Tibetan, many are now opting for standard Chinese schools or the Chinese track in *minzu* schools because they feel that a good knowledge of Chinese is more than ever necessary for finding a job. Some even contend that Tibetan is becoming a useless language. However, in many areas there is clearly a demand for more schools that use Tibetan as the language of instruction, and in some cases this option has been available only at private schools sponsored by monasteries or NGOs. The lack of funding has obviously been an important factor, but the politicization of the language issue may also have made local educators and officials reluctant to demand more teaching in Tibetan in public schools lest they be accused of local nationalism.

Education is taking on greater importance for Tibetans who wish to participate in the economic development of their region and avoid being marginalized in decision-making processes. In order to play a part in these processes, however, Tibetans currently have no choice but to become fluent in the Chinese language, study subjects taught only in Chinese within the standard Chinese educational system, and finally to work through the institutions of the Chinese state. For those who choose this path, the challenges are considerable and leave them few opportunities to learn to read and write Tibetan. Quite a few educated Tibetans resent this situation.

There seems to be little if any disagreement that the Tibetan language constitutes a vital aspect of Tibetan culture and that the survival of written Tibetan is important for cultural survival. But opinions begin to diverge when it comes to practical measures to ensure the preservation of the Tibetan language and how to combine this attempt with the equally important effort to provide opportunities for Tibetans in a social setting in which Chinese is evidently the most important language. Some tend to see the promotion of the Tibetan language and culture through the educational system as their main priority, whereas others argue that a strong emphasis on the Tibetan language at the expense of other subjects serves only to diminish opportunities for Tibetans to take part in the development of their communities.

4 / In Search of Tibetan Culture

When Chinese leaders give themselves credit for developing Tibetan culture, they are often referring to advances in publishing and broadcasting in Tibetan. A Chinese white paper of July 2000 characteristically describes not only government spending on education and "cultural relics" (Ch: *wenwu*),[1] including monasteries, but also the development of mass media such as broadcasting, cinema, and newspapers and artistic production within modern literature, painting, and performing arts. In addition, the publication describes the further development of Tibetan medicine, museums, archives, and archaeological surveys and the celebration of traditional Tibetan festivals, concluding that both traditional and modern aspects of Tibetan culture are being encouraged and supported: "While developing and promoting its traditional culture, Tibet is also developing modern scientific and technological education and news dissemination at an unprecedented rate. It deserves careful reflection that, although Tibetan culture is developing continuously, the Dalai Lama clique is clamoring all over the world that Tibetan culture has become extinct, and, on this pretext, is whipping up anti-China opinions with the backing of international antagonist forces."[2]

In order to counter these claims of the Dalai Lama "clique," the white paper redefines Tibetan culture to include modern cultural expressions. In so doing, it confronts the very notion of Tibetan culture as an essentially Buddhist culture, which is how Tibetan culture has been represented in some of the publications produced by Tibetan exiles and Western nongovernmental organizations (NGOs). This is a clear example of a struggle to define Tibetan culture, with political implications that involve not only what Tibetan culture is but, even more important, what it should be.

In this chapter, we examine primarily the modern Tibetan culture promoted by Chinese authorities within numerous institutional settings. Publishing and mass media are prominent in communicating this cultural production, which includes contemporary art forms such as literature, theater, photography, and painting. We also discuss the use of the Tibetan language in local governance and daily life, look into the role of "culture departments" (Ch: *wenhuaju*) in promoting institutionalized cultural expressions, and examine the reinstatement of popular festivals within new political contexts.

LANGUAGE AND LITERATURE

During the early 1950s, Chinese Communist Party (CCP) policy was to use Tibetan as the main language in areas inhabited by Tibetans. In eastern Tibetan areas, the first government meeting about the use of Tibetan language took place in 1952.[3] The authorities concluded that Tibetan should be used as the main language at all levels of government within the region, but reports and propaganda materials should be printed in both Chinese and Tibetan. Han cadres were to learn spoken and written Tibetan, Tibetan cadres should learn Chinese, and those who were able to learn quickly would receive prizes.[4] At the national level and in several provinces, "*minzu* publishing houses" (Ch: *minzu chubanshe*) started to publish literature in minority languages, including Tibetan.

The Tibetan exile historian Tsering Shakya, who has researched the development of Tibetan literature since the 1950s, writes that the first stage of the CCP colonizing project in Tibetan areas during the 1950s was directed primarily at establishing an apparatus for governance.[5] As far as language was concerned, translating Communist terminology into Tibetan and creating a new Communist lexicon were of paramount importance. At this stage, Tibetan intellectuals were recruited as patriotic personages to form, in Tsering Shakya's words, "a class of mediators between the past and the present." Literate monks represented one such useful elite for the new rulers.[6]

The skills of the old elite were needed in the first years of the People's Republic of China, but when the Democratic Reforms campaign was introduced, the old elite came under attack, and efforts to support use of the Tibetan language more or less ended. During the worst years of oppression, there was not much in the way of publishing in Tibetan or institutionalized cultural activities in Tibetan areas other than song and dance troupes praising Mao Zedong. With the onset of the Cultural Revolution in 1966,

Tibetan-language publishing consisted of CCP propaganda materials and translations of news reports from Chinese newspapers. The Tibetan language was no longer taught in schools. All Tibetans who were educated during this period were taught in Chinese only, and a generation of Tibetan cadres is unable to read or write their own language.

Not until the Third Plenary Session of the Eleventh Party Congress in 1978 did authorities revise their policies toward ethnic minorities and begin to support the resurrection of minority languages. Around 1980, Chinese authorities began reintroducing the use of minority languages in the government of autonomous areas and sponsoring research and publications on ancient books, folk literature, art, Tibetan medicine, and astronomy. Modern Tibetan novels are being published, although they often are written in Chinese by Tibetan authors and then translated into Tibetan. Painters cooperatives have been established, and Tibetan opera is again being performed at arts festivals. Much of this cultural production is also available to a wider audience through radio and television broadcasting.

Radio broadcasts began in Tibetan areas in the 1950s, and today most local stations in these areas broadcast regularly in Tibetan, offering news and educational and cultural programs, mainly traditional music. Since the early 1980s, television's popularity has grown, and Tibetan-language programs are now transmitted to most areas of the Tibetan Plateau. Outside the Tibet Autonomous Region (TAR), Qinghai TV Station's Tibetan Department, established in 1984, is one of the main producers of Tibetan-language programming. Qinghai TV channels currently broadcast programs in Tibetan to most Tibetan areas and began satellite transmission in 1997. The staff of the Tibetan Department numbered forty-five persons in 1999. It has one department for news and another for features and other programs.[7] We were told that in 1994, the station broadcast in Tibetan for fifteen minutes daily—ten minutes of news and five minutes of cultural programming. By 1999, the broadcast was one hour per day. According to Tibetan viewers, the feature programs presented mostly Tibetan traditional music, dance, and costumes.[8] Programs produced in Qinghai are broadcast in the Amdo dialect, and although they are available in areas of Sichuan, we were told in Sichuan that Tibetans there, who speak the Kham dialect, often ignored the programs because of language problems. However, one Tibetan from Mili (Muli) Tibetan Autonomous County (TAC) in Sichuan said that he always watched the Qinghai channel because it confirmed his Tibetanness.[9] This Tibetan even claimed that minorities in general liked to watch minority programs and that doing this made them feel closer to one another than to the Han.

A large number of feature films have been subtitled or dubbed into Tibetan. For instance, the Qinghai Province Film Translation and Production Factory has translated films into Tibetan since 1975.[10] Most films are dubbed in the Amdo dialect, but some are also dubbed in Kham. Several prefectures and counties in Qinghai have local branch offices that subtitle or dub films into local dialects of Tibetan and other languages, such as Mongolian and Tu.[11]

According to a Chinese government white paper, by the year 2000 the TAR People's Publishing House had published more than 6,600 titles with a total distribution in excess of 78.9 million copies, of which 80 percent were in Tibetan.[12] The Tibet Academy of Social Sciences in Lhasa established the Ancient Book Publishing House, which has recruited a number of specialists, while other institutions published various kinds of dictionaries, reference books, and monographs.[13] The collection, research, editing, and publication of the Gesar epic, still popular among storytellers, was listed as a key scientific research project in the sixth, seventh, and eighth five-year plans of the Chinese state.[14] Tibetan Buddhist literature, including the complete Tengyur (T: bstan 'gyur) and many works on Buddhist philosophy, has been collated, edited, and published as have a number of classic works on history and geography such as *Red Annals* (T: deb ther dmar po), *Blue Annals* (T: deb ther sngon po), *A Feast for Wise Men* (T: mkhas pa'i dga' ston), and *Grand Exegesis of the World* (T: 'dzam gling rgyas bshad). Works on Tibetan medicine include *The Four-Volume Medical Codes* (T: rgyud bzhi) and *Blue Lapis Lazuli* (T: ba' idurya sngon po). Tibetan lunar calendars are published every year by the TAR Tibetan Hospital in Lhasa and were sold in many of the areas we visited.

Most books in China contain a preface written by the author, editor, or other approved person. In a book that deals with anything Tibetan, this preface very often includes a passage about the positive economic and cultural developments in Tibetan areas over the last fifty years, references to Deng Xiaoping's theories, derogatory remarks about the old feudal Tibetan society, or dogmatic explanations of the historical connections between Tibet and China. Not surprisingly, critics have questioned the freedom of expression of Tibetan artists and cultural workers.[15]

TIBETAN NEWSPAPERS AND MAGAZINES

Freedom of expression has also been a major concern in the dissemination of news via broadcasts and printed media. The Tibetan government-in-exile claims that "the majority of publications from Tibet disdain the Tibetan people's perspective on their own history and culture; some of them openly ridicule Tibetan history, culture, and traditional wisdom."[16] The commentary further accuses Chinese mass media of being a tool for spreading Communist Chinese propaganda while China erects a wall to hold back the flow of news from the outside world. In yet another attempt to define what Tibetan culture should be, the exile government claims that neither publishing nor the news media in China further the cause of Tibetan culture. Before discussing the content of Tibetan-language newspapers and journals, let us first look into their availability.

A number of newspapers and periodicals are published in the Tibetan areas within and outside the TAR. In addition to those published in the TAR, Qinghai, Gansu, and Sichuan all have their own Tibetan-language newspapers. Qinghai publishes *Qinghai Tibetan News* (Tso ngön Böke Sargyur),[17] and Gansu and Sichuan publish newspapers that include *Kanlho News* (Kanlho Sargyur) and *Ngaba News* (Ngaba Sargyur).[18] We were also told about a Tibetan edition of a newspaper published in Kandze (Ganzi) TAP but were unable to find a copy during our visit. Qinghai in particular has a good selection of periodicals in Tibetan, such as *Qinghai Education* (Tso ngön Lobso),[19] *Climb* (Tsernyeg),[20] and *Life of the Party* (Tanggi Tsowa).[21] There are also Tibetan editions of *Qinghai Judicial News* (Tso ngön trimlu Sargyur)[22] and *Qinghai Science and Technology News* (Tso ngön Tsenrig dang Trulche Sargyur)[23] and even a children's newspaper, *Snowland Youth* (Gangjonggyi Chonu).[24]

In addition, a number of literary magazines are available in Tibetan. Those published outside the TAR include *Light Rain* (Drangchar)[25] and *Qinghai Folk Arts and Literature* (Tso ngön Mangtso Gyutsal),[26] both published in Qinghai, and *Moonlight* (Daser),[27] published in Kanlho (Gannan) TAP. *Light Rain*, which publishes poetry and literary fiction, was established in 1981 and is one of the first magazines of its kind. The Qinghai provincial government provided subsidies, and the Trace Foundation contributed financial support and computer equipment. The magazine is currently distributed to subscribers in seventeen countries and is said to be the most popular magazine in Tibetan areas. It had a circulation of 8,000 in 1999.

Khampa Culture (Kangba Wenhua) is a Chinese-language magazine published in Dartsedo (Kangding), in Kandze TAP. In 2000, it had a circulation of 1,000 and was issued two to four times a year. The magazine is fully sponsored by the Kandze Prefecture Culture Department and is distributed mainly on an exchange basis with relevant offices and research institutes.[28] The purpose of the magazine, according to an interview with one of the Han editors, is to maintain interest in Tibetan studies and increase local knowledge of Tibetan culture. The topics covered are, as he expressed it, art, literature, Buddhism, monasteries, and opinions and discussions about the Kham area and contemporary society.

The publications described above are available mainly by subscription. Although subscription costs have increased due to rising paper and postage prices, a number of readers have access to these newspapers and periodicals at work. Those who do not may find them at public libraries, which have been established in most prefecture seats and a few county seats. Larger bookstores in locations like Xining, the capital of Qinghai, sometimes stock a small selection of Tibetan periodicals, and Tibetan-language books are available in prefecture and county bookstores. All prefecture seats have a Xinhua Bookstore (Ch: Xinhua Shudian), and most of these sell books in Tibetan on subjects such as Tibetan Buddhism, religious philosophy, Tibetan medicine, literature, language, grammar, folk stories, Tibetan art, and biographies of famous lamas.[29]

All Tibetan-language newspapers are mouthpieces of the CCP at the prefectural or provincial level. This means that the news and opinions presented to readers are carefully selected according to the current policies of the CCP. There are no independent newspapers free to publish unbiased information and criticize the policies of the CCP. News broadcasts on radio and television are also censored by the authorities, and news in Tibetan is usually translated from earlier broadcasts in Chinese.

In fact, almost all news in Tibetan, broadcast and printed, is translated from Chinese. A substantial amount of published Tibetan-language literature, particularly in the natural and social sciences, is also translated from Chinese. Except in Buddhist studies, very little published literature has been translated from Tibetan to Chinese. Government reports and documents in Tibetan are mostly translations from Chinese, since their purpose is to ensure that government regulations are understood by all local officials involved in their implementation.

Literary and cultural magazines make up the clear majority of Tibetan-language periodicals. As far as we know, the only exception, currently published outside the TAR, is *Qinghai Tibetan Science and Technology News*, which was established in 1984 by the Qinghai Province Science and Technology Association. It is a four-page weekly and covers topics of interest to farmers and herders. It is likewise very difficult to find books in Tibetan on natural sciences, although there is a wide selection of Tibetan-language publications on Tibetan medicine, Tibetan literature and linguistics, biographies, Tibetan painting, and folk stories.

MODERN TIBETAN LITERATURE

Fiction has been a popular genre among Tibetan readers since the early 1980s. Authorities encouraged this literary style as a means of conveying political messages to the public. The genre deserves attention for its role in facilitating new interest in the use of the Tibetan language and generating public debate on the current challenges confronting Tibetans. Literary journals are the most important venue for contemporary fiction. Tsering Shakya has analyzed the content of much modern Tibetan literature, paying particular attention to the ideological role of contemporary Tibetan literary production.[30] He views the emergence of new literature in Tibetan in light of the Chinese civilizing mission in Tibet. Chinese leaders have conceived of Tibet as a territory that is culturally as well as economically, socially, and technologically backward. Therefore, the emancipation of the serfs of Tibet meant not only socioeconomic improvements and technological development but also cultural empowerment. Language and literature thus became the main focus of colonial exchange.[31]

The TAR Writers Association started the first Tibetan-language literary journal, *Tibetan Literature and Art* (T: Bod kyi rtsom rig sgyu rtsal), in 1980.[32] The first issue contained four short stories by Tibetan writers. As noted by Tsering Shakya, all four stories were translations from the original Chinese and had been published several years earlier in Chinese journals and reprinted in textbooks. Moreover, the theme of these stories was the dark period of feudal exploitation before the liberation of Tibet by the People's Liberation Army.[33] Nevertheless, the first issue of *Tibetan Literature and Art* was important because it set a standard for the first generation of Tibetan writers educated in China. In the early period, Tibetan literary journals were dominated by stories about the evils of the old Tibetan society. After 1985, it became permissible to expose the crimes of the Gang of Four and praise the Four Modernizations, which led to the publication of a number of stories about the tragedies and sufferings of the people during the Cultural Revolution.[34]

Tashi Dawa (b. 1959), one of the most prominent Tibetan writers today, was the editor of *Tibetan Literature and Art* for several years. In 1992, he became vice-chairman of the TAR Writers Association.[35] Despite this, Tashi Dawa writes in Chinese only. Although his father was a Tibetan cadre,

Tashi Dawa spent most of his childhood with his Chinese mother in metropolitan Chongqing, then part of Sichuan. His literary career began when his story "Reticence" appeared in an early issue of *Tibetan Literature and Art*. Works by Tashi Dawa have been translated into both English and French.[36]

The most influential literary journal in Tibetan, *Light Rain*, is published outside the TAR, in Qinghai. A number of stories that appeared first in this journal were later reprinted in Tibetan-language textbooks. One of *Light Rain*'s most notable contributions is its emphasis on stories originally written in Tibetan rather than translated from Chinese. There is a strong literary tradition in the Amdo region, and it is worth mentioning that some of the most outstanding Tibetan writers have been Amdowas, including the founder of modern Tibetan literature, Dhondrup Gyal (1953–1985), and the first prominent critic of Tibetan society during the Republican period, Gedun Chöphel (1905–1951). The writings of these two authors also figure prominently among the modern texts chosen for the Five Provinces series of Tibetan-language textbooks for junior middle schools. According to Janet Upton's study on education in Tibetan in Ngaba (Aba) Tibetan and Qiang Autonomous Prefecture, the biting style and critical reflections that characterize the writings of these two authors are being held up as models for a new type of Tibetan literary production.[37] However, it is hardly a coincidence that they were also among the strongest advocates of modernism and delivered some of the most radical literary attacks on Tibetan traditionalism in recent history.

Literary production in Tibetan is supported and encouraged by the authorities for the role it plays in political education. Tibetan fiction writers have no opportunity to publish works that openly criticize the authorities or deal with issues that are too far removed from what are considered appropriate themes for the education of the masses. However, one of the characteristics of fiction is its ability to convey multiple meanings and allow many different interpretations. Tsering Shakya suggests that, despite evident Party control and restrictions on freedom of expression, Tibetan writers, intellectuals, and artists have been able through fiction to conduct an autonomous debate on the nature of Tibetan identity.[38]

TIBETAN LANGUAGE IN DAILY LIFE

While it is not difficult to find reading materials in Tibetan, the need or opportunity to use written Tibetan in daily life is limited. There has been debate among Tibetan educators and intellectuals about the viability of Tibetan as a language, and many contend that Tibetan is becoming a "useless" (Ch: *wuyong*) language. Some have argued that knowledge of written Tibetan is becoming unnecessary, while fluency in Chinese is increasingly important for dealing with modern life. According to one Tibetan education specialist in Sichuan, the documents, notes, and certificates in every government department are in Chinese. The post office requires that letters be addressed in Chinese, operator-assisted telephone calls must be placed in Chinese, and the instructions for all types of electrical appliances are in Chinese. Learning Chinese is therefore essential, but the ability to read Tibetan is of little practical value in daily life. In some areas, particularly where Tibetans constitute a small minority, even spoken Tibetan has fallen into disuse. Exposure to the Chinese language in daily life has caused many Tibetans to abandon their native language completely.

Loan words from Chinese are also entering the Tibetan language, especially words for modern appliances and technology and political and administrative terminology. In addition, many Tibetans mix Tibetan and Chinese terms when speaking Tibetan. This mixed language can be heard not only in towns and markets but even in monasteries. For example, at one of the larger monasteries in Qinghai, we were surprised when the monk we interviewed, who had attended the Buddhist college in Beijing, used Chinese terms in speaking of the "Buddhist college" (Ch: *foxueyuan*), "Buddhist ceremony" (Ch: *fahui*), and "tantra" (Ch: *mizong*), although the interview was conducted in Tibetan.

Many Tibetans have recognized the need to counter the trend toward sinicization and language loss by modernizing the Tibetan language, creating a standardized terminology for science and technology, and coining Tibetan terms for a range of new products and techniques. This work has already been initiated, and a system of approving new terminology has been established under governmental supervision. Tibetan has also become a computerized language. Word processing in Tibetan has been available since the early 1990s, and Tibetan software was being developed in the late 1990s. During our fieldwork, we noticed that even some monasteries were making use of Tibetan fonts. For instance, Drango Monastery (Ch: Shouling Si)[39] in Drango (Luhuo) County had access to computers with such fonts, and every image in the side chapels bore a printed label in both Tibetan and Chinese. A local Tibetan cadre told us that the county government did not have computers with Tibetan fonts, implying that this monastery was better equipped.

TIBETAN LANGUAGE IN LOCAL GOVERNANCE

China's Law on Regional Autonomy of Ethnic Minorities (1984) stipulates that ethnic minorities have the right to develop and use their local spoken and written languages. This principle is also recognized in the 1982 revision of China's constitution. In particular, policy statements from Chinese authorities recognized the importance of using minority languages in local government documents and providing public information in minority languages. Despite well-intended policies, implementation has been a different matter. When resources are limited, the use of Tibetan in public affairs is not considered a top priority for local officials. In fact, the use of Tibetan language in local administration is being neglected in most Tibetan areas outside the TAR, especially in areas where Tibetans constitute a minority of the population. Very few Han cadres and officials know Tibetan. Since most government offices have Han officials among the office staff, it is difficult to use Tibetan in administrative work. It is also necessary for Tibetan cadres to use Chinese for communicating with their superiors in higher-level departments. Tibetan can be used to communicate only with other Tibetans in the local community. Socioeconomic and political conditions in Tibetan areas thus create a situation in which written and spoken Tibetan are increasingly becoming obsolete.

In Dechen (Diqing) TAP, for instance, with the exception of bilingual signs, Chinese is clearly the language of administration. During our visit, we were unable to find Tibetan-language newspapers or official documents of any kind in Tibetan. A survey conducted in the 1980s concludes that in Kanlho TAP, Chinese language was used in major sectors of society.[40] Tibetan was used by herding and farming families, in monasteries, and in local commercial relations, but communication between ethnic groups was conducted in Chinese. The same report reveals that in Pari (Tianzhu) TAC, also in Gansu, Chinese was used extensively except within the monastic community, the Tibetan hospital, and *minzu* primary schools. Written Chinese was used in all county government reports, except those related to religion.[41]

In Qinghai, in addition to Chinese, written Tibetan and Mongolian are in ordinary use, and Muslims, such as Salar and Hui, use written Arabic for religious purposes only. After Chinese, Tibetan is the most commonly spoken language in the province, where the registered Tibetan population is 20 percent of the total population according to the 1990 census.[42] In farming and herding regions in several of the Tibetan Autonomous Prefectures, few Tibetans understand Chinese. This is the case in areas such as Jyekundo

(Yushu), Golok (Guoluo), and most of Malho (Huangnan), which were nearly all Tibetan before 1950 and where, according to the 1990 census, Tibetans still constitute a majority (96.5 percent, 88 percent, and 63 percent respectively). Han who arrived in these areas after 1950 are involved mainly in government administration, industry, and services located primarily in towns and along highways. This is also where the influence of the Chinese language is more obvious. We also observed, however, that a considerable number of Hui, who are Chinese-speaking Muslims, had opened restaurants along the main roads in Qinghai and appeared to have picked up some Tibetan language for business purposes.

In Golok and Jyekundo, Tibetan is still used by all Tibetans, including government officials. Generally speaking, village district and county administrations use Tibetan more than do prefectural administrations. Public meetings often are conducted in both Tibetan and Chinese, although some officials may use Chinese only. For example, when the provincial vice-governor delivered the opening speech at the horse race festival in Jyekundo in July 1999, he spoke exclusively in Chinese. Even though he is a Tibetan from Jyekundo and was speaking to a Tibetan audience at a Tibetan cultural event, he spoke in Chinese without translation. His only words of Tibetan were *tashi delek*, or "good luck," with which he ended his speech. Some of the locals who attended the ceremony reported that very few people in the audience were able to understand the vice-governor's speech.

In Tibetan-majority prefectures such as Golok and Jyekundo, Tibetan is used even in the prefectural administration. However, Chinese is the main language of administration in prefectures where Tibetans are less of a majority or in the minority, such as Malho, Tsolho (Hainan), Tsonub (Haixi), and Tsochang (Haibei). The predominance of Chinese became very clear during our visit, in meetings at which both Tibetan and Han officials were present. All meetings with government officials were conducted in Chinese as long as Han officials were present and sometimes even when only Tibetan officials were there. Even second-generation Han in several of these prefectures were unable to understand Tibetan. In the late 1980s, according to a study published in 1994, 95 percent of the herders in Tsochang had no understanding of Chinese, and the situation appeared to be unchanged ten years later.[43] Still, high-level meetings in this prefecture were conducted in Chinese, except those of the religious affairs department, which were reportedly bilingual.

Many Tibetan areas currently have a translation office, which is mainly responsible for translating government documents between Tibetan and

Chinese, providing bilingual signs and stamps for government offices, standardizing translations for the names of government offices, and interpreting into Tibetan during meetings if a participant does not understand Chinese well. Although local governments have used translators since the 1950s, new translation offices were established as recently as the 1990s in some prefectures. In Tsochang TAP, for instance, a translation office was established in 1996 with a staff of five.[44] The office reported that by the end of 1998, 85 percent of government offices in the prefecture had bilingual signs and office stamps. We were also informed that government documents, especially those concerning farmers and herders, were written in both Tibetan and Chinese.[45]

Several translation offices have edited and printed old Tibetan texts as well as folk literature.[46] The translation unit in Malho TAP, established in 1981, has a department that edits old books and manuscripts and another that translates government documents.[47] The Tsolho TAP translation office translated and edited local Tibetan publications and conducted research on local culture, concentrating on folk literature and folk songs but including topics such as local cuisine. Translation units initially were set up to ensure that CCP policies, laws, and regulations were enforced even in areas where nobody knew Chinese. It now appears, however, that several of these units actively promote the use of Tibetan language in local governance, and some are even creating new interest for local cultural traditions.

INSTITUTIONALIZED CULTURAL EXPRESSIONS

At the end of the Cultural Revolution, institutionalized culture resurfaced in a new political context. Nevertheless, government-sponsored work units still employ the majority of artists and cultural workers in China. These cultural workers are organized as members of artists associations set up by the authorities and receive their training primarily in state-run schools or within their work units. This is also true of many producers of Tibetan arts and crafts, such as performers of Tibetan opera, song and dance troupes, modern painters, and even some painters of *thanka* and murals. The song and dance troupes are funded by local government at the county and prefecture level. They perform and compete at cultural festivals, athletic events, and celebrations. Prefecture and county government units such as the cultural relics departments are active in organizing these events and are also involved in a number of other public cultural activities.

Each prefecture seat has a "prefecture cultural house" (Ch: *zhou wen-*

huaguan) or "people's arts palace" (Ch: *renmin yishu gong*). These some-times house exhibits and organize cultural activities such as dance classes, art classes, and musical performances. Culture departments are also respon-sible for administering the local branch of the Xinhua Bookstore and libraries and occasionally publish literature on topics related to local cul-tural life.[48]

Culture departments sponsor popular culture not only for the local popu-lation but also for tourism, which is becoming an important part of the economy. For instance, in 1998, officials in Dechen TAP developed a five-point plan that listed as one of its top priorities the rescue of Tibetan cul-ture, which was recognized as worthy of investment because of tourism. The culture department was key in implementing the plan. During inter-views, we were told repeatedly that cultural resources were still underde-veloped and that the culture department intended to help promote handicrafts and folk arts, such as carving, pottery, drawing, and silverware. The officials explained that a survey of traditional handicrafts had already been conducted in 1997–98 in all minority areas of Yunnan, including Dechen TAP. According to the Center for U.S.-China Arts Exchange, the center's team of advisers designed the survey in collaboration with the Yunnan Folk Arts Center. The survey was conducted in 120 counties in Yunnan by 2,000 cultural cadres trained to use prevailing international research methodologies in combination with their own knowledge of specific *minzu* and villages.[49] Based on this survey, Chinese authorities recognized a number of artists and craftsmen as national treasures.

Thanka *Painting*

For many, Tibetan art has become synonymous with *thanka* painting, and in the Tibetan areas we visited, we found several places where painted and embroidered *thanka* are still being created by local artists. The two most famous areas are Rebkong (Tongren) in Malho TAP, in Qinghai, and Kandze TAP, in Sichuan. In both these areas, the prefecture culture depart-ments have been actively engaged in promoting *thanka* painting.

In Malho, the culture department manages an art gallery and institute that support the revival of the art. The Rebkong area is famous for its painted and embroidered *thanka*, statues, murals, architectural design, and sculp-ture in wood, clay, and stone. At the Rebkong Art Gallery, we were informed that four village districts, all in Rebkong County, have been cen-ters of art production since the early fifteenth century.[50] One of the *thanka* painters at the Rebkong Art Institute explained that the craft used to be passed down from father to son but today the painters learn from teachers rather than within their families. The art institute was started in 1978, after the *thanka* painting tradition had suffered a twenty-year interruption (including the ten years of the Cultural Revolution). Most of the old *thanka* painters passed away during the Cultural Revolution, or escaped abroad, but there were still four famous artists in the area who served as teachers when the art institute was established. Together with many other students from the four village districts, this painter spent years learning from one of these artists. According to his estimate, as of 1999, there were about 1,000 painters in the four districts.[51]

At the time of our visit, the Rebkong Art Gallery was exhibiting several old and new *thanka* paintings and a few small statues. Despite the systematic destruction of all types of religious objects during the Cultural Revolution, some old *thanka* paintings had been preserved. A few were displayed in the art gallery, but the gallery staff reported that the oldest *thanka* paintings had been given back to the monasteries. Despite efforts to revive the painting tradition in Rebkong, the staff of the art gallery informed us that the quality of painting was not as high as it had been before the Cultural Revolution.

Dartsedo, the Kandze Prefecture seat, has become an important center for cultural activity in the Tibetan areas of Sichuan. The culture department established the Thanka Research Institute (Ch: Zanghua Yanjiuyuan) in 1986–87 and also finances its work. When we visited the institute, it had three employees. The newly arrived Tibetan office leader was an established painter himself and had received his training from an old master. In 1985–86, he worked directly under the tenth Panchen Lama. He designed the emblem of the Tibet Development Fund and the main door of the Buddhist college in Beijing. He also produced a number of paintings and scrolls for restored monasteries.[52]

We were told that Kandze TAP is the only Tibetan area that has such a project. The main tasks of the institute is to register artists of traditional Tibetan paintings, both secular folk art and sacred paintings, and to inform the public about their work. The institute's researchers travel extensively within Kandze, collecting sample artworks and interviewing artists. In their opinion, Derge County has the highest concentration of folk artists and the highest artistic level of traditional painting in the prefecture. Painting is still taught in the traditional way, by master to students, but at present it can also be studied at the "Tibetan school" (Ch: *Zangwen xuexiao*) in Dartsedo, the only known school with a department that concentrates on Tibetan art traditions. This school is administered by the provincial Ethnic Affairs Commission and thus recruits students from all of Sichuan. Its art department teaches *thanka* painting, Tibetan interior decoration, furniture decoration, and textile painting. All teachers are graduates of the school.

The first large-scale exhibition of *thanka* paintings, featuring sixty of the contemporary *thanka* registered by the institute, was organized in the spring of 2000. The exhibition revealed great interest among the general public and was visited by a large number of both locals and non-residents. Some Tibetan viewers were said to have prostrated themselves in front of the sacred *thanka*. The leader of the institute informed us that the idea behind the exhibition was to display the exceptional level of artistic talent within the prefecture. Local Han artists who had studied the *thanka* painting tradition had made a few of the paintings in this exhibition.

Kandze and Malho TAPs are not the only places where *thanka* painting has been revived. Labrang Monastery in Kanlho TAP is a center for cultural activity in Tibetan areas of Gansu. During our visit, we observed the work of one local artist who had studied painting during his youth, before the Cultural Revolution. In addition to *thanka* paintings, this artist had also created a number of murals for local monasteries.

Both Kumbum Monastery and Labrang Monastery regularly practice *gyegu* during important religious festivals. We were able to witness one such event at Kumbum Monastery, which has several giant *thanka* that are displayed for different occasions.

Cultural Sites and State-Sponsored Museums

Culture departments are responsible for the management of "key historical and cultural sites under state protection" (Ch: *zhongdian wenwu baohu danwei*). The government is obligated to provide financial support for preserving and maintaining such sites. Support could come from any level of government—national, provincial, prefectural, or county. For instance, Labrang Monastery in Sangchu (Xiahe) County, Kanlho TAP, is a national-level cultural site, and Sangchu County also supports several other sites.[53]

Culture departments are also in charge of museums. In 1999, we visited the Hainan Prefecture Museum, in Tsolho TAP, which is a history, folk, and relics museum. At that time, we interviewed its leader, a researcher and archaeologist who often worked in the excavation grounds. The exhibitions mainly displayed artifacts from archaeological excavations, but the museum had been closed for a long time. Most of the archaeological materials were said to be from pre-Han cultures along the Yellow River. The leader of the museum told us that the museum contained no "Tibetan" objects, although we were informed that 333 tombs from the "Qiang culture" were excavated in 1994.[54]

The Zhongdian Museum in Gyelthang is another historical and cultural museum. It opened in 1997 and contains eight large halls. Exhibits cover the history, development, natural resources, religions, folk costumes, flora and fauna, prehistory, and ancient history of the area. During our visit, the museum was featuring photographs of natural landscapes in Dechen and from the fashion show at the Khampa Arts Festival. Several other institutions also promoted the idea of Khampa culture. The Chinese-language *Khampa Culture* magazine is published in Dartsedo. We were also told about a museum in Dartsedo that was exhibiting "Kham material culture," but it was not open during our visit in spring 2000.

Kunming and Chengdu both have *minzu* museums that exhibit costumes collected during the 1950s along with cultural objects such as jewelry, musical instruments, utensils, tools, and other traditional objects made and used by the different minority ethnic groups. One museum in Chengdu is located on two floors of the Southwest Nationalities Institute administration building. The upper floor, which opened in 1991, resembles the prayer hall of a temple and contains a replica of a Tibetan Buddhist altar. The carved altarpiece was made in Sichuan in the 1930s. The room has elaborate woodcarvings, and on the walls are rare antique *thanka* paintings. We were told that it took three years to construct this floor and cost ¥60,000 (US$7,600) in 1991. About 1,000–2,000 guests visit the museum every year. Admission is ¥1 (US$0.12) for students, ¥2 (US$0.25) for others, and free for official guests. We were told that approximately half the visitors are university students.

Minzu *Song and Dance Troupes*

Almost every Tibetan autonomous prefecture and county has its own "*minzu* song and dance troupe" (Ch: *minzu gewutuan*), which performs at local festivals.[55] Some troupes also tour nationally and internationally, and in areas where tourism is a growing business, folk songs, folk dances, and music have been singled out as cultural products for tourist consumption. In a meeting with the culture department in Tsochang TAP, we were told that the members of the prefecture's song and dance troupe had been trained at the Army Art University, where the prefecture had sent thirty young students in the early 1990s. These students became the main members of the group, which in 1999 consisted of fourteen performers. The officials complained that the best dancers and singers left the prefecture and joined ensembles in large cities such as Guangdong and Shanghai. Since good artists were few, the prefecture planned to sponsor another twenty students who were to be trained in Beijing in Tibetan opera, or *namthar,* as it is called in the Amdo region. Members of government song and dance troupes in this area evidently need to go to Beijing to learn Tibetan opera.

The song and dance troupes also give theatrical performances. In Machen (Maqin) County, Golok TAP, we saw an evening performance commemorating the forty-fifth anniversary of the establishment of the prefecture in 1954. Two performers narrated in both Chinese and Tibetan. Most songs were in Chinese, but the theatrical sections were performed in Tibetan, without translation. This part of the show was very popular with the mostly Tibetan audience, which participated actively in the performance, shouting, laughing, and singing loudly. Interestingly, tickets for the show were distributed through government units and were not for sale to the general public.

Horse Race Festivals

The "horse race festival" (Ch: *saimahui*) is a popular event in all the Tibetan areas. In Golok TAP, the government sponsored a horse race festival for the first time in 1998. We attended the second festival in 1999, which coincided with the forty-fifth anniversary of the founding of the prefecture. Local song and dance troupes from different counties performed at the festival grounds during the one-week celebration, and fashion shows were held. Festival participants dressed in traditional Tibetan costume, or *chuba,* rather than in modern Western-influenced outfits. Traveling traders gathered to sell inexpensive consumer goods. Government officials and local entrepreneurs closed their offices for one week and worked out of tents at the festival grounds; we conducted several of our interviews with prefecture officials in such tents. Socializing is an important aspect of the celebrations, with participants consuming large quantities of food and alcohol in one another's tents.

Jyekundo TAP also has an annual horse race festival. It was organized in 1981 to commemorate the thirtieth anniversary of the founding of the prefecture. The festival was held occasionally throughout the 1980s, and since the fortieth anniversary of the prefecture in 1991, it has been held regularly during one week in late July. Tibetans from the entire prefecture gather at

FIG. 4.1. Opening ceremonies at the horse race festival in Jyekundo, 1999. In this year, the festival marked the fiftieth anniversary of the founding of the People's Republic of China.

a site on the grasslands near Jyekundo Town to be entertained with competitions between county song and dance troupes, Gesar storytelling, horse and yak races, games, and other contests. At the festival we visited, the yak races were a favorite event and received the most attention from the crowd.[56]

A display of "trades" (Ch: *hangye*) was a prominent feature at several of the festivals we attended. For instance, twenty-five work units and organizations—including schools, military and security forces divisions, banks, various government departments, the Women's Federation, and, surprisingly, two monasteries—were represented in the parade at the opening ceremony of the Jyekundo horse race festival. The monasteries had also prepared their sacred relics for exhibition in the city.[57]

FIG. 4.2. Staff of a government-run tent hotel near Xihai Town, Tsochang.

Government departments sponsored the popular Khampa and Neighboring Regions Arts Festival. In 1997, the fourth Khampa festival was held
in Dechen TAP. The event takes place every four years in different parts of
the Kham region, and the festival in Dechen included fashion shows and
horse racing. From the photos displayed in the local museum, we could see
that the fashion show featured grossly exaggerated forms of traditional
Tibetan costumes. We were told that some of the costumes were so heavy
that the models had difficulty walking. The old jewelry worn by the models was collected from many families, since no single family could have owned
such a large collection.

Most of the participants at the festivals we attended were dressed in *chuba*,
some of which were lined with the fur of endangered animals such as leop-

ard and otter. Children were likewise dressed in expensive and elaborate *chuba,* matching their parents. In towns, a *chuba* is worn only for special occasions, and Western-style clothes are worn for everyday life.[58] The price of a *chuba* depends largely on the fur lining and the quality of cloth. The most expensive might cost at least ¥10,000 (US$1,270), equivalent to the annual income of a government worker.

As we have seen, there is a wealth of evidence to support the claim that Tibetan culture is being developed in China today. However, what kind of Tibetan culture is being developed? Most Tibetan cultural expressions clearly are organized within a political setting in which popular culture is used to advance the political goals of the authorities. The horse race festivals are a typical example. These popular folk festivals retain many aspects of local traditions that have been reinterpreted within the current political setting. The combination of horse racing, folk culture, and commemorations of what is referred to as the "peaceful liberation" of these areas is striking. It appears that local officials are appropriating popular culture in order to disseminate the political propaganda of the CCP. Or could it be the other way around? Could it be that some local cadres are actually using political rhetoric as an excuse for promoting popular cultural expressions? One could at least argue that many local participants at these events are not only enjoying themselves but also making a conscious effort to revive Tibetan culture.

In the Reform era, government policy has allowed for the open expression of many traditional rituals and customs, but as Richard Madsen points out, "Many members of the indigenous communities have forgotten such customs and the younger generation never had a chance to learn them. So as they revive certain community rituals and customs, they are not so much carrying on tradition as *inventing* tradition. They are selectively taking partially remembered elements of the past and recombining them in new ways to meet the needs of the present."[59] The Tibetan situation is no exception. What we observed in the Tibetan areas we visited may well be interpreted as a self-conscious reinvention of Tibetan culture.

The persecution of Tibetan culture during the Cultural Revolution left a void that the Chinese government has been attempting to fill in a politically controlled manner. The state thus actively promotes the revitalization of Tibetan and other minority cultures and at the same time tries to regulate cultural expressions and define what culture is and should be. This is done primarily through the establishment of cultural institutions that both stimulate cultural activities and guide cultural workers to comply with CCP ideas on the social role of cultural expressions. Yet, it is difficult, if not impossible, for the authorities to control every aspect of even the most institutionalized expressions of Tibetan culture. A case in point is the ability of contemporary Tibetan writers to convey multiple meanings and conduct an autonomous debate on Tibetan identity through literature.

5 / Culture As a Way of Life

Religion and literary heritage have played a vital role in the formation of Tibetan identity, both within and outside of Tibet. However, a new vision of Tibetanness has been emerging in the People's Republic of China. This is a vision of authentic Tibetan culture as the culture of the grasslands.[1] Life on the grasslands is being eulogized in songs and paintings, poems and karaoke videos, glossy magazines and promotional tourist materials. This image of the grasslands is one of nomads and their herds roaming a beautiful landscape of snow-capped peaks and green pastures, blue skies, and crystal-clear waters. It is an image of Tibet that attracts increasing numbers of tourists from the crowded urban centers of eastern and southern China. Moreover, this image also appeals to many urban Tibetans, giving them a sense of identity not simply as members of a backward and superstitious nationality dominated by religion but as a people of the high plateau who have their roots in the very landscape of Tibet. This grasslands Tibet is precisely where they can find the greatest contrasts to life in the Chinese city.

Tibetan exiles have similarly identified the preservation of the grasslands and other environmental issues as important for the survival of Tibetan culture. In a number of statements, the Tibetan government-in-exile has held Chinese in-migration responsible for eroding Tibetan culture. For instance, in response to a Chinese white paper on Tibetan culture, the Tibetan exile government argued that China's Develop the Western Region campaign aims to exploit Tibet's natural resources and escalate the migration of Chinese settlers to Tibet, which poses a new and greater threat of extinction to Tibet's unique culture and national identity.[2] Similar concerns are voiced in a recent report on environmental and development issues from the Central Tibetan Administration, the bureaucratic arm of the Tibetan government-in-exile: "Beijing is only interested in grabbing Tibet's natural resources for its own advantage and, in the process, is destroying an ancient lifestyle and culture through environmental degradation and population transfer of Chinese settlers."[3]

Not surprisingly, the Chinese authorities regard the campaign as entirely positive for the development of Tibetan culture. The following statement is a typical example of Chinese government rhetoric:

> At present, as mankind has marched into the new millennium, economic globalization and informationization [sic] in social life are developing rapidly, increasingly changing people's material and cultural lives. With the deepening development of China's reform and opening-up and the modernization drive, especially the practice of the strategy of large-scale development of the western region, Tibet is striding toward modernization and going global with a completely new shape, and new and still greater development will certainly be achieved in Tibetan culture in this process.[4]

These and a number of other similar statements give the unfortunate impression that neither party has given careful thought to the issues. In their rhetoric at least, both the Chinese government and the Tibetan government-in-exile tend to ignore the very real dilemmas of finding sustainable and culturally appropriate paths to development in the Tibetan areas. This chapter takes the concerns raised by Tibetan exiles as its point of departure and examines the effects of changing settlement patterns and environmental degradation on the viability of traditional lifestyles and means of subsistence in the areas under study.

CHANGING SETTLEMENT PATTERNS

We have seen in the preceding chapters that demographic patterns influence the availability of bilingual schooling in Tibetan areas and that Tibetan language seems to become increasingly obsolete in areas where Tibetans no longer constitute a majority of the population. Changing settlement patterns also have negative consequences for Tibetans in terms of access to cultivable land, pasturage, water, and forest resources. Since the great majority of Tibetans still are farmers and herders (some 85–90 percent according to most estimates), these factors are crucial for the viability of their current lifestyles. Let us therefore take a closer look at some of the demographic changes that have taken place in the areas under study since the early 1950s.

Since the earliest years of the People's Republic of China, political strategy has been to move excess population to frontier areas and extract natural resources from these same "underdeveloped" areas. During the 1950s, the government urged people to move to the frontier areas, among them Qinghai, to help "build socialism" in the minority regions. This policy was first implemented in 1956, with the launching of the *xiafang* (rustication) campaign. One of the aims of this campaign was to transfer millions of people from the overpopulated areas of eastern China to frontier areas in the north and west. By resettling Han in minority regions, the campaign also sought to facilitate the integration of ethnic minorities and strengthen China's borders against invasion.[5] In the course of the first two years of the campaign, some 600,000 settlers were sent to Qinghai, Gansu, Ningxia, Xinjiang, and Inner Mongolia.[6] At least 40,000 were sent to Qinghai during 1956 alone.[7] Many of the rusticated youth managed to return to their homes in the interior during the 1959–62 famines caused by the Great Leap Forward (1958), but the *xiafang* movement accelerated again during the socialist education campaigns of the mid-1960s.

Most of the voluntary in-migration of farmers took place in areas with the most favorable conditions for cultivation, such as the river valleys of Kham (Ch: Kangba) and eastern parts of Amdo. In addition to voluntary resettlement, Qinghai has been singled out for the establishment of large "prison labor camps" (Ch: *laogai*). The town of Terlenkha (Delingha) was originally a prison camp, and the Ge'ermu Prison Farm played an important role in the construction of Golmud (Ge'ermu). Between 1950 and 1990, a total of 160,000 prisoners were transferred to Qinghai from eastern China, according to internal sources.[8] As a result, prisoners make up 5.2 percent of the population of Tsonub (Haixi) Mongolian and Tibetan Prefecture and as much as 18 percent of the population of Dulan County, the largest concentration of prisoners of any county in China.[9]

Dulan is also the move-in site for the controversial Qinghai component of the Western Poverty Reduction Project, a large-scale land reclamation project that involves the resettlement of at least 58,000 poor farmers from eastern parts of Qinghai, mainly Muslims and Han from Haidong. Initially, the World Bank was to provide funding, but Chinese authorities withdrew from the project on 7 July 2000, because of strong opposition from the bank's board of directors. This occurred after an independent inspection panel criticized the bank's managers for breaking a number of their own regulations during the planning process. The inspection panel concluded in its report that assessments made by World Bank staff failed to consider many of the most significant social and environmental impacts on ethnic minorities.[10] Panel members reported that although the inspection team recorded many positive comments about the proposed project during its field visit, it also discovered some disturbing and dramatic examples of "what can only be described as a climate of fear, through which some individuals neverthe-less managed, at great perceived risk, to express their opposition to this project." During our visit to Qinghai, we were approached by Tibetans who wanted to give their views on this project. We were told that, although they were afraid to express their true opinions, "no Tibetans want the World Bank project in Dulan to be implemented."

Chinese policy makers still seem to regard the Tibetan Plateau as a poten-tial site for the resettlement of people from overpopulated regions of China. These planners apparently disregard the conditions on the Plateau, where only about 2 percent of the land is suitable for cultivation. Demographic changes have already affected patterns of land use, particularly availability of pasturage and forest resources.

LOSS OF GRAZING LAND

Beginning in the 1950s, state farms were established in some of the most fertile grazing areas on the Tibetan Plateau, initially to reclaim wilderness areas for agricultural purposes, including animal husbandry and forestry. These farms were first administered directly by the Ministry of State Farms and Land Reclamation in Beijing and employed People's Liberation Army (PLA) soldiers as workers. At present, the provincial governments manage these farms, and the Ministry of State Farms and Land Reclamation is a department of the Ministry of Agriculture. State farms are also managed by other departments within the Ministry of Agriculture as well as by the PLA and the Public Security Bureau. The Public Security Bureau uses pris-oners as workers. In some Tibetan areas, such as Dzoge (Ruo'ergai) County in Ngaba (Aba) Tibetan and Qiang Autonomous Prefecture, state farms cur-rently employ up to 8 percent of the population.[11] As of 1991, state farms performed 10 percent of wool production in all of China.[12]

Reports indicate that more areas in Qinghai came under cultivation by prisoners in labor camps during the 1990s.[13] In their study of the history of the Chinese gulag, James D. Seymour and Richard Anderson describe the economic importance of labor camps in Qinghai.[14] They conclude that while the number of camps and prisoners has been decreasing since the early 1980s, and the overall market shares of *laogai* enterprises have been declining, production has been rising in some areas.[15] Since the 1980s, the Laogai Bureau has been excluded from the most promising new industries, such as electrical power generation, oil drilling and refining, aluminum smelting, and chemical production. The bureau tried to compensate by making large investments in agriculture.[16] In Tsonub, *laogai* still play a major role in the economy, and the prefecture's camps are described as among the most modern and productive in China.[17] In 1987, the grain delivered to the prefectural grain bureau by *laogai* enterprises amounted to 51.3 percent of the prefecture's total.[18] Among agricultural products, however, rapeseed (canola) for cooking oil has the highest market share, accounting for almost 10 percent of the province's total output in 1987. Rapeseed is becoming increasingly important, and since 1987 the policy of Qinghai's Laogai Bureau has been to emphasize rapeseed at the expense of grain. In 1995, prison farms increased the area under cultivation.[19]

For state farms and other enterprises engaged in large-scale rapeseed and grain cultivation, high-yield grasslands are an important asset. The widespread use of pasturelands for rapeseed cultivation can easily be observed as one travels across the Qinghai countryside, particularly around Qinghai Lake. The growing yields of rapeseed in recent years also testifies to a considerable increase in the use of grazing land for state farm cultivation. This is causing a serious shortage of pastureland for herders. Since the 1950s, new roads and transport facilities have accelerated the establishment of agricultural settlements on former grazing lands, particularly in the low-lying eastern parts of the province and the Tsaidam Basin in Tsonub. State farms, including army farms, were established on some of the grasslands best suited for cultivation. Overall in Qinghai, some 4,670 square kilometers of new agricultural land were registered between 1958 and 1989, including prime irrigated land.[20]

The Tibetan Plateau has about 480,000 square kilometers of land designated as "nature reserve" (Ch: *ziran baohuqu*), mainly in the Tibet Autonomous Region (TAR). The largest in Qinghai is the Hoh Xil Nature Reserve, which, at more than 47,740 square kilometers, covers 6.5 percent of the province. Although these areas are designated as protected, gold prospectors and poachers have encroached on some of them. In Hoh Xil Nature Reserve, an estimated 20,000 Tibetan antelope are killed annually, according to local sources, and only about 50,000 were said to remain in 1999.[21] The degree of wildlife protection afforded by nature reserve status is ques-

FIG. 5.1. Nomad tent and herder, Dashi County, Tsochang. Nearby are the remnants of one of China's major nuclear research bases, which closed down in the early 1990s.

tionable, but such a designation may in some cases further dispossess Tibetan and Mongolian herders, who may be prohibited from using these areas as pasturelands.

The government policy on pastoralism since the 1950s has been to locate nomadic herders in permanent settlements. Under a program with the slogan "fixed habitation and nomadic herding," the government set up veterinary stations and built schools, shelter sheds for livestock, and simple dwellings.[22] This policy is actively implemented today, and several counties recently set goals for fencing grasslands and constructing housing for herders. For example, we found that Derge (Dege) County, in Kandze (Ganzi) Tibetan Autonomous Prefecture (TAP), initiated a long-term strategy during the 1980s aimed at settling the nomads in permanent dwellings by the year 2000.[23] In Machu (Maqu) County, Kanlho (Gannan) TAP, the

FIG. 5.2. A Golok boy in front of prayer flags, next to a Nyingmapa temple.

eighth Five-Year Plan (1991–95) set yearly goals for fenced acreage and new dwellings.[24] In Kanlho, more than 50,000 *mu* of grasslands were fenced by 1992 and 450 dwellings built for the purpose of settling nomads.[25] In addition, herders have been encouraged to plant fodder crops and build storage structures for hay and other winter fodder.

Before collectivization, pasture was communally or tribally owned, but after the onset of economic reforms in 1979, land rights were redistributed to individual families. In principle, households are assigned the right to use certain pastures, as specified in contracts with local authorities.

Since the implementation of the Household Responsibility System in 1980, overstocking has been blamed for pasture degradation and desertification. It has been argued that market forces may contribute to overstocking because herders now have the opportunity to generate cash profits from their livestock and, given increased access to consumer goods, have new incentives for maximizing the size of their herds. Some experts, however, question the actual increases in herd size and argue that the traditional grazing and management patterns that have reemerged result in the optimum and sustainable use of grazing land.[26] Others claim that fencing, irrigation, and the use of hybrid seeds are inappropriate measures for raising the productivity of grasslands.[27] Some researchers even claim that these policies may increase the potential for overgrazing and grassland degradation by reducing herd mobility.[28] These and other policies may therefore be contributing to rangeland degradation rather than solving the problems. For instance, a report by a delegation of American experts on rangeland management suggests that pasture degradation may be caused by government attempts to manage common resources through ill-equipped centralized bureaucracies and inappropriate regulations.[29]

Another significant problem is the loss of grazing land due to state expropriation and encroachment by Chinese settlers. In addition to the actual loss of the land, such expropriation often obstructs migration routes between pastures and blocks access to drinking water. It is not surprising that we are now seeing evidence of popular resistance to these policies, such as the 1991 demonstrations in the Qinghai capital Xining demanding that grasslands be returned to the herders.[30] Similar concerns were voiced by Tibetan cadres as well as civilians during our visit to Qinghai in 1999. Tibetan government officials told us in informal conversations that "the Chinese always destroy the grasslands."

The traditional herding practices developed by Tibetan nomads were rational responses to the resources and risks of the grasslands, and as such they have proved successful over the centuries.[31] Yet herders are now prevented from participating in the formation of policies that affect them. Animal husbandry as a school subject is currently taught only in Chinese, and according to our experience, the majority of the veterinary station staff in herding areas are Han. It is evident from the way animal husbandry is taught and from the lack of Tibetan experts on pastoralism that indigenous knowledge about herding is not sufficiently put to use. On the contrary, we have the impression that the knowledge of herders is considered inferior.

LOSS OF FOREST RESOURCES

The depletion of forest resources is also a serious problem in many Tibetan areas, particularly in Kham. During fieldwork, we observed large areas where the forest cover had been completely removed and soil erosion was causing serious damage. According to Chinese officials, by 1998 Sichuan had lost almost all its forest reserves as a result of several decades of excessive logging.[32] These conditions are also evident in the neighboring Tibetan areas of Gansu, Yunnan, and Qinghai. Chinese sources reported that government policies in Ngaba produced an annual timber harvest up to five times higher than natural production.[33] Provincial authorities have been the driving force behind irresponsible forest practices, since forestry departments were compelled to meet their annual timber procurement quotas. In addition, this timber often had to be sold below production cost, forcing the forestry departments to cut even more in an effort to balance their losses and secure income for active and retired employees. Dictated low prices commonly made reforestation impossible.[34]

Timber was processed for the most part by provincial government enterprises, and very few jobs were created locally. Due to excessive logging, Tibetans have been deprived of their traditional forest resources, such as medicinal herbs. During our talks with Tibetan government officials, it became clear that some Tibetans are deeply resentful about this situation. They told us that although the forests are vanishing, locals are not benefiting economically. In one interview, an official claimed that "if we were only given the opportunity to use our forest resources ourselves, we would be the richest county in China."

Nonetheless, taxes paid by the provincial enterprises provided an important source of income for many local governments. For instance, in the 1990s, about 70 percent of Ngaba Prefecture's income came from revenues from logging managed by the Sichuan Province Forestry Department. Neighboring Kandze TAP has the second-largest forest area in China, covering about 10 percent of the prefecture.[35] Before 1998, logging was the major source of income in several of the prefecture's counties. The highest forestry-based income in the prefecture could be found in Drango (Luhuo) County, where as much as 87 percent of the county income once came from forestry.

In the summer of 1998, there was serious flooding of the Yangzi River and its tributaries. Extensive clear-cutting by the timber industry was given the blame, and the central government decided to stop logging on the upper reaches of the Yangzi and Yellow Rivers in Yunnan, Sichuan, and Qinghai. Sichuan authorities subsequently issued their own ban on logging in natural forests in Ngaba and Kandze Prefectures and neighboring Liangshan Yi Autonomous Prefecture. Logging was banned by the end of 1998 in most Tibetan areas outside the Tibet Autonomous Region (TAR). Tibetan officials explained to us that the new policies were created to protect the lives of the people living downstream, not to save the remaining forests in Tibetan areas. One official commented starkly that "if those people down-stream had not 'bled' [i.e., suffered from the flooding], we would not have been allowed to keep what is left of our forests." It is clear, however, that many Tibetan areas, especially in Kham, lost a vital income source with the loss of forestry revenues. These areas are currently struggling to find alter-native sources of income.

Local officials in Tibetan areas of Sichuan confirmed in interviews that Chinese authorities have announced a range of reforestation schemes for affected areas. According to the Xinhua News Agency, the central govern-ment announced a massive forest-conservation project for all of China, at the cost of more than US$2.3 billion for the first phase, from 1998 to 2000.[36] In Sichuan and the TAR, tens of thousands of former loggers are to be trained in tree planting. If these schemes are well planned and implemented, they could have a very positive effect on the environment in these areas. There are indications, however, that even reforestation may cause problems. For instance, the Sichuan government has announced that an area of nearly 90,000 square kilometers in western Sichuan that is now being used pri-marily for livestock grazing, covering approximately 38 percent of the total area of Ngaba and Kandze Prefectures, will be closed in order to facilitate reforestation projects.[37] It is still not clear which areas will be off-limits for grazing, but there is a risk that many Tibetan herders in western Kandze and Ngaba will lose valuable pasture, which would constitute a serious hard-ship. There have been no announcements regarding possible compensation.[38]

INDUSTRIALIZATION AND THE POVERTY OF PLENTY

In addition to the adverse effects of deforestation and the rangeland degrada-tion described above, industrialization is taking its toll on the environment. In the name of the Develop the Western Region policy, industrialization and the extraction of mineral and energy-based resources are currently being stepped up. What are the particular consequences of these developments for the livelihoods of local Tibetan communities, and to what extent are they providing economic benefits to Tibetans?

Recent exploration indicates that Qinghai has very large oil reserves, and the Tibetan Plateau and the Tsaidam Basin are rich in mineral resources.[39] Although the western provinces of China are seen as underdeveloped regions, their resource potential is fully recognized.[40] In the areas we vis-ited, county and prefecture officials often gave us information about rapid increases in industrial output, yet the same officials told us that they cannot support themselves but must depend on support from the provincial and central governments. The main reason for this apparent contradiction is that in China, all natural resources belong to the state.

A report by two Chinese researchers, published in English in 1991, gives an unusually precise description of the current situation in the so-called undeveloped border regions of China, at least if we disregard the derogatory term "backward": "The poverty of life in the backward regions is staggering, yet even more astonishing is the wealth of natural resources to be found in the same regions. But what really gives pause for thought is what happens when the poverty-stricken inhabitants of backward regions are faced with rich resources. In a situation where gains should be proportional to effort, they get no return on their efforts."[41]

Neither is the environmental degradation caused by industrial development a secret to the Chinese authorities. For instance, in a symposium on the Qinghai Tibetan Plateau in Xining in 1998, researchers delivered a paper detailing the serious condition of the environment in the Tsaidam region.[42] Environmental problems presented in the report include deforestation, lack of measures to prevent pollution, contamination of waterways by pollutants, and chronic leaks from oil pipelines. According to the researchers, existing laws regulating the extraction of mineral resources are not implemented.

On several occasions during our fieldwork, Tibetans expressed doubts about the Chinese development of Tibetan areas. Civilians also commented on the problems of industrial development. They reported that herders had lost their lands because of industrial construction and that pollution from industrial plants was giving local people and their livestock previously unknown diseases. We were also told that people are afraid to complain about such problems and that, in particular, talking to foreigners about these issues is done at considerable risk. We therefore suspect that environmental problems connected to resource exploitation are much more widespread than has so far been made known to the outside world.[43]

While logging is facing problems of resource exhaustion, hydroelectricity is a renewable resource that is gaining more and more attention and is currently regarded as a key industry for the development of the mountainous Tibetan areas. It has been estimated that more than half of China's exploitable hydroelectric potential lies within the Plateau region.[44] Qinghai already has a number of large-scale dam projects, and Tibetan areas of Sichuan and Yunnan have been targeted for more. Hydroelectricity is a potential income source for local governments. However, large state-owned power sta-

tions are favored, in that county power stations are allowed to sell their surplus only after the power from state-owned stations has been fully utilized.
Surplus power is then sold at a fixed price as contracted with other counties.
This limits the ability of county governments to earn a stable income from
hydroelectric power.[45]

In addition to these economic issues, there are several other local disadvantages to generating electricity with large-scale dam projects. Local communities often are displaced and fertile valley grounds flooded. Mountain
rivers often carry a high sediment load, which causes sediment accumula-
tion in reservoirs. Dams and reservoirs lead to stagnation of rivers, which
in turn destroys fish stocks. By controlling flooding, dams deprive agricultural areas downstream of fertile soil. In addition, because much of Tibet
is a seismically active zone, all people living downstream from dams are
potentially endangered. Despite these disadvantages, local people are sel-
dom included in the planning phase of hydroelectric projects or addressed
as beneficiaries.[46]

The Tibetan intellectual Tsering Dundrup has argued that not only does
help with development flow from the Han to the minority populations in
China but a considerable contribution goes the other way, from the minorities to the Han.[47] In his book, Dundrup gives an account of how minority
peoples have helped China by protecting the borders and supplying natural
resources to the Chinese state. The populations living in the border areas
have served as an active buffer at the gate of the country. This is especially
true in the case of the Tibetans. In Dundrup's opinion, this kind of support
cannot be estimated in monetary terms, but he refers to statistics for Kandze
TAP, where the central government in the period 1958–87 took out more than
12 million cubic meters of timber in addition to large amounts of gold and
medicinal herbs. Dundrup challenges the image of the passively receiving
minorities and creates a new image of actively contributing minorities.

DEVELOP THE WESTERN REGION

In March 2000, the central government announced a new plan, Develop
the Western Region, which applies to the TAR and the four provinces that
comprise Tibetan areas.[48] Although its effects were not apparent during our
visits in 1998–2000, we suspect that the campaign will be a continuation of
the current practice of resource exploitation in the name of development,
which has been going on since the 1950s. One new aspect of the current cam-

paign is that multinational corporations are being invited to join in the exploitation, making the scale of operations potentially much greater and the consequences for the local environment and society much more serious. As of June 2000, more than 60 of the world's top 500 industrial enterprises had already invested in western China, including Ford Motor Company, BP Amoco, and Glaxo Holdings Ltd.[49] Two out of ten key projects are located in Tibetan areas. One of these is the construction of a new pipeline from the Tsaidam Basin to Lanzhou in Gansu. The other key project is the establishment of a potash fertilizer plant that exploits the resources of the Cha'erhan Salt Lake deposit. Human rights organizations claim that pipeline construction and development of oil reserves in the Tsaidam Basin will result in the resettlement of large numbers of Han workers into traditionally nomadic areas.

As of 2002, the news media were reporting on new plans to develop the Tibetan region. One such plan was to construct a railway line between Golmud (Ge'ermu) and Lhasa. Another was for building a giant hydroelectric power station at Metok (Motuo) on the Yarlung Tsangbo River.[50] With a capacity of 38 million kilowatts, this would be the world's largest power plant. In comparison, the capacity of the Three Gorges plant is 18 million kilowatts. Construction of this plant would probably require nuclear explosions to blast a tunnel through Namcha Barwa, a mountain in the Himalaya range. A series of large dams and reservoirs is also planned for the Mekong River. The potential downstream impacts are so serious that the Vietnamese government has protested. Also currently on the drawing board is a plan to divert water from the upper reaches of the Yangzi River system, mainly in Sichuan, to the northern provinces of Ningxia, Inner Mongolia, and Shanxi.[51] The concurrent construction of the new gas pipeline from the Tsaidam Basin to Lanzhou will greatly facilitate the exploitation of oil and gas reserves in the Tsaidam Basin. All these large-scale development projects may have detrimental consequences for the fragile Plateau environment. In addition, Chinese authorities admit that the development plan requires the transfer of additional workers and technicians from other parts of China. The Ministry of Personnel announced in June 2000 that it was outlining preferential policies to attract professionals to the western region and planned to train thousands of senior technicians and civil servants for work in the west during the coming year.[52]

In several Tibetan areas, regulations are already in place to encourage outside investors to set up enterprises. For instance, in Dechen (Diqing) TAP, in Yunnan, the central, provincial, prefectural, and county governments established preferential policies, including tax concessions, priority in obtaining loans, and lenient land use fees.[53] These policies are explicitly aimed at speeding up the exploitation of resources and opening up the market in areas inhabited by the Tibetan people.[54] Such regulations are expected to become more and more common with the implementation of the Develop the Western Region campaign and China's entry into the World Trade Organization.

As mentioned earlier, all natural resources in China, above and below ground, belong to the state, including the land itself, which is not owned by groups or individuals but is leased or obtained by assignment. Land use regulations do not preclude reallocation of land used for farming or herding to industrial or commercial enterprises, even without the consent of those who are already using the land. Farmers and herders would then have the right to be reassigned new land or otherwise compensated; however, the amount of compensation would be decided by local authorities. According to regulations, wasteland is preferred for commercial crop cultivation, but the definition of wasteland, as opposed to grazing land, is open to interpretation. This makes herders, who are dependent on grazing rights, especially vulnerable to encroachment by commercial enterprises.

ALTERNATIVE PATHS TO DEVELOPMENT

Local communities are finding their own ways of adapting to changes in the larger society, such as by increasing their participation in the new market economy. In some areas, raw materials for the manufacture of Tibetan medicine have become important trade goods, in both the domestic and the international market. In other areas, tourism has become a promising income source.

In Tibetan areas of Sichuan and Yunnan in particular, tourism is now a major sector, especially in the more accessible areas where communications are reliable. Sungchu (Songpan) and Namphel (Nanping)[55] Counties in Ngaba opened to foreign tourists as early as 1986 and have already established themselves as popular tourist destinations. The beautiful Jiuzhaigou Nature Reserve in Namphel was designated a state nature reserve in 1978, and in 1982 it became a state key scenic area. The reserve was officially opened to tourists in 1984 and by 1995 was receiving about 160,000 tourists a year, most of them Han. Tourism is also of growing importance in other parts of Ngaba. In 1999, a large skiing facility, with downhill tracks and lifts, was being planned in Tashiling (Lixian) County, targeting mainly domestic (urban Chinese) tourists.

In Kandze TAP, Chaksam (Luding) and Dartsedo (Kangding) Counties were opened for tourism as early as 1988, but the rest of the prefecture remained closed until December 1998.[56] The Kandze Prefecture Tourism Department was established in 1991 and has since been involved in surveying the prefecture and selecting potential sites for tourism. A team from the Sichuan Province Tourism Department conducted research for one year in various parts of Kandze, and this work resulted in an internal tourism plan for the prefecture.[57] The Kandze Tourism Plan includes a study of ecology and ecological tourism and covers the period 2000–2015. By 2015, tourism is intended to replace logging as the primary source of income for the prefecture. Tourism is booming, and between January and May 2000 alone, some 50,000 tourists visited the prefecture. The majority are Han, primarily from Sichuan's capital, Chengdu. The planners regard the natural environment, with its glaciers and hot springs, as the main attraction. However, they also see Tibetan Buddhist sites and local Tibetan (Khampa) culture as attractions, especially for tourists from outside the province. The Kandze Prefecture Tourism Department clearly wishes to promote Khampa identity and to establish Kandze as the place to experience the attractions of Kham (Kangba):

> Kangba, the natural park!
> Kangba, the last Pure Land!
> Kangba, the happy land of rare birds and animals!
> Kangba, the collection of Tibetan culture!
> Kangba, the paradise of artists!
> Kangba, the last homeland for human beings!
> Come to Kangba, my dear friends. This is a place beyond your imagination. Here you will enjoy natural scenery. Here you will find yourself. Here you will obtain dignity of life and then you will enter into a higher realm.[58]

It is interesting to note that Tibetan culture is one of Kham's tourist attractions. In Tibetan areas of Yunnan, we found that Tibetan culture was promoted as a resource worthy of investment for the sake of tourism. As early as 1998, officials in the Dechen Prefecture government made the rescue of Tibetan culture a top priority. We were repeatedly told during interviews that natural scenery and culture were the two attractions for tourists in Dechen and that cultural resources were still underdeveloped.

Although tourism has significant advantages compared to resource exploitation, it is not without its problems. Western critics have pointed out the absence of religious and cultural sensibility in tourism development. Tourism not only influences the local economy but also affects religious sites. Local officials actually control the use of monasteries as tourist attractions. This entails providing access to monasteries for increasing numbers of tour groups. For instance, in Kanlho TAP, state-sponsored tourism is centered around Labrang Monastery, where the residence of the former abbot has been converted into a hotel.[59] Package tours to Labrang have been available to foreign tourists since the 1980s, and during our visit there in 1999, monks were working as tour guides and selling tickets, generating revenue not only for the monastery but also for the government. Other monasteries, such as Kumbum Monastery in Qinghai, are also experiencing what some would describe as an invasion of tourists. In some monasteries, one can see signs asking tourists not to spit or smoke on the premises.

Another potential problem with tourism is the uneven distribution of profits. Many tourist services are provided by government-run hotels and travel agencies, which are managed by local tourism departments or other government agencies. Government officials also play a significant part in planning tourism development and sometimes have dual roles as administrators and entrepreneurs in private enterprises. Since they are working within the vestiges of a party-controlled, planned-economy system, their positions as officials give them a good opportunity to benefit financially from tourism. Still, at least some locals can profit from small-scale private enterprises such as renting ponies, vending, and operating private hostels and restaurants. Tourism also creates a market for handicraft and other souvenir items.

A range of cultural products is sold to tourists in the Tibetan areas, such as audio and video recordings of folk music and dances, *thanka* paintings, carpets, knives, jewelry, and wooden bowls. Those working in the tourism industry often dress in Tibetan costumes and may perform Tibetan music and dances. Tibetan festival tents accommodate tourists in so-called tent hotels. A variety of glossy magazines, postcards, and coffee-table books on aspects of Tibetan culture is produced for tourist consumption. A marketable and somewhat "folkloric" version of Tibetan culture is one of the main items on sale to tourists.

While the potential economic benefits for local communities are obvious, there are also several significant challenges connected to the development of tourism. One problem is that tourism may lead to disputes between

local farmers and herdsmen who do not depend on tourism for their livelihood and those for whom Tibetan culture has become a commodity. For
instance, in a recent study of the impact of tourism on local pilgrimage practices in Jiuzhaigou, Peng Wenbin concludes that tourism has created economic disparities among villagers and is introducing new strains and
conflicts into local Tibetan communities.[60]

Where culture is a major attraction, there are inherent conflicts between
the goal of preserving culture and the goal of promoting tourism. One of
the major issues in the study of the impact of tourism on ethnic minority
communities has indeed been whether tourism is a destructive force that
causes the collapse of cultural meanings or is an aid to cultural survival.[61]
Whereas some studies are deeply critical of cultural commoditization, a number of works question the importance of tourism as an agent of change, and
others emphasize that people (re)discover their own history and traditions
by marketing their culture and begin to realize their own worth.[62] In the
case of Tibet, for instance, some of the cultural products on sale to tourists
have become popular with Tibetans as well. In this sense, cultural production linked to tourism is a very important factor in the revitalization of
Tibetan culture.

The rediscovery of culture through tourism may be particularly evident
in situations that involve ethnic tourism, in which ethnic minorities are promoted as a major tourist attraction. In Tibetan areas, this creates a new awareness among local people of what their ethnic identity implies. As noted by
Peng Wenbin, for example, Tibetan village leaders at the tourist site where
he conducted fieldwork had become "keenly interested in constructing an
'authentic' image of Tibetans" and invited a dance teacher from another
area to teach locals how to perform the most authentic dances in the newly
opened Ethnic Culture Village. Peng concludes, "It is fair to say that with
the advent of tourism, local village identity in Jiuzhaigou now has wider
implications. It is being connected to areas perceived by the locals of
Jiuzhaigou to be the core of Tibetan history and culture."[63]

As described by Mary L. Cingcade, ethnic tourism offers those involved
the opportunity to represent their vision of Tibet. They do not necessarily
have the same agendas, but certain representations constitute points of
converging interests, such as in the production of folk culture: "Tourists get
their fill of Tibetan folk culture while the Chinese government capitalizes
on Tibetan folk life to boost tourism and finds an audience for its propaganda on harmonious political and ethnic relations."[64]

When tourists find their vision of authentic Tibet at sacred sites, this may also be an important asset for Tibetans who need funds to rebuild monasteries. Charlene E. Mackley, who has studied one such site, concludes that tourism there has created an outlet for the resurgence of traditional culture in the off-hours.[65] This suggests that, regardless of whether or not Tibetans are benefiting economically from tourism, Western tourist demands for experiences of authentic Tibet have provided incentives for the restoration of sacred sites and offered Tibetans an opportunity to rearticulate Tibetan identity.

Mary Cingcade claims that the single most defining feature of the ethnic tourism agenda in Tibet is the search for Shangri-la, with Tibet seen as a peaceful, harmonious land untouched by the evils that plague developed civilizations and hence a symbol of those values that modernization has supplanted.[66] The journey away from modernity is a phenomenon that may be catching on among Chinese urbanites as well as Western tourists. For instance, Louisa Schein cites the following remark made by two students of Chinese traditional painting, who had come to the Miao-minority village of Qiangdongnan to conduct research for their graduate thesis: "We chose Qiangdongnan because it is so *fengfu* [abundant, presumably in ethnographic novelty]. There's too much modernization in the cities! Do you know which places are really good, ones that preserve a lot of traditional customs [*baoliu chuantong de dongxi*]?"[67]

The difficulty with such a search for the premodern in Tibetan and other ethnic minority areas is that when tourism becomes the mainstay of local economies, the needs of tourists, rather than the needs of the local people, may dictate cultural preservation. This may give rise to conflicts between modernization efforts and the preservation of traditional lifestyles. When tourists demand experiences of an authentic Tibetan area unspoiled by the presence of anything modern, the needs of local people may even be forfeited. At the same time, the development of tourism may bring too-rapid modernization, causing cultural meanings to collapse by breaking down the socioeconomic ties that knit local communities together. This effect is noted by Peng Wenbin in his study on tourism in Jiuzhaigou, in which he argues that tourism can lead to an erosion of traditional values. Nevertheless, he acknowledges that tourism may "offer a space for Tibetans to reaffirm their cultural differences from the dominant group, thus reconstructing their ethnic identity."[68]

One established way of understanding culture is to tie it directly to the way of life of a particular group of people. In line with this view, many Tibetans believe that nomadic life on the grasslands defines the uniquely Tibetan and represents real Tibetan culture. As the Tibetan exile government and Tibet support groups have claimed, recent efforts to develop the Tibetan region may pose serious challenges to the nomadic lifestyle and other traditional means of subsistence. It is likely that recent policies intended to increase resource extraction and construct new infrastructure will cause an influx of large numbers of Han workers into Tibetan areas, which would further economically marginalize Tibetans. The environmental effects of these policies are also cause for concern. In addition, authorities are implementing plans to settle the nomadic population, fence the grasslands, and increase the output of agricultural products. One important consequence of these policies is that herders find themselves increasingly reliant on market forces.

As a means of increasing income levels and alleviating poverty in Tibetan areas, tourism represents an interesting alternative to resource exploitation. Tourism may benefit Tibetan communities economically and may also provide an important source of inspiration for those who want to revitalize Tibetan culture. Yet, the development of tourism may also aggravate economic disparities and lead to cultural commoditization. It is difficult to judge whether tourism in Tibetan areas is becoming a cause of cultural deterioration or a source of cultural revitalization. This depends not only on particular circumstances but on what is meant by "culture." It is clear, however, that tourism already has had significant effects on the understanding of Tibetan culture. These effects are becoming more evident as an increasing number of Tibetan communities find themselves in the midst of tourism development projects.

6 / Tibetan Culture on the Margins: Destruction or Reconstruction?

I n trying to answer our question about the survival of Tibetan culture, we have at least been able to identify some of the controversies related to the definition of Tibetan culture and the evident problems related to studying it, whether in quantitative or qualitative terms. Clear-cut answers have not been found to even the most basic questions, such as the number of monasteries that have been reconstructed and how many Tibetan students are able to learn the Tibetan language in school. It is of course even more difficult to draw conclusions about the qualitative aspects of Tibetan cultural life. In order to deepen our understanding, it has been necessary to draw on the works of others who have done extended research on particular topics related to our study. We have also had many discussions about Tibetan culture with Tibetans currently living in and outside of China. Even so, we do not claim to have answers to the more complex and ambiguous questions, such as what motivates people to rebuild monasteries, how Tibetan children are influenced by the school system, and how people understand the Tibetan poetry or news reports they read and the cultural events in which they participate.

As described in our introduction, the concept of culture has been under intense debate within the field of anthropology and related disciplines. In the course of this debate, a number of scholars have criticized the very notion of culture, aptly questioning whether there was ever such a thing as traditional culture, the possible meaning of pure or original culture, or under which circumstances, if any, culture might remain unaffected by change. Change is no longer seen as a contradiction but as an inevitable part of the process of (re-)creating or (re)inventing culture, however the concept may be understood. It has also been pointed out that the concept of culture has had a profound impact on the ways in which people throughout the world have come to understand themselves and explain their beliefs, rituals, and customs. In fact, the very notion of cultural survival has become an important political tool for indigenous peoples and ethnic minorities who are struggling to keep their identities alive, to achieve autonomy or self-determination. This context is important to keep in mind when we discuss current conditions for Tibetan cultural survival.

Tibet support groups, the Tibetan government-in-exile, and other Tibetan refugee representatives have voiced strong criticisms of the Chinese government, accusing Chinese authorities of wantonly destroying Tibetan culture and implementing a policy of cultural genocide in Tibet. Chinese government media countered these accusations by publishing extensive reports on the development and flourishing of Tibetan culture under Communist rule and taking every opportunity to document conditions favorable to Tibetan cultural life in China. A recent white paper from the Chinese government on the development of Tibetan culture and a response to this white paper from the Tibetan exile government are striking expressions of two opposing views on the fate of Tibetan culture. Looking back to the early years of the People's Republic of China, the Chinese white paper describes the Democratic Reforms campaign as "marking the advent of a brand-new era in the social and cultural development of Tibet, [that] ended the monopoly exercised over Tibetan culture by the few upper-class feudal lamas and aristocrats, making it the common legacy for all the people of Tibet to inherit and carry on."[1] In the Tibetan exile government's response, the reforms are seen as marking the advent of an era that has reduced Tibet to a "cultural wasteland, where even the survival of the Tibetan language is in question."[2]

Realities are of course not as black and white as they appear above. On the one hand, there is little reason to celebrate the Democratic Reforms campaign, which was probably one of the greatest tragedies in recent Tibetan history. On the other hand, it would be equally incorrect to describe contemporary Tibet as a cultural wasteland, and moreover it would be unfair to all the Tibetans who have contributed to the rebuilding of religious sites, supported the use of Tibetan in the schools, and involved themselves in contemporary Tibetan literature and arts. In fact, vigorous cultural reconstruction is taking place in several important spheres in Tibetan areas today.

First, Tibetans have made great efforts to revive religious life, within and outside of the monastic communities. In the two decades since the early 1980s, Tibetans have accomplished the amazing feat of reconstructing thousands of Tibetan Buddhist and Bön monasteries, temples, and other religious sites that were originally built over a period of several centuries. The Tibetan people deserve recognition for the enormous amount of work and funds they have contributed to restoration projects, particularly if we take into account their economic and political conditions. The great majority of Tibetans have participated in this revival, and it should be understood not only as a religious revival but also as a revival of Tibetan and local identities.

Second, educated Tibetans are making a considerable effort to preserve and develop the Tibetan written language, concentrating in particular on the Tibetan literary heritage. Publishing is one of the main outlets for this type of cultural production, while textbooks for learning Tibetan language make classical as well as modern Tibetan literature known to new generations of Tibetans. There was a time, during both the Democratic Reforms period and the Cultural Revolution, when the Tibetan language was suppressed by Chinese authorities. Important changes have taken place since then. As we have seen, a substantial number of literary works in Tibetan are being published, a system of approving new terminology has been established, and Tibetan has even become a computerized language.

Third, entrepreneurs and local culture brokers are manufacturing Tibetan tradition by developing a range of new cultural products for the tourist market. If Tibetan culture is becoming interesting to many Tibetan cadres, this may be due largely to its heightened sales potential. Tourism is a growing business, and local Tibetans are also eager to take part in the economic benefits it offers. This already affects their awareness of what Tibetan culture is.

Finally, Tibetan urban youth are shaping their own modern Tibetan identity based on key traditional symbols and expressing this identity through such media as popular music and visual arts, creating a kind of Tibetan urban subculture. These new cultural creations are available in most township markets in the form of audiotapes and video CDs and are particularly popular among young Tibetans. During our many long-distance car rides in Tibetan areas, we noticed that the most popular music tapes among local drivers featured Tibetan singers performing Tibetan pop songs although with mainly Chinese lyrics.[3] These lyrics are immensely popular among young Tibetans and often describe Tibetan natural scenery or topics related to Tibetan cultural traditions and a search for Tibetan identity. At cultural festivals, one can experience a blend of old and new modes of expression— commercial and noncommercial, modern, self-consciously folkloric, and traditional— in which Tibetan culture is revived and celebrated by young and old.

On the negative side, Tibetans involved in these four fields of cultural reconstruction are struggling with a number of difficulties and dilemmas. The problems faced by Tibetans engaged in practicing and promoting religion are discussed in chapter 2. To sum up the main points, the reconstruction of living monasteries where ceremonies and religious study are revived has been accomplished in spite of restrictions and not because of government support. There is evidence that the authorities not only regulate the number of monks and nuns and the reconstruction of monasteries but even attempt to control the number of monks allowed to pursue curricula of Buddhist studies, the regimens of examination, and the financial affairs of the monasteries.[4] Regulations also affect the recognition of tulkus and the performance of rituals and ceremonies. Whereas Chinese authorities have invested resources in the preservation and reprinting of ancient Buddhist texts, they simultaneously condemn the daily practices and beliefs of Tibetan Buddhists as superstitious and backward. During recent years, new campaigns to control the monasteries and nunneries (in particular the Patriotic Education campaign) have posed great threats to religious freedom. The religious revival of the 1980s has in effect been halted, and there are reasons to fear that the future will bring even more repression of religious practice.

As noted in chapter 4, writers and publishers of Tibetan-language works face the problem of freedom of the press. Political rhetoric is included in one way or another in most Tibetan-language publications. Perhaps more surprisingly, we also found that marketization poses problems for Tibetan-language publishing. As books and journals, including school textbooks, become increasingly expensive, Tibetan literature becomes less accessible to many potential readers. Needless to say, if people are unable to afford magazines or books, it makes little difference to them whether or not such publications are available in Tibetan. Likewise, if people do not have access to a computer or television set, it makes no difference whether software is available in Tibetan or Tibetan-language broadcasts are transmitted by satellite. Another important problem involves the limited range of topics selected for publications in Tibetan. Nonfiction materials in Tibetan concentrate on humanities topics rather than on the natural and social sciences, and this may be one of the reasons why many young Tibetans find Chinese-language publications more interesting than Tibetan ones.

The viability of Tibetan as a written language depends more than anything else on the school system. As explained in chapter 3, many Tibetan children do not attend school at all, and a large number of those who do lack the opportunity to learn their native language. This is especially the case in areas where Tibetans now constitute a minority in the population. There are many indications that the situation is worsening, owing to in-migration, marketization, insufficient funding, and educational policies that in effect reduce the availability of bilingual education. The concerns expressed by Tibetan educators are not unwarranted.

It is interesting to compare the problems of Tibetans in China with those of Tibetan exiles on the Indian subcontinent who are also a minority group with limited rights. English was for many years the main language in schools in Tibetan exile settlements in India because it is the lingua franca of Indian society. It has been difficult to obtain clearance from the Indian government to change the language of instruction in Tibetan schools from English to Tibetan. Primary schools run by the Tibetan Children's Village implemented teaching in Tibetan as early as 1985, but other Tibetan pri-mary schools had to wait until 1994, when all schools governed by the Department of Education (DOE) of the Tibetan government-in-exile were finally allowed to use Tibetan as the language of instruction at the primary level (grades one to five). In the sixth grade, however, English continues to be the language of instruction. This is because the curriculum for Tibetan schools in India, Nepal, and Bhutan must be approved by a board of edu-cation that is recognized by each national government. Tibetan secondary schools in India, for example, use textbooks in English published by the Indian National Council for Educational Research and Training. These text-books are based on the curriculum prescribed by the Central Board of Secondary Education in New Delhi.[5]

During the past decade, the Tibetan exile government developed a pro-gram to modernize the Tibetan language by inventing new words for mod-ern technologies and appliances and has made efforts to strengthen the role of the Tibetan language in the exile community. It is obvious, however, that the use of Tibetan language is threatened by the very pressures of surviv-ing as refugees in a foreign country. The situation for Tibetan exiles is thus similar to the situation of Tibetans in China. Whereas Tibetans in China are picking up loan words from Chinese, young Tibetans in India are pick-ing up more and more Hindi and English loan words.[6]

In chapter 5, we discussed the cultural brokers of the tourist and tourism-related markets and their reliance on notions of Tibetanness as something exciting and exotic for the sale of their products, whether these products are a destination or an audio recording. This trend represents a growing commoditization of Tibetan culture that may be unavoidable but is cer-tainly not unproblematic. As defined here, culture is inherently contested and continuously reconstructed. This implies that cultural expressions will change as different people find new reasons for defining and promoting a particular identity. Within such an understanding of culture, it is difficult to talk about the authenticity of cultural expressions. What we can say, however, is that the economic role of Tibetan cultural expressions is changing as Tibetanness becomes increasingly marketable. This process can be observed not only in China but to an even greater extent in Tibetan settlements in India and Nepal. It may in fact be considered part of a global process of commoditization of exotic ethnic cultures.[7] It is still too early to grasp the implications for the understanding of Tibetan culture in local communities that are being developed for tourism, but it is clear that this process will represent a major force for change in the years to come.

Young urban Tibetans who are attempting to forge a secular Tibetan identity are also facing some dilemmas. Those who are actively involved in these attempts, such as writers and artists, may discover that they are walking a political tightrope. On the one hand, their efforts to reshape Tibetan identity may gain them the support of the authorities, who wish to promote a modern secular and preferably socialist Tibetanness. On the other hand, if they accept this support, they face criticism from Tibetan traditionalists who fail to see the need for renewing Tibetan identity and regard these modernists as somehow betraying Tibetan traditions. It appears that some Tibetan exile cultural institutions also have a vested interest in a particular notion of authentic Tibetan culture that they attempt to preserve. Clare Harris, in her book on visual arts, describes how representatives of the refugee community tend to see it as their duty to preserve the authentic Tibetan culture as it was prior to 1959, when the Dalai Lama and the first large groups of refugees left Tibet.[8] Tibetan exiles often refer to 1959 as an important historical marker, and Harris claims that Tibetan artists are considered more "authentic" if they received their training before 1959. There is also an expectation that artists should remain faithful to the ancient traditions of religious art rather than experiment with new styles of painting.[9]

Representatives of the Tibetan exile government have similarly criticized young Tibetans within China who deviate from their view of authentic Tibetan culture. They claim that the Chinese Communists have nurtured an entirely new, socialist version of Tibetan culture in China, a campus culture that is neither Tibetan nor Chinese:

> While the traditional spiritual culture is denounced as the culture of feudal lords, the campus culture is touted as the culture of the new, socialist Tibet.

Although campus culture is taught from primary school to university level, it has absolutely no relevance to the reality of Tibetan society. The knowledge of this shallow campus culture may help one make a living as a poet, writer, translator, or journalist or administrative clerk under the Chinese government. But it does not empower him or her to further the development of Tibetan culture.[10]

This kind of criticism poses interesting questions about who should have the authority to define Tibetan culture. It nevertheless fails to acknowledge the contemporary challenges faced by young Tibetans living and working in China and the subtle ways in which they try to promote their visions of a new secular Tibetan identity without attacking religion or traditional values or necessarily praising Communism. There appears to be a conflict of perspectives, perhaps even an ideological divide, between these young urban Tibetans and members of the exile elite who dismiss the very idea of a secular Tibetanness and see themselves as the preservers of Tibetan culture at a time when that culture is being extinguished in Tibet. Conflicting views about the importance of preservation versus modernization also manifest themselves in debates within the exile community as well as among Tibetans in China. These debates are to a certain extent informed by the particular conditions for cultural expression provided by the framework of Chinese cultural and *minzu* policies. When Chinese authorities intervene in religious matters or limit specific cultural expressions and encourage others, this obviously influences how Tibetans come to define their culture and seek to reconstruct or preserve their Tibetanness.

PRESERVATION AND PROGRESS

Tibetan culture is by definition contested, but it is negotiated in China under specific conditions provided by the Chinese state and influenced by government policies and regulations. In other words, as Tibetans struggle to maintain and modernize Tibetan culture, they are doing so in response to the conditions created by Chinese authorities, whether they are adapting to or opposing these conditions. One might therefore argue that in the process of developing modern expressions of Tibetanness, Tibetan culture is contested and reconstructed on Chinese rather than on Tibetan terms.

In China, ethnic minorities are often depicted as backward and in need of help from the central government to develop. The basic view of the Chinese Communist Party (CCP) is that widespread religious belief among many of the minorities is an impediment to progress and, at best, an obstacle to be overcome. In addition to this ideological standpoint, the CCP fears the rise of Tibetan religious institutions as focal points of Tibetan separatism. As described in policy guidelines such as Document 19 (1982), the Party has maintained that the tendency to believe in religion will diminish gradually as people achieve a higher standard of living and economic prosperity takes hold. However, the importance of religion in Tibetan areas does not seem to have diminished but rather has increased since the beginning of the Reform era. Similar trends are also evident among other religions and spiritual movements in China, such as Islam and the Falun Gong movement. This has caused Chinese leaders to tighten control over institutionalized religion all over China, including the Tibetan areas. Contrary to the guidelines described above, Chinese authorities repeatedly used force against religious communities during the 1990s, implementing Patriotic Education to suppress "separatism" in Tibetan monasteries and nunneries and cracking down on the Falun Gong movement beginning in 1999.

Is there really a contradiction between economic progress and religious revival? In the so-called developed world, many people are in fact returning to religion and spirituality to find a deeper sense of meaning in their lives. A number of people have found this sense of meaning in Tibetan Buddhism, and some of them have even contributed to the revival of Tibetan monasteries and nunneries in China. One of the reasons authorities regard religious revival as a threat may be that it provides a moral alternative to the ideology of the current regime. However, ethical choices and value judgments cannot be changed by the use of force and ideological pressure. This will only strengthen the resistance of many Tibetans toward government policies and reinforce the role of religion as a marker of Tibetan identity. Moreover, as long as Chinese authorities intervene in religious affairs for political purposes, it should come as no surprise that Tibetans and other minorities will use religion as a political tool.

Regardless of whether Chinese authorities continue their campaigns against religion, local Tibetan communities will have to consider the appropriate numbers of monks and nuns in Tibetan monasteries and nunneries. Chinese authorities could influence the size of the Tibetan clergy by increasing funding for schools in Tibetan areas, making these schools less expensive, and revising the curriculum in primary and secondary schools so that basic education is relevant to the needs of Tibetans.[11] Education in Tibetan, made available at all levels and with a wider selection of courses, could give all Tibetan children the opportunity to learn Tibetan. This would not only provide a good alternative for parents who would otherwise send their children to the monasteries but also make public education much more attractive, ensure the future viability of the Tibetan language, and improve Tibetans' capacity to take care of their own affairs.

Chinese authorities have made efforts to redefine Tibetan culture as non-Buddhist and have allowed if not actively supported a wide range of secular cultural expressions. This can only be understood as a conscious political strategy to secularize Tibetan culture. This strategy is in line with the CCP view of religion as an essentially detrimental social force and with associated modernist notions of the need to fight superstition and backwardness in order to achieve progress and scientific development. Yet the Tibetan language has clearly become a language for publishing special interest books within the arts and humanities, particularly in what might broadly be called Tibetan cultural studies. Books in Tibetan on natural science subjects are few and far between. The selection of subjects taught in Tibetan in colleges and universities reflects the same bias. Consequently, the Tibetan language has become irrelevant for the very development efforts Chinese authorities wish to promote, and Tibetans who want to participate in developing their economy must do so in Chinese. This is not only a problem for the viability of the Tibetan language but also represents a serious obstacle for development efforts in Tibetan areas.

The image of Tibetan culture as the culture of the grasslands corresponds very well with the CCP view of Tibetan culture as a secular culture of the people. This image may however represent more than just a secularization of Tibetanness. It raises important questions about cultural survival that go beyond the celebration of traditional festivals, the publication of poetry in Tibetan, and the broadcast of ethnic song and dance performances. Although young educated Tibetans still see the Tibetan language and the revival of religious life as important to the survival of Tibetan culture, there is a growing recognition that issues such as land rights and environmental degradation may be even more crucial.

Chinese legislation protects the rights of Tibetans and other ethnic minorities in China to develop their own culture and upholds the principle of autonomy for minorities. A different and much less promising picture emerges, however, if we look at the actual rights this autonomy allows. Unfortunately, in contemporary China, minorities do not have distinct rights to natural resources or even the power to make decisions about the very land on which they live.

If Tibetans were given the chance to manage their own resources, they might not keep their traditional lifestyles unchanged, but they would have to find their own balance between preservation and progress. For the sake of future generations, they need sustainable development that preserves the fragile Plateau environment and also creates prosperity.

Administrative Divisions in
the People's Republic of China

The highest level within the Chinese system of administrative division is the "province" (Ch: *sheng*). Apart from the regular provinces, province-level areas include the Beijing municipal area and the five "autonomous regions" (Ch: *zizhiqu*). The Tibet Autonomous Region (TAR) is thus a province-level administrative unit.

Within each province, there are "prefectures" (Ch: *zhou*) and prefecture-level "municipal areas" (Ch: *shi*). Some prefectures are "autonomous prefectures" (Ch: *zizhizhou*) assigned to one or more ethnic minorities. However, within an autonomous region, there are no autonomous prefectures, since the higher-level administrative unit is already assigned to an ethnic minority.

Within each prefecture, there are "counties" (Ch: *xian*), some of which are "autonomous counties" (Ch: *zizhixian*). Counties are explicitly designated autonomous only when they are located within a prefecture that either is not autonomous or is assigned to an ethnic group other than the one for whom the county is designated. A municipality may also be a county-level administrative unit, but there are no autonomous municipalities.

Within each county, there are "village districts" (Ch: *xiang*) and "townships" (Ch: *zhen*). In some areas, the older designation "district" (Ch: *diqu*) is still in use. Since the early 1980s, village districts and townships have been administered by their own governments. Some village districts with large minority populations located outside autonomous counties or within autonomous counties assigned to other ethnic minorities have since been assigned the status of autonomous village district.

APPENDIX 2

Demographic Composition in
the Autonomous Prefectures

All information is from 1990 census figures.

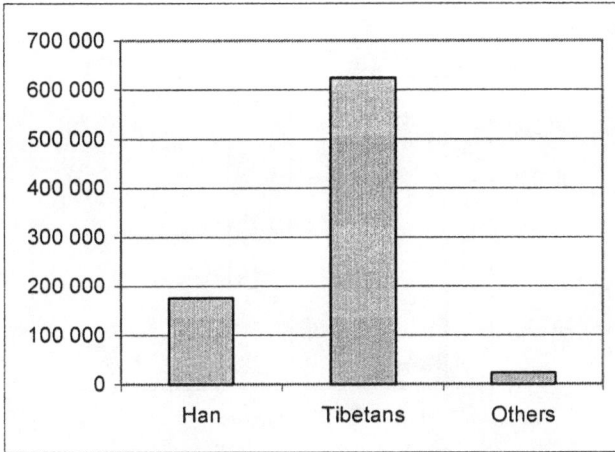

CHART A2.1. Kandze (Ganzi) Tibetan Autonomous Prefecture

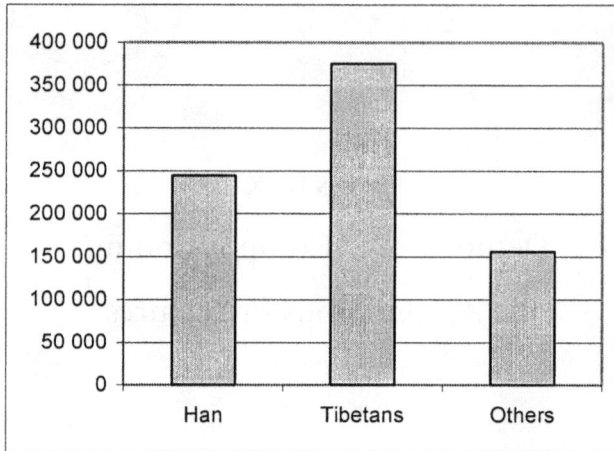

CHART A2.2. Ngaba (Aba) Tibetan and Qiang Autonomous Prefecture

GANSU

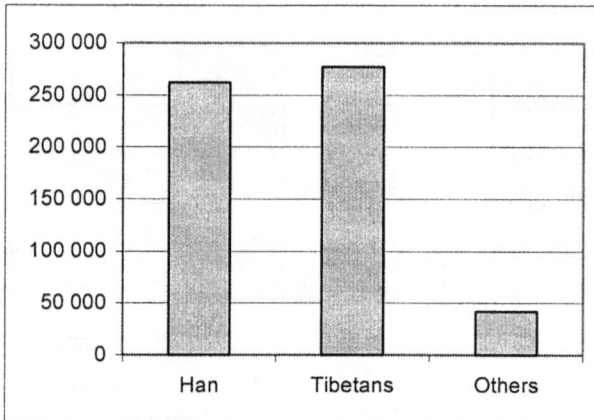

CHART A2.3. Kanlho (Gannan) Tibetan Autonomous Prefecture

YUNNAN

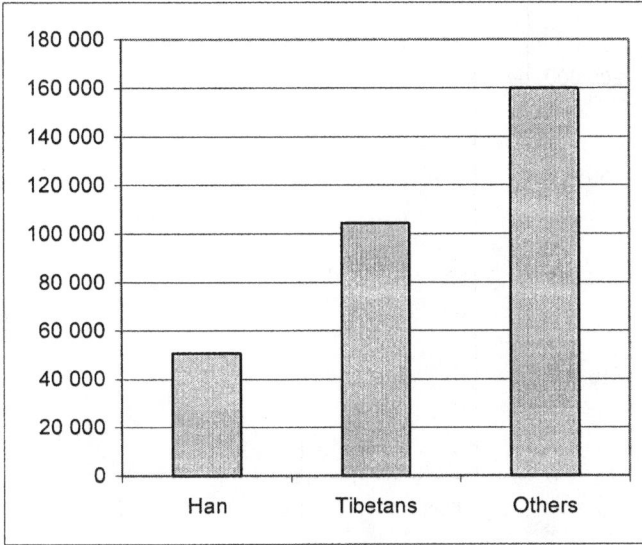

CHART A2.4. Dechen (Diqing) Tibetan Autonomous Prefecture

QINGHAI

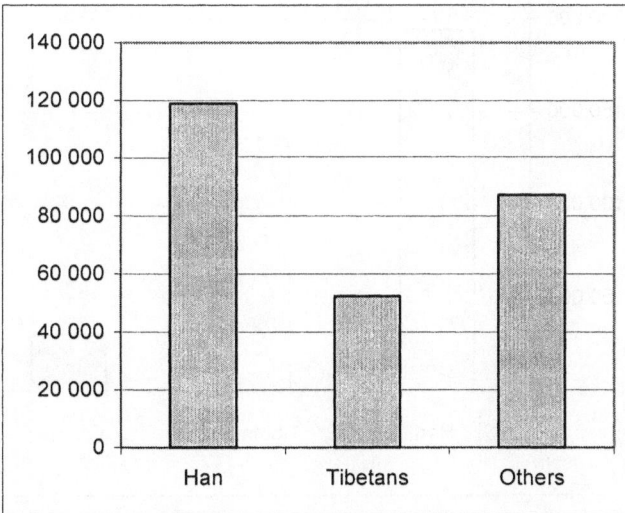

CHART A2.5. Tsochang (Haibei) Tibetan Autonomous Prefecture

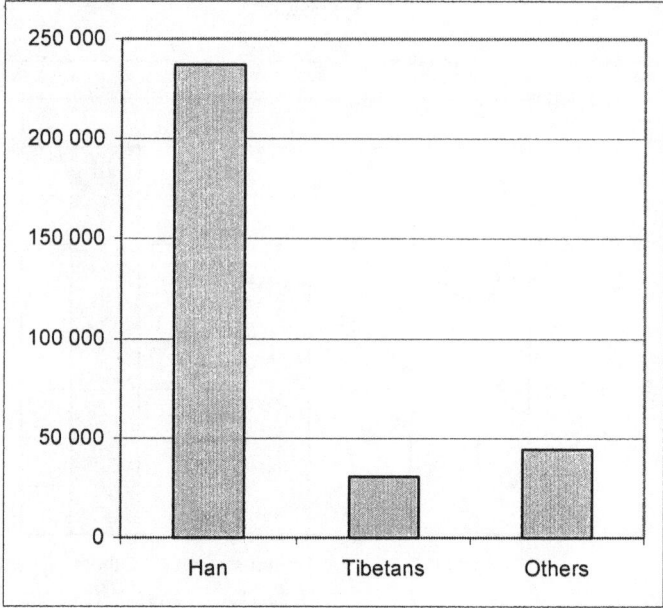

CHART A2.6. Tsonub (Haixi) Mongolian and Tibetan Autonomous Prefecture

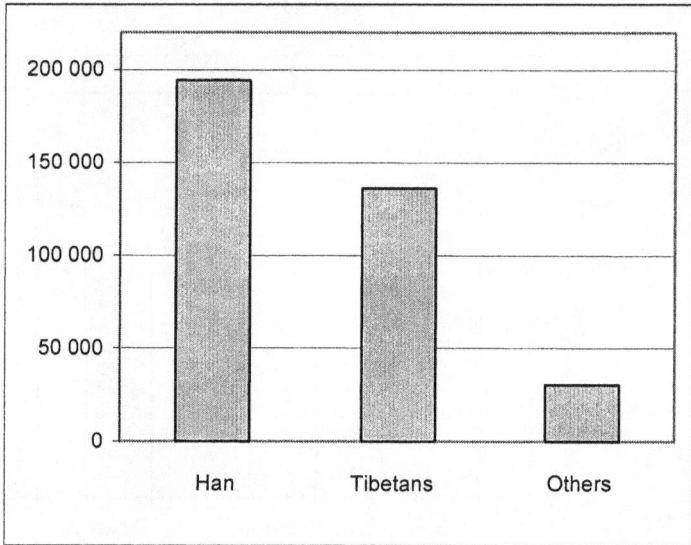

CHART A2.7. Tsolho (Hainan) Tibetan Autonomous Prefecture

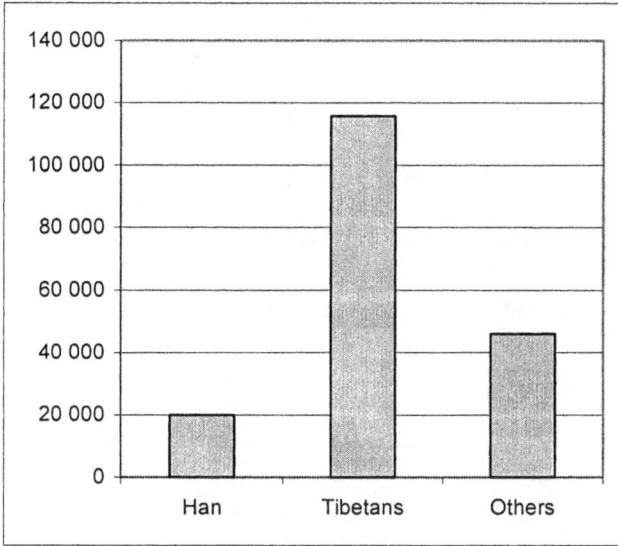

CHART A2.8. Malho (Huangnan) Tibetan Autonomous Prefecture

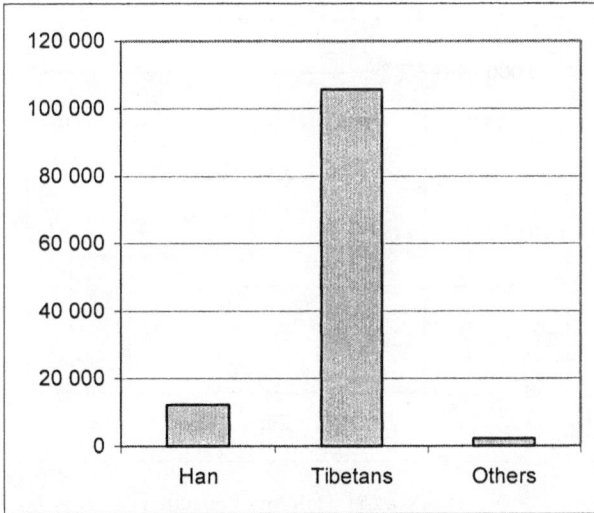

CHART A2.9. Golok (Guoluo) Tibetan Autonomous Prefecture

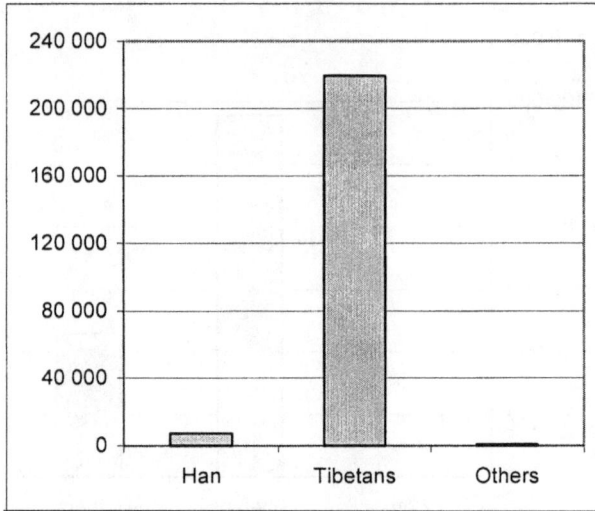

CHART A2.10. Jyekundo (Yushu) Tibetan Autonomous Prefecture

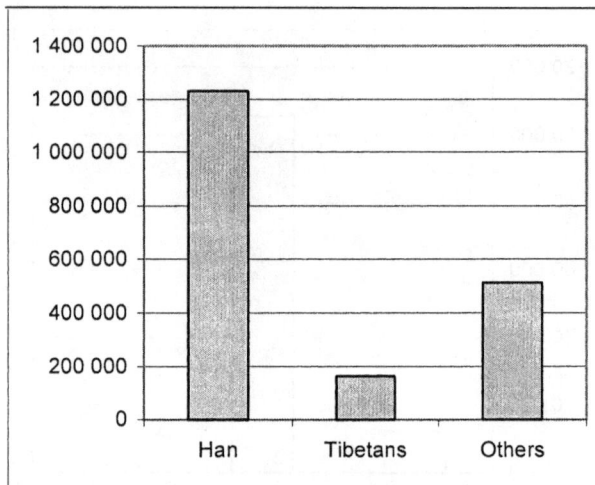

CHART A2.11. Haidong Prefecture

APPENDIX 3

Data on Religion

SICHUAN

Sichuan has two Tibetan-designated prefectures, Ngaba (Aba) Tibetan and Qiang Autonomous Prefecture (T and Q AP) and Kandze (Ganzi) Tibetan Autonomous Prefecture (TAP), and one Tibetan-designated county, Mili (Muli) Tibetan Autonomous County (TAC) in Liangshan Yi Autonomous Prefecture. Written sources give inconsistent information on the number of monks and monasteries in these areas in the 1950s. For instance, Ran Guangrong writes that Ngaba Prefecture had 207 monasteries, with a total of 14,400 monks, but the Ngaba Prefecture History states that Ngaba had as many as 343 monasteries and 26,226 monks before the implementation of Democratic Reforms.

In an interview with officials in the Sichuan Province Religious Affairs Department, we were unable to obtain exact numbers on monasteries in Sichuan because of the "difficulties" of defining a monastery. According to the officials, there were more than 900 Tibetan monasteries in Sichuan in the 1950s, compared to more than 780 in 1999. Exact figures for monasteries of the different orders were unavailable, but a list of approximate numbers, which was read to us during the interview, indicated the following breakdown as of 1999: more than 300 Nyingmapa, more than 200 Gelugpa, about 100 Sakyapa, 40 Kagyupa, and more than 20 Jonangpa. We were also told that there were 4 or 5 "not belonging to a specific order" and more than 90 Bön monasteries. As for their locations, the officials stated that about 250 were located in Ngaba Prefecture, more than 500 were in Kandze, and 16 were in Liangshan Yi Autonomous Prefecture. Among the latter, 15 (all Gelugpa monasteries) were said to be located in Mili (Muli) TAC. Another 2 Tibetan Buddhist monasteries were reportedly located in Yuanyuan and Baoxing Counties.

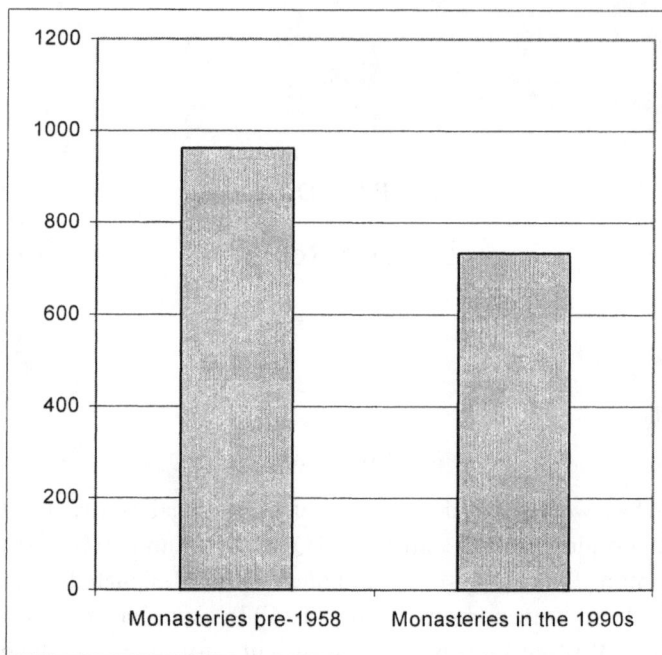

CHART A3.1. Monasteries in Sichuan

The Sichuan Province Religious Affairs Department did not want to comment on the number of monks in the 1950s but claimed that the approximate number in 1999 was more than 50,000, which included 8,000 lamas, more than 40,000 *draba*, 3,000 nuns, and 500 tulkus. Officials informed us that Ngaba Prefecture had 10 nunneries at present, while Kandze TAP had more than 20 nunneries.

After comparing different sources and evaluating the amount of detail they provide, we regard the figures in table A3.1 as the most reliable.

TABLE A3.1. Monasteries and Monks in Sichuan

	Monasteries pre-1958	Monks pre-1958	Monasteries in the 1990s	Monks in the 1990s
Kandze (Ganzi)	564	80,000	516	43,000
Ngaba (Aba)	343	26,226	201	19,982
Mili (Muli)	15		15	
TOTAL	922	106,226	732	62,982

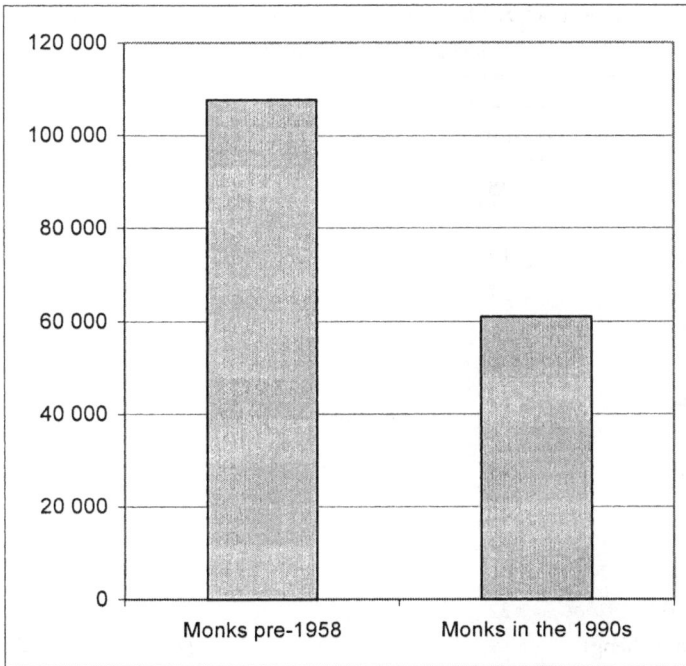

CHART A3.2. Monks in Sichuan

A number of different sources give information on the situation in Kandze TAP. The Kandze TAP Religious Affairs Department claimed that the prefecture had as many as 597 monasteries in the early 1950s, but, as did the provincial authorities, they pointed out that the definition of a monastery was wider than it is today. They also reported that the prefecture had 80,000 monks, nuns, and tulkus in the 1950s, comprising 15 percent of the population. Even more detailed information on the numbers of monasteries in Kandze prior to 1958 can be found in a report published by the Sichuan Province Ethnic Affairs Commission. These figures are listed in table A3.2 in the section on Kandze below.

The Kandze Prefecture Religious Affairs Department provided further information about 516 Tibetan Buddhist monasteries, 3 Christian churches, and 1 mosque in 1999. The churches and mosque were all located in Dartsedo (Kangding) County. The department reported that there were 41,000 monks, 2,000 nuns, and 453 tulkus in Kandze, with 87 of those tulkus officially recognized by the authorities since 1980. When comparing the

TABLE A3.2. Monasteries and Monks in Kandze (Ganzi)
Tibetan Autonomous Prefecture

County	Monasteries pre-1958	Monks pre-1958	Monasteries in 1990	Monasteries in 1999	Monks in 1999
Dartsedo (Kangding)	28		26	31	
Chaksam (Luding)	–		–	–	
Nyachukha (Yajiang)	17		26	33	
Lithang (Litang)	27		30	30	
Bathang (Batang)	46		16 (18)	17	
Tawu (Daofu)	41		27	31	
Drakgo (Luhuo)	32		22	22	
Kandze (Ganzi)	40		35 (36)	45	
Nyakrong (Xinlong)	79		52	54	
Pelyül (Baiyu)	41		33	35	
Derge (Dege)	57		57	57	
Sershül (Shiqu)	55		46	46	
Gyesur (Jiulong)	22		3	4	
Chathreng (Xiangcheng)	9		24	27	
Derong	10		6 (4)	6	
Dabpa (Daocheng)	20		12	13	
Rongdrak (Danba)	21		29	35	
Serthar (Seda)	19		30	30	
TOTAL	564	80,000	474 (475)	516	43,000

SOURCE, MONASTERIES PRE-1958: Sichuan Sheng Minzu Shiwu Weiyuanhui, *Zangchuan fojiao siyuan ziliao xuanbian,* 28–53. *Note:* One alternative source, *Ganzi Zhou zhi,* refers to 495 monasteries in 1956 (319), and a second, Ran, *Zhongguo Zangchuan fojiao siyuan,* reports 540 monasteries prior to 1958 (117).

SOURCE, MONKS PRE-1958: Interview with the religious affairs department in Kangding, May 2000. *Note:* An alternative source, Ran, *Zhongguo Zangchuan fojiao siyuan,* gives a total of 79,300 monks prior to 1958 (117).

SOURCES, MONASTERIES IN 1990: *Ganzi Zhou zhi,* 319–35. *Notes:* Alternative figures, in brackets, are from Kangding Minzu Shizhuan Bianxiezuo, *Dangdai Ganzi,* 113–25. Three sources give different information about the number of monasteries in Derong: Kangding Minzu Shizhuan Bianxiezu, *Dangdai Ganzi,* gives 1990 figures of 4 monasteries, 1 Gelugpa and 3 Kagyupa; *Ganzi Zhou zhi,* gives information on 6 monasteries based on 1990 statistics, 1 Gelugpa, 3 Kagyupa, and 2 Nyingmapa (335); and Sichuan Sheng Minzu Shiwu Weiyuanhui, *Zangchuan fojiao siyuan ziliao xuanbian,* gives the preceding figures, probably based on sources from the early 1950s, and an incomplete list of 10 monasteries, including reference to 2 Gelugpa monasteries, 1 Kagyupa, 4 Nyingmapa, 1 Bön, and another 3 monasteries with orders not listed (39).

SOURCE, MONASTERIES IN 1999: Interview with the religious affairs department in Kangding, May 2000. *Note:* An official in the Sichuan Province Religious Affairs Department confirmed that Kandze had more than 500 Tibetan monasteries in 2000.

SOURCE, MONKS IN 1999: Interview with the religious affairs department in Kangding, May 2000. *Note:* In comparison, *Ganzi Zhou zhi* reports the current number of monks and nuns as 54,000, comprising 13 percent of the population (319–35).

figures from the Kandze Prefecture Religious Affairs Department in 2000 with interviews we conducted in four of the prefecture's counties, we find that the numbers of monasteries reported by the county and the prefecture governments are identical. The Kandze Prefecture History contains information about the number of monasteries in the prefecture in 1990. Compared to that information, it appears that from 1990 to 2000, the number of monasteries increased by 42, from 474 to 516. The prefecture government figure on Derong County (17 monasteries) is probably inaccurate, because no other identified source refers to more than 10 monasteries in the county. Most probably the total figure should have been 6, including only 2 Nyingmapa monasteries instead of 13, since this number corresponds with the total number of Nyingmapa monasteries listed in the Kandze Prefecture History.

We do not have as much detailed information about the number of monasteries in the neighboring prefecture of Ngaba. Several written sources provide information on the numbers of monks and monasteries in Ngaba Prefecture, but all of them give different figures. The Ngaba Prefecture History gives a comprehensive list of monasteries, by order, before 1958: 108 Gelugpa, 116 Nyingmapa, 18 Sakyapa, 34 Jonangpa, and 62 Bön. This adds up to 338 monasteries, although presumably at least 5 rebuilt Kagyupa monasteries should be added to the list, since they most likely existed in the 1950s. This would give a total of 343 monasteries. *China's Tibet* (no. 1, 1998) reports that 201 monasteries were reopened in the prefecture: 60 Gelugpa, 70 Nyingmapa, 13 Sakyapa, 18 Jonangpa, 5 Kagyupa, and 35 Bön. The article also states that Ngaba had 120 tulkus at that time. These two sources are the most detailed we have been able to find, and we regard them as the most reliable. Unfortunately, neither of them compares the situation today with that prior to the destruction that took place during the Democratic Reforms campaign.

According to the Ngaba Prefecture Religious Affairs Department, there were a total of 280 religious sites in the prefecture in 1999, including mosques, and 18,000 monks and clerics. The department was unable to give us further details about the number of Tibetan Buddhist and Bön monasteries and monks in the prefecture. However, we collected an almost complete set of county histories from Ngaba, which in most cases contain information on the situation before 1958 and in the 1990s. The county histories list a total of 248 monasteries before 1958, with more than 17,710 monks. They also list altogether 195 monasteries in the 1990s, with more than 13,068 monks. Unfortunately, these sources are too incomplete to provide information on the prefecture as a whole, although some give detailed information for both the pre-1958 period and the 1990s, which enables us to compare the figures for each county from the same source. The information drawn from these county histories is listed in table A3.3.

TABLE A3.3. Monasteries and Monks in Ngaba (Aba)
Tibetan and Qiang Autonomous Prefecture

County	Monasteries pre-1958	Monks pre-1958	Monasteries in the 1990s	Monks in the 1990s
Barkham (Ma'erkang)	73	1,026+	53	813+
Ngaba (Aba)	50	8,247	33	6,486
Kakhok (Hongyuan)	7+	1,000+	7	200
Throchu (Heishui)	16			
Namphel (Nanping)	9	542		
Dzoge (Ruo'ergai)	45	4,703	29	1,470
Dzamthang (Rangtang)			48	3,292
Chuchen (Jinchuan)	37	1,760	20	807
Tsenlha (Xiaojin)	7	282	5	
Tashiling (Lixian)	4	150		
Lunggu (Wenchuan)			0	
Maowün (Maowen)	0		0	
TOTAL	248	17,710	195	13,068

SOURCES, MONASTERIES PRE-1958: *Aba Zhou zhi*, 248, and Ran, *Zhongguo Zangchuan fojiao siyuan*, 117.

SOURCES, MONASTERIES IN THE 1990S: *China's Tibet*, no. 1 (1998), and the Ngaba Prefecture Religious Affairs Department. *Note:* The Third Office of the Sichuan Province Religious Affairs Department, which is in charge of Tibetan Buddhism, reported in 2000 that Ngaba prefecture had about 250 Tibetan monasteries.

SOURCES, MONKS PRE-1958: *Aba Zhou zhi*, 344, and Ran, *Zhongguo Zangchuan fojiao siyuan*, 117.

SOURCES, MONKS IN THE 1990S: Ngaba Prefecture Religious Affairs Department and *Aba Zhou zhi*, 344.

GANSU

Gansu has two areas designated as Tibetan autonomous: Kanlho (Gannan) Tibetan Autonomous Prefecture and Pari (Tianzhu) Tibetan Autonomous County in Wuwei Prefecture. According to Pu Wencheng, there were 369 Tibetan monasteries in Gansu prior to 1958, with 16,900 monks and 310 tulkus. Of these, 196 monasteries were located within Kanlho TAP: 8 Nyingmapa, 2 Sakyapa, 9 Bönpo, and 177 Gelugpa. Pu does not indicate the number of monks in Kanlho before the Democratic Reforms campaign. In fact, none of the available sources provides complete information on the number of monks in Kanlho before 1958. However, Pu reports that there were 108 Tibetan monasteries and around 5,000 monks in Gansu in 1990. Of these, Kanlho had 89 monasteries and 4,700 monks. According to information from the Kanlho Prefecture government, by 1998 Kanlho had 121 monasteries and

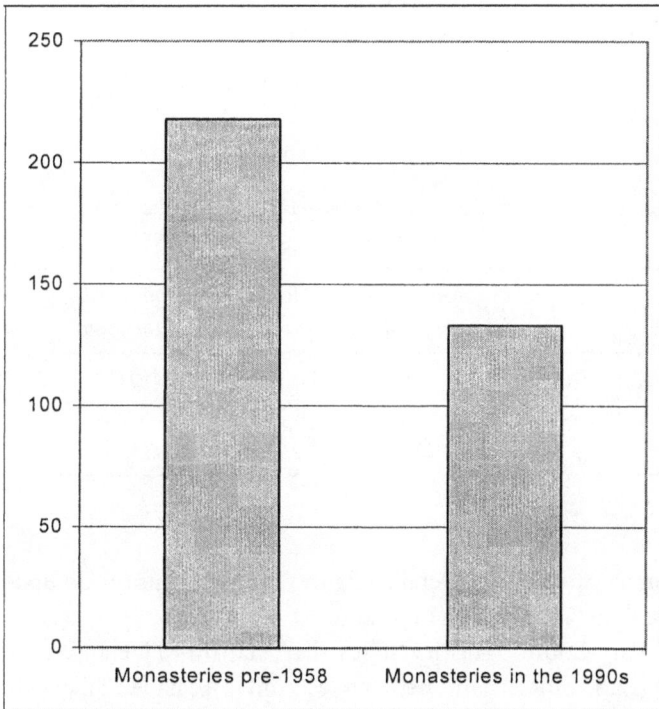

CHART A3.3. Monasteries in Gansu

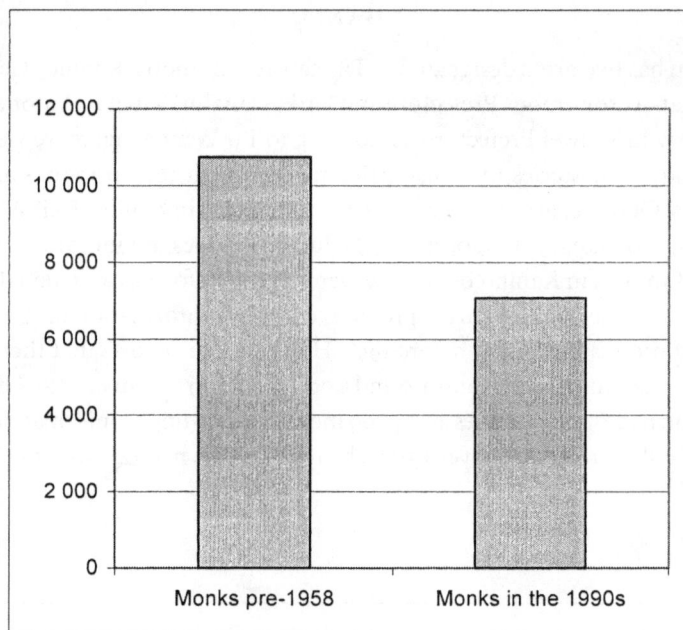

CHART A3.4. Monks in Gansu

TABLE A3.4. Monasteries and Monks
in Gansu Tibetan area

County	Monasteries pre-1958	Monks pre-1958	Monasteries in the 1990s	Monks in the 1990s
Kanlho (Gannan)	196	9,562	121	7,006
Pari (Tianzhu)	22	1,203	12	70
TOTAL	218	10,765	131	7,076

more than 6,300 monks. Detailed figures for each county add up to a total of more than 7,006 monks in Kanlho.

The Pari County History states that Tianzhu Tibetan Autonomous District (Pari's official name between 1950 and 1956) had 14 Tibetan Buddhist monasteries in 1950. Establishment of Tianzhu TAC and related changes in boundaries in 1956 added 8 more monasteries, and the county then had 22

TABLE A3.5. Monasteries and Monks in Kanlho (Gannan)
Tibetan Autonomous Prefecture

County	Monasteries pre-1958	Monks pre-1958	Monasteries in the 1990s	Monks in the 1990s
Sangchu (Xiahe)	63	4,324+	36	3,200
Luchu (Luqu)	8	1,030	8	773+
Chone (Zhuoni)	10 (?)		19	1,000+
Batse (Lintan)	3		3	112+
Thewo (Diebu)	23	2,237	20	670
Drukchu (Zhouqu)			21	201+
Machu (Maqu)	8	1,971	12	1,050+
TOTAL	196 (115)	9,562+	121(119)	6,300 (7,006+)

SOURCE, MONASTERIES PRE-1958: Pu, *Gan Qing Zangchuan fojiao siyuan*, 503–63, provides details on 115 monasteries in six of Kanlho's seven counties.

SOURCE, MONKS PRE-1958: Pu, *Gan Qing Zangchuan fojiao siyuan*, 503–63.

SOURCE, MONASTERIES AND MONKS IN THE 1990s: Pu, *Gan Qing Zangchuan fojiao siyuan*, and interview with the Kanlho Prefecture Religious Affairs Department in Tsö (Hezuo), April 1999. Note: The total number of monasteries was said to be 121, whereas the county-level figures add up to only 119. Alternative figures are in parentheses.

monasteries, 1,203 monks, and 35 tulkus. Pu Wencheng reports that in 1989, permission was given to reconstruct 12 monasteries in Pari. According to Pu, only 7 out of the original 173 monasteries had been rebuilt outside of Kanlho and Pari by 1990. In comparison, at least 101 out of 218 monasteries were rebuilt within the Tibetan autonomous areas. If this is correct, the Tibetan autonomous areas have much higher rates of reconstruction than does the rest of the province. Despite this, we have limited our comparisons to Tibetan autonomous areas of Gansu only. Specific information on pre-1958 and 1990s numbers of monasteries and monks in Kanlho TAP is in table A3.5. A breakdown of monasteries and monks in Pari TAC for the same time periods is in table A3.6.

TABLE A3.6. Monasteries and Monks in Pari (Tianzhu)
Tibetan Autonomous County

Monasteries pre-1958	Monks pre-1958	Monasteries in the 1990s	Monks in the 1990s
22	1,203	12	70

SOURCE, MONASTERIES AND MONKS PRE-1958: *Tianzhu Xian zhi*, 766.
SOURCE, MONASTERIES AND MONKS IN THE 1990S: Pu, *Gan Qing Zangchuan fojiao siyuan*, 503–63.

YUNNAN

Yunnan has only one Tibetan-designated area, Dechen (Diqing) TAP. The most comprehensive information, historical and contemporary, on the numbers of monks and monasteries in Dechen can be found in a study on Tibetan Buddhism in the prefecture edited by Sonam Dolkar. According

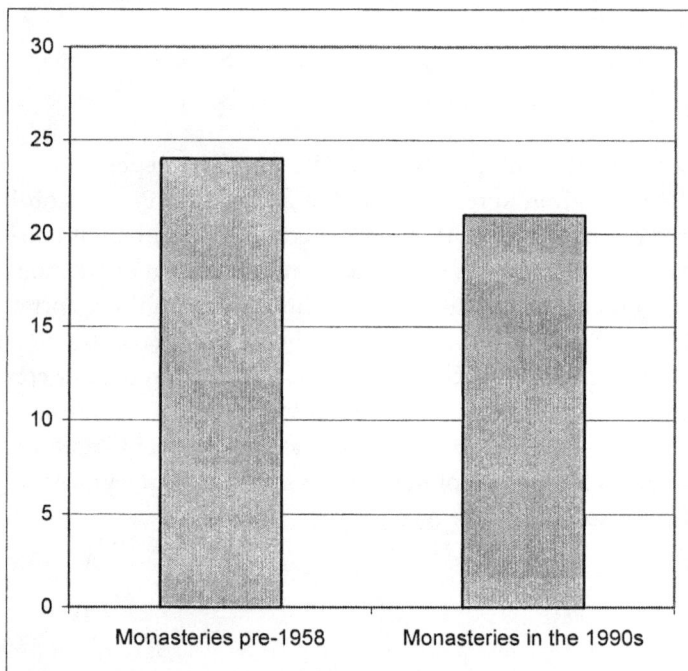

CHART A3.5. Monasteries in Yunnan

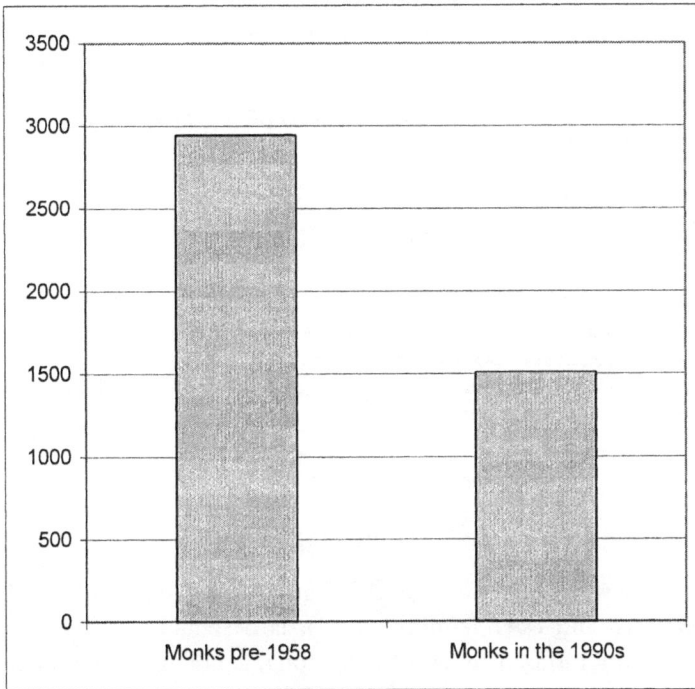

CHART A3.6. Monks in Yunnan

to the study, there were a total of 24 monasteries in Dechen in 1949: 13 Gelugpa, 7 Kagyupa, and 4 Nyingmapa. Gyelthang (Zhongdian) County had 3 monasteries, Dechen (Deqin) County had 17 monasteries, and Balung (Weixi) Lisu Autonomous County had 4 monasteries. By 1994, at least 20 of these monasteries were being rebuilt. Many were still undergoing reconstruction at the time of our visit in 1998, although rebuilding began in the mid-1980s.

According to a 1998 Xinhua news report (BBC Summary of World Broadcasts, 4 April 1998), Yunnan then had 25 Tibetan monasteries. Local sources confirmed that at least 1 Tibetan monastery outside Dechen Prefecture had been rebuilt, the Karma Kagyupa monastery of Tashi Chomphelling, located in Lijiang Naxi Autonomous County. Because we had only limited knowledge of this monastery and other monasteries located outside Dechen, our statistics for Yunnan cover only the Tibetan autonomous area of Dechen TAP.

TABLE A3.7. Monasteries and Monks in Dechen (Diqing)
Tibetan Autonomous Prefecture

County	Monasteries pre-1958	Monks pre-1958	Monasteries in the 1990s	Monks in the 1990s
Dechen (Deqin)	17	1085+	16	756
Gyelthang (Zhongdian)	3	1470+	3	648
Balung (Weixi)	4	390	2	104
TOTAL	24	2,945+	21	1,508

SOURCE, MONASTERIES AND MONKS PRE-1958: Dolkar, *Zongjiao zhi*, 20–28.

SOURCES, MONASTERIES AND MONKS IN THE 1990S: Dolkar, *Zongjiao zhi*, 20–28; *Deqin Xian zhi*, 321–23; unpublished government documents; and interviews with the Dechen Prefecture Religious Affairs Department, Gyelthang, July 1998.

QINGHAI

There are seven prefectures in Qinghai. Five are designated Tibetan autonomous, and one, Tsonub (Haixi), is designated Mongolian and Tibetan autonomous. The seventh, Haidong, is not an autonomous prefecture, but it encompasses several counties with village districts that have Tibetan autonomous status. It also has a large number of Tibetan monasteries, including Kumbum, which is one of the six major monasteries of the Gelugpa tradition. In addition, several Tibetan monasteries are located within Xining Municipality. Since we have reliable information for the province as a whole, these figures are presented in our data on Qinghai Province, even though we do not present data on Xining Municipality in the tables below. Note that we have conducted interviews in Tibetan autonomous prefectures only.

According to Pu Wencheng, Qinghai had 722 Tibetan Buddhist monasteries prior to the 1958 Democratic Reforms campaign, with approximately 57,647 monks and 1,240 tulkus. By 1990, there were about 627 monasteries in Qinghai, with a total of 19,640 monks and 360 tulkus. Of these, 343 monasteries belonged to the Gelugpa school, with a total of 10,169 monks and 158 tulkus. There were 135 Nyingmapa monasteries, with a total of 4,875 monks and 129 tulkus; 101 Kagyupa monasteries, with 2,868 monks and 47 tulkus; and 29 Sakyapa monasteries, with a total of 1,056 monks and 14 tulkus.

The Qinghai Province Ethnic Affairs Commission reported in an interview in 1999 that there were 2,085 religious sites altogether in Qinghai in

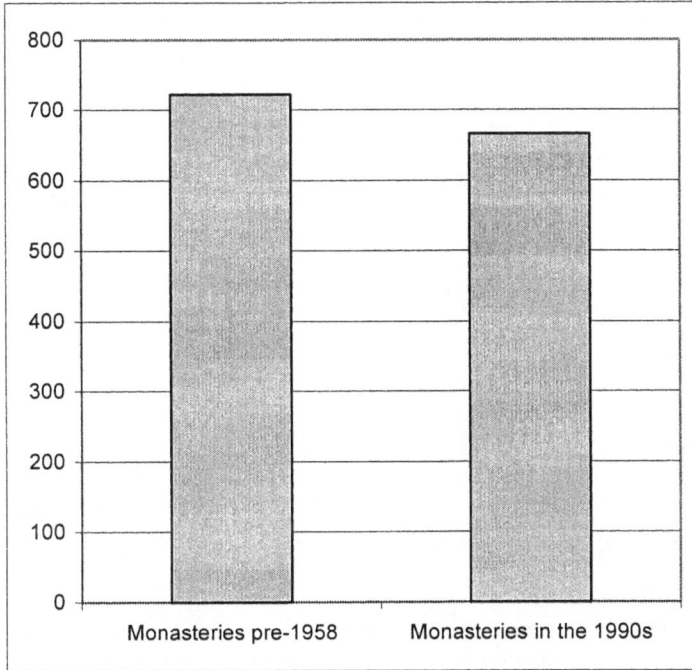

CHART A3.7. Monasteries in Qinghai

1996, with a total of more than 26,000 religious personnel (including monks and nuns, imams, and priests). These included Chinese Buddhist monasteries (19 sites with 28 monks), Muslim mosques (1,339 sites with 2,234 religious personnel), Christian churches (36 sites with 9 priests), Taoist monasteries (12 sites with 58 monks), and Tibetan Buddhist and Bön monasteries (666 sites with 24,478 monks). In addition, there were 3,650 monks who "travel from one monastery to another." The total number of Tibetan Buddhist and Bönpo monks in the province was thus 28,128. There were 497 tulkus in the province, 73 of whom had been recognized since 1978.

The Ethnic Affairs Commission provided the following breakdown of Tibetan Buddhist and Bön monasteries: 343 Gelugpa monasteries with 12,800 monks; 170 Nyingmapa monasteries with 5,885 monks; 105 Kagyupa monasteries with 3,643 monks; 28 Sakyapa monasteries with 975 monks; 9 Jonangpa monasteries with 872 monks; and 11 Bön monasteries with 303 monks. At the time of our interview, the Qinghai Province Ethnic Affairs Commission had not yet compiled statistics on nuns. However, according to Pu, there

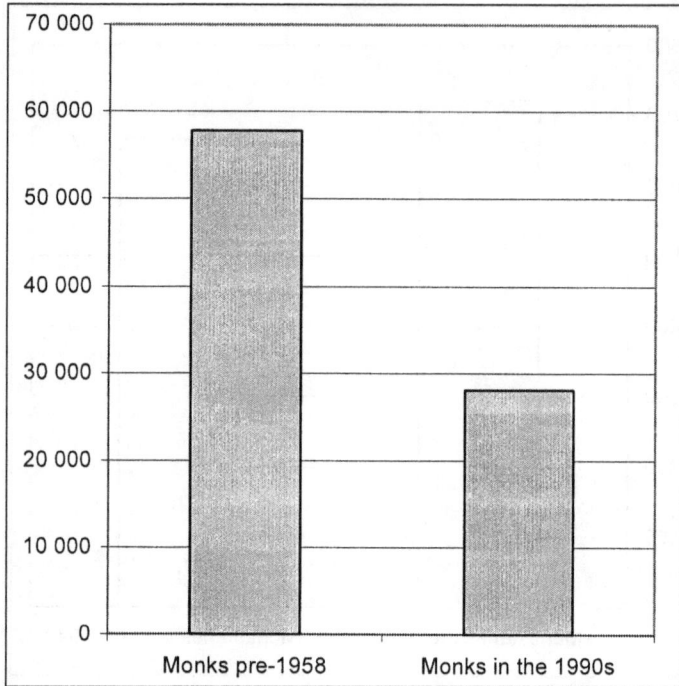

CHART A3.8. Monks in Qinghai

were 2,500 nuns in Qinghai before 1958, whereas by 1990 there were 18 nunneries and 700 nuns in the province (only 28 percent of the 1958 figure).

Our total figures for Qinghai cited in chapter 2 are drawn from Pu on
the pre-1958 situation and from the Qinghai Province Ethnic Affairs
Commission on conditions in the 1990s.

TABLE A3.8. Monasteries and Monks in Qinghai

Monasteries pre-1958	Monks pre-1958	Monasteries in the 1990s	Monks in the 1990s
722	57,647	666	28,128

Detailed information on each prefecture is presented in the sections below.
The following table, A3.9, contains a summary of the prefectures for comparison (Xining Municipality excluded).

TABLE A3.9. Monasteries and Monks in Qinghai, by Prefecture

Prefecture	Monasteries pre-1958	Monks pre-1958	Monasteries in the 1990s	Monks in the 1990s
Tsochang (Haibei)	24	1,575	26	669
Tsonub (Haixi)	20	1,150	16	318
Tsolho (Hainan)	118	7,306	130	5,643
Malho (Huangnan)	80	8,984	74	3,700
Golok (Guoluo)	63	10,669	61	7,279
Jyekundo (Yushu)	190	25,554	168	5,600
Haidong	218	5,800	151	2,364
TOTAL	713	61,038	626	25,573

TABLE A3.10. Monasteries and Monks in Tsochang (Haibei)
Tibetan Autonomous Prefecture

County	Monasteries pre-1958	Monks pre-1958	Tulkus pre-1958	Monasteries in the 1990s	Monks in the 1990s	Tulkus in the 1990s
Dashi (Haiyan)	2	220	10	2	30	3
Kangtsa (Gangcha)	11	680	10	9	170	0
Dola (Qilian)	6	430	28	4	60	0
Semnyi (Menyuan)	5	245	6	2	17	0
TOTAL	24	1,575	54	17 (26)	277 (669)	3 (10)

SOURCE, MONASTERIES AND MONKS PRE-1958 AND 1990S: Pu, *Ganqing Zangchuan fojiao siyuan*, 410–28.
Notes: Figures in parentheses are from an interview with the Tsochang Prefecture Religious Affairs Department, July 1999. According to the Kangtsa County Religious Affairs Department, this county alone had 13 Tibetan monasteries with 430 monks in 1999, considerably higher figures than those reported by Pu.

TABLE A3.11. Monasteries and Monks in Tsonub (Haixi)
Mongolian and Tibetan Autonomous Prefecture

County	Monasteries pre-1958	Monks pre-1958	Monasteries in the 1990s	Monks in the 1990s
Themchen (Tianjun)	7	400	1 (8)	134 (126)
Ulan	7	500+	4	104
Dulan	6	250	4	88
TOTAL	20	1,150+	9 (16)	326 (318)

SOURCE, PRE-1958 AND 1990 FIGURES: Pu, *Gan Qing Zangchuan fojiao siyuan*, 243–58.
NOTE, 1999 FIGURES: Figures in parentheses are from an interview with the Themchen County Religious Affairs Department, July 1999. Total figures including this information are also in parentheses.

TABLE A3.12. Monasteries and Monks in Tsolho (Hainan)
Tibetan Autonomous Prefecture

County	Monasteries pre-1958	Monks pre-1958	Monasteries by 1990	Monks by 1990	Monasteries in 1999	Monks in 1999
Chabcha (Gonghe)	16	1,066	19	540	24	828
Tsigorthang (Xinghai)	13	1,430	15	1,424	17	780
Mangra (Guinan)	18	972	15	407	15	651
Gepa Sumdo (Tongde)	14 (17)	1,690	15	556	16	1,162 (2,679
Thriga (Guide)	54	2,148	56	1,357	58	705
TOTAL	115 (118)	7,306	120	4,284	130	4,126 (5,643

SOURCE, PRE-1958 AND 1990 FIGURES: Pu, *Gan Qing Zangchuan fojiao siyuan*, 162–242.
SOURCE, 1999 FIGURES: Interview with the Tsochang Prefecture Religious Affairs Department, July 1999. *Notes* Figures provided by the Gepa Sumdo County Religious Affairs Department are in parentheses. Total figures including this information are also in parentheses. An alternative source, Marshall and Cooke, *Tibet Outside the TAR*, report that the prefecture had 113 Tibetan monasteries and 8,256 monks prior to 1958 and about 116 monasteries and 4,63 monks in 1995.

TABLE A3.13. Monasteries and Monks in Malho (Huangnan)
Tibetan Autonomous Prefecture

County	Monasteries pre-1958	Monks pre-1958	Monasteries by 1990	Monks by 1990	Monasteries in 1999	Monks in 1999
Rebkong (Tongren)	37	4,564	35	1,269	35 (36)	(1,819)
Chentsa (Jianza)	25	2,038	18	708	11 (25)	(882)
Tsekhok (Zeku)	14	1,400	13	317	9	
Yülgennyin (Henan)	4	982	4	254	4	
TOTAL	80	8,984	70	2,548	59 (74)	3,700

SOURCE, PRE-1958 AND 1990 FIGURES: Pu, *Gan Qing Zangchuan fojiao siyuan,* 429–95.
SOURCE, 1999 FIGURES: Interview with the Malho Prefecture Religious Affairs Department, Rebkong, July 1999.
Note: Figures provided by the county governments are in brackets as are total figures including this information.

TABLE A3.14. Monasteries and Monks in Golok (Guoluo)
Tibetan Autonomous Prefecture

County	Monasteries pre-1958	Monks pre-1958	Monasteries by 1994	Monks by 1994	Monasteries in 1999	Monks in 1999
Pema (Banma)	23	2500	22	1,358	23	1,443
Chikdril (Jiuzhi)	12		10	1,135	11	1,414
Darlak (Dari)	10	2,000	11	945	9	1,604 (1,659)
Gade (Gande)	8	2,093	6	565	8	1,836
Matö (Maduo)	4	277	4	166	4	233 (148)
Machen (Maqin)	6	1,568	5	565	6	779
TOTAL	63	10,669	58	4,734	61	7,308 (7,279)

SOURCES, PRE-1958 FIGURES: Pu, *Gan Qing Zangchuan fojiao siyuan,* 260–300, and Marshall and Cooke, *Tibet Outside the TAR.*
SOURCE, 1994 FIGURES: Xie, *Guoluo Zangzu shehui,* 155–57. *Note:* Number of monasteries by Buddhist order: Nyingmapa, 39; Jonangpa, 7; Gelugpa, 6; and Kagyupa, 1.
SOURCE, 1999 FIGURES: Interview with the prefecture government, July 1999. *Note:* Number of monasteries by Buddhist order: Nyingmapa, 46; Jonangpa, 8; Gelugpa, 6; and Kagyupa, 1. Information from county governments is in parentheses as are total figures including this information.
NOTES: An alternative source, *Dari Xian zhi,* 241–42, reports that in the 1950s Darlak had 5 monasteries and 8 tent monasteries with 1,840 monks, including 76 tulkus. Out of a population of 11,500 persons in 1956, about 13.7 percent were involved with religious work. In comparison, in 1985 the county had only 765 religious personnel.

TABLE A3.15. Monasteries and Monks in Jyekundo (Yushu)
Tibetan Autonomous Prefecture

County	Monasteries pre-1958	Monks pre-1958	Monasteries in 1999	Monks in 1999
Jyekundo (Yushu)	45	10,642	44	
Nangchen (Nangqian)	81	6,094	51	
Trindu (Chengduo)	27	4,625	22	
Dzatö (Zaduo)	24	2,388	42	
Dritö (Zhiduo)	1		3	
Chumarleb (Qumalai)	12	1655	6	
TOTAL	190	25,554	168 (169)	5,600

SOURCE, PRE-1958 FIGURES: Pu, *Gan Qing Zangchuan fojiao siyuan,* 301–409.

SOURCE, 1999 FIGURES: Interview with the prefecture government, July 1999. *Notes:* Information from the prefecture government is in parentheses. Prefecture officials reported the quota for monks was 3,616 but said that this figure was much lower than the actual figure. They expected the quota to be 5,600–6,000 within the year, which gives a strong indication that the actual number of monks in Jyekundo was at least 5,600.

NOTE: One alternative source, Pu, *Gan Qing Zangchuan fojiao siyuan,* 301–409, reports that Jyekundo had a total of 184 monasteries by 1990, with 5,383 monks, and a second, Marshall and Cooke, *Tibet Outside the TAR* (citing *Bright Mirror of Tibetan Buddhist Monasteries in Qinghai,* 14), reports that there were 195 monasteries in Jyekundo TAP prior to 1958 and 169 reopened monasteries by 1990 (2395).

TABLE A3.16. Monasteries and Monks in Haidong Prefecture

County	Monasteries pre-1958	Monks pre-1958	Monasteries by 1990	Monks by 1990
Huangyuan	6	341	4	42
Huangzhong	29	1,788	11	
Xunhua	33	1,507	27	530
Hualong	46		34	1,410
Huzhu	15	665		
Pingan	4	81	3	7
Ledu	31	428	17	54
Minhe	54	990	55	321
TOTAL	218	5,800	151	2,364

SOURCE: Pu, *Gan Qing Zangchuan fojiao siyuan,* 16–161.

APPENDIX 4

Data on Bilingual Education

Percent

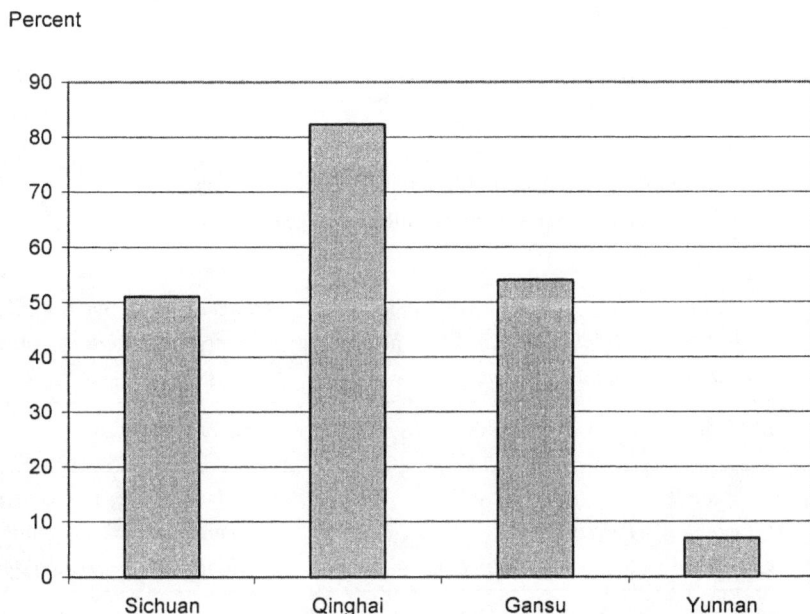

CHART A4.1. Tibetan Children Who Attend Bilingual School, by Province

NOTES: The figures above are for Tibetan Autonomous Prefectures only. Information is from interviews with prefecture education departments. Percentages of Tibetan schoolchildren out of total numbers of schoolchildren in each area are calculated on the basis of the 1990 national census figures. These may not be completely accurate, since it is possible that fewer Tibetan children go to school than, for example, Han children and that non-Tibetan schoolchildren, including Han children, sometimes attend bilingual (Tibetan) schools.

SICHUAN

TABLE A4.1. Data on Bilingual Education in Kandze (Ganzi)
Tibetan Autonomous Prefecture, 2000

Primary schools	Pupils in primary schools	Middle schools	Students in middle school	Bilingual primary schools	Pupils in bilingual primary schools	Bilingual middle schools	Students in bilingual middle schools
1,216	81,336	40	13,756	821	50,386	28	5,412

Schools	Bilingual schools	Percent bilingual	Students	Students in bilingual schools	Percent in bilingual	Percent Tibetans in population (1990 census)
1,256	849	68	95,092	55,798	59	76

TABLE A4.2. Data on Bilingual Education in Ngaba (Aba)
Tibetan and Qiang Autonomous Prefecture, 1999

Primary schools	Pupils in primary schools	Middle schools	Students in middle school	Bilingual primary schools	Pupils in bilingual primary schools	Bilingual middle schools	Students in bilingual middle schools
1,418	113,000	70	29,400	233	16,500	20	3,500

Schools	Bilingual schools	Percent bilingual	Students	Students in bilingual schools	Percent in bilingual	Percent Tibetans in population (1990 census)
1,488	253	17	142,400	20,000	14	48

NOTE: Figures for bilingual schools and students are approximate.

GANSU

TABLE A4.3. Data on Bilingual Education in Kanlho (Gannan)
Tibetan Autonomous Prefecture, 1999

County	Schools	Bilingual schools	Students	Students in bilingual schools	Percent in bilingual	Percent Tibetans in population (1990 census)
Chone (Zhuoni)	143	26	11,190	1,621		
Batse (Lintan)	145	3	20,760	121		
Machu (Maqu)	16	14	2,853	2,097		
Luchu (Luqu)	33	31	2,866	2,302		
Thewo (Diebu)	105	30	7,854	2,149		
Drukchu (Zhouqu)	163	30	16,209	1,939		
Sangchu (Xiahe)	102	87	19,154	10,553		
TOTAL	707	221	80,886	20,782	26	48

YUNNAN

TABLE A4.4. Data on Bilingual Education in Dechen (Diqing)
Tibetan Autonomous Prefecture, 1998

County	Schools	Bilingual schools	Students	Students in bilingual schools	Percent in bilingual	Percent Tibetans in population (1990 census)
Dechen (Deqin)	225	10		309		
Gyelthang (Zhongdian)	324	18		795		
Balung (Weixi)	435	2		36		
TOTAL	984	30	48,425	1,140	2.4	33

APPENDIX 4

QINGHAI

TABLE A4.5. Data on Bilingual Education in Tsochang (Haibei)
Tibetan Autonomous Prefecture, 1999

County	Schools	Bilingual schools	Students	Students in bilingual schools	Percent in bilingual	Percent Tibetans in population (1990 census)
Dashi (Haiyan)	34	5	3,221	723		
Kangtsa (Gangcha)	24	9	3,167	1,086		
Semnyi (Menyuan)	154	0	23,572	0		
Dola (Qilian)	45	12	5,502	766		
TOTAL	257	26	35,462	2,575	7.3	20

NOTES: The number of students reported for the prefecture as a whole was much lower than the total for the four counties combined. Bilingual schools include both Chinese-Tibetan and Chinese-Mongolian schools.

TABLE A4.6. Data on Bilingual Education in Tsonub (Haixi)
Mongolian and Tibetan Autonomous Prefecture, 1999

County	Schools	Bilingual schools	Students	Students in bilingual schools	Percent in bilingual	Percent Tibetans in population (1990 census)
Delingha		0				
Ulan		0				
Dulan		4				
Gormo (Ge'ermu)		1				
Mangya		0				
Dachaidam		0				
Themchen (Tianjun)		14				
TOTAL	209	19	52,671	2,966	5.6	9.9

NOTE: Information on bilingual schools applies only to Chinese-Tibetan schools and not to Chinese-Mongolian schools.

TABLE A4.7. Data on Bilingual Education in Tsolho (Hainan)
Tibetan Autonomous Prefecture, 1999

Schools	Bilingual schools	Percent bilingual	Students	Students in bilingual schools	Percent in bilingual	Percent Tibetans in population (1990 census)
446	283	63	54,704	28,802	53	59

TABLE A4.8. Data on Bilingual Education in Malho (Huangnan)
Tibetan Autonomous Prefecture, 1999

County	Schools	Bilingual schools	Students	Students in bilingual schools	Percent in bilingual	Percent Tibetans in population (1990 census)
Rebkong (Tongren)	94	61 (85)	11,277 (10,484)	6,213 (7,684)		
Chentsa (Jianza)	79	31 (66)	7,010	3,787		
Tsekhok (Zeku)	30	17	3,631	3,541		
Yülgennyin (Henan)	10	9	2,220	1,777		
TOTAL	213 (219)	118	24,138 (24,857)	15,318	62	64

NOTES: There are quite a few inconsistencies between the figures given to us in our interview with prefecture officials (in parentheses) and the written information we received after the prefecture officials had telephoned each county government for more detailed information. Also, the numbers provided by officials in two of the counties do not match those provided by the prefecture officials. Figures from interviews with county governments are in parentheses.

TABLE A4.9. Data on Bilingual Education in Golok (Guoluo)
Tibetan Autonomous Prefecture, 1999

Schools	Bilingual schools	Percent bilingual	Students	Students in bilingual schools	Percent in bilingual	Percent Tibetans in population (1990 census)
89	88	99	10,068	9,596	95	88

TABLE 4.10. Data on Bilingual Education in Jyekundo (Yushu)
Tibetan Autonomous Prefecture, 1999

Schools	Bilingual schools	Percent bilingual	Students	Students in bilingual schools	Percent in bilingual	Percent Tibetans in population (1990 census)
142	142	100	23,342	23,342	100	97

APPENDIX 5

Place-Names in Chinese and Tibetan

Chinese (pinyin)	Tibetan (phonetic)	Tibetan (Wylie)
	SICHUAN	
Aba Q and TAP	Ngaba	rnga ba
Aba	Ngaba	rnga ba
Heishui	Throchu	khro chu
Hongyuan	Kakhok	rka khog
Jinchuan	Chuchen	chu chen
Lixian	Tashiling	bkra shis gling
Ma'erkang	Barkham	'bar khams ('bar gams) ('ba' khams)*
Maowen	Maowün	ma'o wun
Nanping	Namphel	rnam 'phel
Rangtang	Dzamthang	'dzam thang (dzam thang)
Ruo'ergai	Dzoge	mdzod dge
Songpan	Sungchu	zung chu
Wenchuan	Lunggu	lung dgu
Xiaojin	Tsenlha	btsan lha (btsen lha)

Chinese (pinyin)	Tibetan (phonetic)	Tibetan (Wylie)
Ganzi TAP	Kandze	dkar mdzes
Baiyu	Pelyül	dpal yul
Batang	Bathang	'ba' thang
Danba	Rongdrak	rong brag
Daocheng	Dabpa	'dab pa
Daofu	Tawu	rta'u
Dege	Derge	sde dge
Derong	Derong	sde rong
Ganzi	Kandze	dkar mdzes
Jiulong	Gyesur	brgyad zur
Kangding	Dartsedo	dar rtse mdo
Litang	Lithang	li thang
Luding	Chaksam	lcags zam
Luhuo	Drango	brag 'go
Seda	Serthar	gser thar
Shiqu	Sershül	ser shul
Xiangcheng	Chathreng	cha phreng
Xinlong	Nyarong	nyag rong
Yajiang	Nyachukha	nyag chu kha
Muli TAC	Mili	
Muli	Mili	rmi li

GANSU

Gannan TAP	Kanlho	kan lho
Diebu	Thewo	the bo
Hezuo	Tsö	gtsos
Lintan	Batse	ba tse
Luqu	Luchu	klu chu

Chinese (pinyin)	Tibetan (phonetic)	Tibetan (Wylie)
Maqu	Machu	rma chu
Xiahe	Sangchu	bsang chu
Zhouqu	Drukchu	'brug chu
Zhuoni	Chone	co ne
Tianzhu TAC	Pari	
Tianzhu	Pari	dpa' ris (dba' ris)

QINGHAI

Guoluo TAP	Golok	mgo log
Banma	Pema	bad ma (ped ma)
Dari	Darlak	dar lag
Gande	Gade	dga' bde
Jiuzhi	Chikdril	gcig sgril
Maduo	Matö	rma stod
Maqin	Machen	rma chen
Haibei TAP	Tsochang	mtsho byang
Gangcha	Kangtsa	rkang tsha (rka tsha)
Haiyan	Dashi	mda' bzhi
Menyuan Hui Autonomous County	Semnyi	sems nyid
Qilian	Dola	mdo la
Hainan TAP	Tsolho	mtsho lho
Gonghe	Chabcha	chab cha
Guide	Thriga	khri ga
Guinan	Mangra	mang ra
Tongde	Gepa Sumdo	gad pa sum mdo
Xinghai	Tsigorthang	rtsi gor thang

Chinese (pinyin)	Tibetan (phonetic)	Tibetan (Wylie)
Haixi Mongolian and TAP Tsonub		mtsho nub
Dulan	Dulan	tu'u lan
Ge'ermu	Gormo	gor mo
Tianjun	Themchen	them chen
Ulan	Ulan	wu lan
Huangnan TAP	Malho	rma lho
Henan/Mongolian Autonomous County	Yülgennyin	yul rgan nyin
Jianza	Chentsa	gcan tsha
Tongren	Rebkong	reb gong
Zeku	Tsekhok	rtse khog
Yushu TAP	Jyekundo	skye rgu mdo
Chenduo	Trindu	khri 'du
Nangqian	Nangchen	nang chen
Qumalai	Chumarleb	chu dmar leb
Yushu	Jyekundo	skye rgu mdo
Zaduo	Dzatö	dza stod
Zhiduo	Dritö	'bri stod
	YUNNAN	
Diqing TAP	Dechen	bde chen
Deqin	Dechen	bde chen
Weixi	Balung	'ba' lung
Zhongdian	Gyelthang	rgyal thang

NOTE: TAP = Tibetan and Qiang Autonomous Prefecture
TAC = Tibetan Autonomous County

APPENDIX 6

Guide for Semi-Structured Interviews

1 / RELIGIOUS SITE

County?
Name of the site (a) in Tibetan and (b) in Chinese?
Number of monks?
Number of tulkus?
Number of teachers?
Which subjects are taught?
Which scriptures do they have?
Which rituals are performed and when?
When was the site (first) built?
Who built it and for what purpose was it built?
When was it destroyed?
When was it rebuilt?
Was it rebuilt in the same place or in a different place?
Who rebuilt it, and who paid for the rebuilding?
Where did the workers and artists come from?
Who paid them?
Who supplied or paid for materials?
Who uses the site now?
For what purposes?
On what occasions?

2 / RELIGIOUS AFFAIRS DEPARTMENT

Name of county or prefecture?
How many religious sites are there in your district?

How many Buddhist monasteries?

Name of the most important monasteries (a) in Chinese and (b) in
    Tibetan and which sect they belong to, how many monks they have,
    whether they are a main or branch monastery, what subjects are taught
    if any, and how many tulkus they have if any.

Names of holy mountains or mountain god temples in the area, and the
    number of pilgrims they receive each year.

3 / EDUCATION DEPARTMENT

County or prefecture?

How many primary schools in total?

How many primary school students?

Bilingual primary schools?

Bilingual primary school students?

Middle schools?

Middle school students?

Bilingual middle schools?

Bilingual middle school students?

Tertiary schools?

Tertiary school students?

Bilingual tertiary schools?

Bilingual tertiary school students?

Name the schools that have Tibetan on the curriculum.

(a) Primary? (b) Middle? (c) Tertiary?

Is Tibetan the language of instruction in other subjects in these schools?

What are the regular tuition fees?

Are there any government scholarships for students?

Where is teachers training available?

Percentage of children who enter primary school?

Middle school?

Percentage of children who complete primary school?

Middle school?

Teacher-to-student ratio in primary school?

Middle school?

4 / CULTURE DEPARTMENT OR LOCAL HISTORY UNIT

Cultural relics (sites) in the district?
Production of folk arts and crafts?
Cultural festivals or sports meets?
Song and dance troupes?
Any books published?
Any films made?
Any historical and cultural museums?

5 / SCHOOL

County?
Name of the school?
Number of students?
Number of teachers?
Ethnic groups of teachers?
When was the school started?
When was Tibetan language first taught in the school?
How many Tibetan-language teachers?
How many Tibetan students?
How many of the students study Tibetan?
In which grades do they study Tibetan?
How many hours per week of Tibetan (in the different grades)?
Other subjects?
How many hours per week of other subjects (in the different grades)?
What is the daily language of instruction in other subjects (excepting
    languages)?
Which exams must the students pass at the end of their education?
In which language?
Where are textbooks in Tibetan published?
Yearly tuition fee or other expenses per student?
Does the school receive funding from sources outside the local
    government?
Which sources?
What do these funds cover?

NOTES

INTRODUCTION

1. See, e.g., Goldstein and Kapstein, Buddhism in Contemporary Tibet.
2. Department of Information and International Relations, Destruction of Tibetan Culture.
3. Information Office of the State Council, Development of Tibetan Culture.
4. Department of Information and International Relations, Destruction of Tibetan Culture.
5. See Verdery, "Ethnicity, Nationalism, and State-Making," 33–58.
6. Geertz, Interpretation of Cultures, 10; Barth, "Enduring and Emerging Issues," 11–32; and Wagner, Invention of Culture.
7. See, e.g., Clifford, Predicament of Culture; Keesing, "Theories of Culture Revisited," 301–12; Wallerstein, Unthinking Social Science; Abu-Lughod, "Writing against Culture," 137–62; Ingold, "Art of Translation," 210–32; and Wagner, Invention of Culture.
8. Keesing, "Theories of Culture Revisited," 301–12.
9. Madsen, "Social Change."
10. Information Office of the State Council, Development of Tibetan Culture.
11. See, e.g., Korom, Constructing Tibetan Culture.
12. J. Norbu, "Dances with Yaks," 21.
13. Tibet Information Network, News Update, 15 August 1997.
14. Department of Information and International Relations, Destruction of Tibetan Culture.
15. Shakya, "Tibet and the Occident," 20–23.
16. During fieldwork, we also collected maps and place-name indexes as source material for a future systematic study of place-names. The material includes extensive lists of place-names in Chinese, Tibetan, and Roman characters and large-scale county maps. Since 1950, administrative divisions have been redrawn and existing

place-names changed on a massive scale in minority areas. This makes the study of Tibetan place-names especially challenging.

17. For a discussion of ethnology in China, see Harrell, "Anthropology and Ethnology," 3–6, and Lemoine, "Ethnologists in China," 83–112. See also Harrell, "History of the History of the Yi," 63–91, and "Nationalities Question," 274–96.

18. Particularly influential works have been Engels, The Origin of the Family, Private Property, and the State (1883), and Morgan, Ancient Society (1877).

19. Clarke, "Research Design," 217–40.

20. Figures that are almost but not completely the same may in fact be considered more accurate.

21. The exceptions are Tsonub (Haixi) and Ngaba (Aba) Prefectures.

22. In Sichuan, we paid a visit to office no. 3 of the Sichuan Province Religious Affairs Department, which is responsible for keeping records on Tibetan Buddhism in Sichuan.

23. Pu, Ganqing Zangchuan fojiao siyuan. Pu Wencheng is a researcher at the Qinghai Academy of Social Sciences, Department of Tibetology. During our visit to the Qinghai Academy of Social Sciences in Xining, July 1999, Pu was introduced as "Qinghai's most famous Tibetologist."

24. Ran, Zhongguo Zangchuan fojiao siyuan.

25. On Dechen, see Dolkar, Zongjiao zhi; on Golok, see Xie, Guoluo Zangzu shehui. Three sources give different information about the number of monasteries in Kandze: Kangding Minzu Shizhuan Bianxiezu, Dangdai Ganzi; Ganzi Zhou zhi; and Sichuan Sheng Minzu Shiwu Weiyuanhui, Zangchuan fojiao siyuan ziliao xuanbian.

26. Michael, Rule by Incarnation, 133.

27. The relationship between mother monasteries and branch (literally, "son") monasteries is referred to as (T) ma bu.

28. For a critique of Chinese demographics, see Banister, China's Changing Population; Dreyer, China's Forty Millions; and Clarke, "Research Design."

29. See, e.g., Gladney, "Question of Minority Identity," 50–54.

30. See, e.g., Gladney, "Representing Nationality in China," 92–123. Gladney notes that the idea of Han ren, or Han person, has existed for many centuries and identifies descendants of the Han dynasty. However, he contends that the notion of Han minzu or Han min (Han ethnic group) is an entirely modern phenomenon that arose with the shift from empire to nation and gained its greatest popularity under Sun Yat-sen's Republican revolution in 1911.

31. Chinese historians connect the Han dynasty with the beginning of trade along the Silk Route and the formation of the Chinese state. Important aspects of this state formation were the standardization of written language, weights, measures, and currency, the establishment of a banking system, and the creation of a system of official exams for recruiting civil servants.

1 / THE SETTING

1. Harrell, "Introduction," 3–36.

2. From a pamphlet published by the Assembly of Tibetan People's Deputies.

3. Information Office of the State Council, *Tibet.*

4. The two most important Tibetan sources on the geography of the Tibetan Plateau are *deb ther rgya mtsho* (Ocean annals), sometimes referred to as *Chronicle of the Spread of Buddhism in the Domed Region,* written by Lama Konchog Tsanpa Rabgye in 1865, and *dzam gling chen po'i rgyas bshad snod bcud kun gsal me long zhes bya ba* (The mirror that illuminates all inanimate and animate things and explains fully the great world), written by Lama Tsanpo in 1820.

5. On the use of the terms "political Tibet" and "ethnographic Tibet," see, for example, Richardson, *Tibet and Its History.*

6. The province of Qinghai was not established until 1928, by the Nationalist government.

7. Bushell, "Early History of Tibet," 466, citing the State Historiographer's Office official Chinese history of the Tang dynasty, Hanlin College of Literature.

8. W. Smith, *Tibetan Nation,* 75.

9. Ibid., 138.

10. Teichman, *Travels of a Consular Officer,* 2.

11. This is the representation of events given in Chinese histories. Tibetan histories may not agree.

12. Clarke, "Movement of Population," 225.

13. Ibid.

14. Ibid., 227.

15. Rock, *Amnye Ma-chen Range.*

16. W. Smith, *Tibetan Nation,* 141.

17. Goldstein, *Snow Lion and the Dragon,* 26–28, and W. Smith, *Tibetan Nation,* 168–81.

18. Lamb, *McMahon Line,* 275–76.

19. Located in present-day TAR.

20. W. Smith, *Tibetan Nation,* 226.

21. In addition to the convention itself, Britain and Tibet signed and ratified a note (the Anglo-Tibetan Declaration of 3 July 1914) stating that "so long as China withholds signature to the aforesaid convention she will be debarred from the enjoyment of all privileges accruing therefrom."

22. The main autonomous areas were identified during the 1950s, but many changes have been made, including renaming *minzu* designations and redrawing boundaries. Borders between several counties, prefectures, and even provinces are contested to this day.

23. Goldstein, *History of Modern Tibet,* 734.

24. Shakya, *Dragon in the Land of Snows*.

25. Goldstein, *History of Modern Tibet*, 717, citing FO371/84454, telegram dated 10 November 1950, from the Commonwealth Relations Office in London to the UK High Commissioner in India. The text reads as follows:

> (a) We consider that Tibetan autonomy is sufficiently well established for her to be regarded as a state within the meaning of the United Nations Charter.... Assuming that India takes this attitude we should be prepared to do so too, though the implications are far reaching. (b) If this view of Tibet's status is conceded and validity of her appeal is upheld in debate, it follows that Chinese action constitutes aggression against Tibet, and in the Security Council which would presumably follow two obvious possibilities would present themselves: (i) the Council might content itself with a condemnation of the Chinese action; (ii) it might call on China to withdraw her forces from Tibet and to restore the status quo. (c) We should hope that Security Council action would be restricted to (i) above. We should particularly wish to avoid action on lines of (ii) above, which would at best be likely to lead to a resolution which China would defy and which could only be enforced by armed action which neither we, nor we assume India or anyone else, e.g., the United States, would be prepared to take. In the result the United Nations would lose prestige.

26. The formal title of this agreement is "The Agreement of the Central People's Government and the Local Government of Tibet on Measures for the Peaceful Liberation of Tibet," signed 23 May 1951.

27. The full text of the agreement is reproduced in Union Research Institute, *Tibet: 1950–1967*, 19–23.

28. Anderson, *Imagined Communities*.

29. Mongolia is an exception, having signed the Treaty of Friendship and Alliance with Tibet at Urga, on 11 January 1913.

30. For instance, the Chinese government white paper *New Progress in Human Rights in the Tibet Autonomous Region* argues: "One of the fundamental commandments of Buddhism forbids the spreading of falsehoods. The Dalai Lama's wanton fabrication of lies and his violation and trampling of this commandment serve only to expose him in all his true colors: He is waving the banner of religion to conduct activities aimed at splitting the motherland." This view was reiterated by Legqoq, chairman of the TAR government in a response to statements made at a U.S. congressional hearing by Paula Dobriansky, the Tibet coordinator for the U.S. State Department. According to *China Daily* (11 March 2002), Legqoq maintained that "the Dalai did nothing to help Tibetans while he was in office and has never stopped his efforts to split the motherland since he fled Tibet in 1959." Legqoq reportedly claimed, "The Dalai has neither abandoned his separatist activities nor given up his pro-independence stance. Instead, he has exploited the negotiation issue to serve his own purposes."

31. Harrell, "Nationalities Question," 276. The term *Zhonghua minzu* was used by writers as diverse as Chiang Kai-shek in his *China's Destiny* (1947) and Communists who equated it with the Soviet Russian word *natsiya*.

32. Ibid., 276–77; the term *minzu* in this sense is equated with the Soviet Russian term *natsionalnost*.

33. On the Chinese civilizing project, see Harrell, "Introduction," 3–36.

34. See Lemoine, "Ethnologists in China," 83–112. Translations of Edvard Westermarck's *The History of Human Marriage* and Emile Durkheim's *Règles de la méthode sociologique* (Rules of sociological method) first appeared in Chinese as newspaper serials. Evolutionism was introduced to the youthful Chinese intelligentsia by Ts'ai Yuan P'ei, who studied philosophy, literature, and anthropology at the University of Leipzig during 1908–11. On a second stay in Europe during 1924–26, he represented China in Stockholm at the International Ethnology Congress on Pre-Columbian America and the Amerindians and studied ethnology at the University of Hamburg. After his return to China, he published an article titled "On Ethnology" in the review *Yiban zazhi,* in which the word "ethnology" was translated for the first time as *minzuxue.* Interestingly, the article stressed the value of reading Chinese historical documents from an ethnological point of view but denounced the "class-conscious" nature of Western ethnology, seen as a "colonialist's examination of subjugated peoples," 89.

35. For a discussion of how Morganian evolutionism resonates with Confucian moralism in viewing people at the "backward" end of the evolutionary scale as primitive and exotic, see McKhann, "The Naxi," 39–62.

36. Ibid., 39. Mao Zedong himself did two studies, one of peasant movements in Hunan (1927) and another titled "Glimpses of Hsing-Kuo" (1930), both inspired by Marxist sociology.

37. This process has been described in Harrell, "Nationalities Question," 274–96; Fei Xiaotong, *Towards a People's Anthropology;* Gladney, *Muslim Chinese;* and Heberer, *China and Its National Minorities,* 30–33. See also, on the Utsat, Pang, "Being Hui, Huan-nang, and Utsat," 190–91; on the Yi, Harrell, "History of the History of the Yi," 66; and on the Ge, Cheung, "Representation and Negotiation of Ge Identities," 240–44.

38. This massive research effort led to the publication of a large series of white papers (Ch: *baipishu;* literally, white-covered books).

39. Over the past fifteen to twenty years, a number of research institutes specializing in Tibetan studies have been established, and several universities and *minzu* institutes currently have Tibetan departments. Research institutes without students include branches of the Chinese Academy of Social Sciences in Tibet, Qinghai, Gansu, and Yunnan, and a national research institute for Tibetan Studies, the China Tibetology Research Centre, is located in Beijing and staffed primarily by Tibetan scholars.

40. Tibetology in China has been dominated by the study of classical Tibetan

texts, the history of Tibet before and after 1949, and Tibetan language and literature. There are two main periodicals on Tibet research: *Tibetan Studies,* published
by the Tibet Academy of Social Sciences in Lhasa, and *China Tibetology,* from Beijing.
Both are published in Chinese and Tibetan editions, while *China Tibetology* has an
English edition as well. There are also Chinese-language periodicals on "Tibetan
Buddhism" (*Xizang fojiao*), "Tibetan education" (*Xizang jiaoyu*), "Tibetan litera-
ture and arts" (*Xizang wenyi*), and "Tibetan culture" (*Xueyu wenhua*). Research on
Tibet conducted in the 1950s–70s was edited and compiled in the ten-volume
Chinese-language *Xizang shehui lishi diaocha ziliao congkan* (*Series of survey data
on Tibetan social history*). There is also a Chinese series about foreign scholars on
Tibet, which has so far published at least fifteen volumes. Most of the research is
Chinese language only.

41. See, for example, Gladney, "Question of Minority Identity," 50–54, com-
menting on the revival of Manchu identity.

42. Although identification work was discontinued with the onset of the Cultural
Revolution, many of these grievances reemerged when the work resumed in the late
1970s. A number of groups have since applied for recognition as separate *minzu*.
However, it seems unlikely at the present time that any new groups will be approved,
since only one additional *minzu* has been recognized, the Jinuo, in 1979.

43. See Wellens, "What's in a Name?" 17–34, and Harrell, "Nationalities Question,"
274–96.

44. Wellens, "What's in a Name?" citing Dai, *Zang-Mian yuzu yuyan yanjiu,*
422–33.

45. Zhongguo Shehui Kexueyuan, *Zhongguo shaoshu minzu yuyan,* 415–21.

46. Information Office of the State Council, *National Minorities Policy.*

47. Kangding Minzu Shifan Zhuanke Xuexiao Ketizu, *Sichuan Zangqu shuangyu
jiaoyu yu jiaoxue yanjiu,* 3.

48. Zhongguo Shehui Kexueyuan, *Zhongguo shaoshu minzu yuyan,* 282–83. It is
unclear how many actually use the script, since the same source reports that only 7
percent of Tu people "knew their own language" in the mid-1980s, 818. This would
amount to approximately 13,000 Tu in Qinghai.

49. Dwyer, "Texture of Tongues."

50. For example, in Tawu (Daofu) County, Kandze TAP, teachers told us that
local dialects differed to the extent that pupils and teachers could hardly communicate in Tibetan.

51. In Dartsedo (Kangding), four such dialects were described: Ergong, Yutong,
Minya, and Quyu.

52. See Upton, "Notes towards a Native Tibetan Ethnology," 3–26.

53. Muge Samten, "On the Question of the 'Dwags Po' Nationality," cited in
Upton, "Notes towards a Native Tibetan Ethnology," 3–26. Muli is now designated
a Tibetan Autonomous County within Liangshan Yi Autonomous Prefecture in
Sichuan Province.

54. Upton, "Notes towards a Native Tibetan Ethnology," 3–26.

55. D. Norbu, "'Otherness' and the Modern Tibetan Identity," 10.

56. Ekvall, *Religious Observances in Tibet*, 95, describes "religion system one" (T: *chos lugs gcig*) as the true and final criterion for a Tibetan in determining his real fellows. Corlin, *Nation in Your Mind*, 150–53, distinguishes between the concepts of *bod* as the area of the Tibetan way of life (the people of *bod* being the maximal endogamous category) and *chos* as the cultural instrument that provides the symbols of collective identification.

57. E.g., Harrell, "Introduction," 1–18, and Gladney, "Question of Minority Identity," 50–54.

58. However accurate these descriptions may be, it is important to remember that individuals still risk becoming victims of prejudice and discrimination after being classified as minorities.

59. See, e.g., Harrell, *Cultural Encounters*, and Brown, *Negotiating Ethnicities*.

60. Although a complete, direct registration census of the TAR was not undertaken until the year 1990, direct registration censuses of Tibetan areas outside the TAR were conducted in 1964 and 1980.

61. Harrell, "Introduction," 3–36.

2 / RELIGIOUS SITES AND THE PRACTICE OF RELIGION

1. Tibet Information Network, News Update, 15 August 1997.

2. Information Office of the State Council, *Development of Tibetan Culture*, 16–25.

3. Statement made by Samdhong Lobsang Tenzin, prime minister of the Tibetan government-in-exile, in his inauguration speech on 5 September 2001. Issued by the Department of Information and International Relations of the Tibetan government-in-exile.

4. According to W. Smith, *Tibetan Nation*, 339, the Red Army resorted to force to get supplies during the Long March in eastern Kham, capturing livestock and taking grain supplies from monasteries.

5. Goldstein, *History of Modern Tibet*, 683.

6. Ibid., 643–44, copied and translated from the original document in Tibetan.

7. For a description of the implementation of the Democratic Reforms campaign in Kham and Amdo, see W. Smith, "Nationalities Policy of the Chinese Communist Party," 51–75.

8. Pu, *Ganqing Zangchuan fojiao siyuan*, 4, 504.

9. J. Norbu, *Warriors of Tibet*, 132, 133.

10. Ibid., 134–35.

11. See, e.g., Pu, *Ganqing Zangchuan fojiao siyuan*, 4.

12. Ibid., 4, 504.

13. Choedon, *Life in the Red Flag People's Commune*, 64.

14. Lopez, "Monastery As a Medium," 61–64.

15. Pu, *Ganqing Zangchuan fojiao siyuan,* 4, 504.

16. Ibid., 4.

17. See, e.g., Makley, *Embodying the Sacred.*

18. Interview at the county religious affairs department, July 1999.

19. The government also expanded facilities for publishing books in Tibetan and increased the number of hours devoted to Tibetan-language radio broadcasts. It introduced a new policy, known as Four Basic Freedoms, which covered the freedom to practice religion, to trade, to lend money at interest, and to keep servants.

20. Minority Rights Group, *Tibetans,* 10.

21. Complete references for the figures are provided in appendix 3.

22. Whereas the figures for Yunnan, Gansu, and Sichuan are for Tibetan-designated areas only, the figures for Qinghai are for the entire province.

23. Due to the lack of reliable pre-1958 population figures, we did not compare the monastic population in proportion to the total population in the two periods.

24. Since the Council for Religious and Cultural Affairs lists monasteries and monks outside the TAR according to the traditional Tibetan regions of Amdo and Kham, it is difficult to make direct comparisons with lists that use the contemporary administrative divisions in Chinese sources.

25. Ruo'ergai Xian Renmin Zhengfu Zongjiao Shiwuju.

26. We were told that all reports on these details went to the "prefecture archives" (Ch: *dang'an guan*) in 1990 and therefore are no longer available at the department.

27. China Exploration and Research Society, *Buddhist Monasteries.* This publication describes the current condition of eighteen monasteries in Kandze TAP.

28. Ibid., 17. The original amount was ¥50,000 (US$6,345), and ¥210,000 (US$26,650) was later allocated to build a Buddhist college, which was moved to Kandze County. The monastery was allowed to keep the surplus.

29. Ibid., 38.

30. Ibid., 47.

31. The monks we interviewed about this emphasized that payment for services was estimated according to the family's income.

32. Interview, July 1999.

33. During the Sixth Month Festival in Thriga, we even saw Tibetans burning spirit money for the *yul lha,* evidently borrowing a custom that is usually considered Han.

34. The name of the mountain god in Tibetan is *gzhi bdag nag rdog.*

35. Guanyin is the Chinese name for the Bodhisattva of Compassion (Skt: Avalokitesvara; T: Chenrezig). This bodhisattva is very popular in China.

36. This information was provided by the keeper of the temple, who also explained that Saban was a teacher from Sakya Monastery in Tibet during the Yuan dynasty (1279–1368) and was known as the teacher of Kublai Khan. According to the legend, he was the first person to come to this site, bringing a bag of pearls from which he made the first image of the Buddha.

37. The dead body is destroyed, ritually served to the vultures, conveying the idea that the spirit moves on to a new incarnation and the body has no better use than to be shared with other living beings.

38. The only requirements are obtaining a tourist visa and making arrangements through a local tourist agency.

39. Some sources transcribe the term as *glu rol*, with *glu* translated as "music."

40. For a detailed description of the Lurol Festival in Rebkong, see Epstein and Peng, "Ritual, Ethnicity, and Generational Identity," 120–38.

41. Interestingly, the local Tibetan who made this comment explained the Tibetan *klu* (spirits of the underworld who often inhabit springs and waters) by referring to the Chinese *long* (dragon).

42. Zhongguo Shehui Kexueyuan, *Zhongguo shaoshu minzu yuyan*, 284.

43. "Tibetan Buddhist Scriptures Said Well Preserved," Xinhua News Agency, 29 August 1996, transcribed by FBIS.

44. We were told that the printing academy had the Kangyur, consisting of 36,000 woodblocks, and the Tengyur, consisting of 67,000 woodblocks. The price of producing a new woodblock was said to be ¥120 (US$14.50). A recent publication about Derge Sutra Printing Academy is J. Yang, *Dege Yinjingyuan*. The book is richly illustrated with high-quality color photos and is published as a trilingual edition in Tibetan, Chinese, and English.

45. Though the complete Kangyur and Tengyur appeared to be available in most Gelugpa monasteries, the situation may be different in monasteries of other traditions. For instance, in a Drigung Kagyupa monastery in Dechen TAP, we were told that the monks used texts specific to the Drigung Kagyupa tradition for recitation but did not have the Tengyur and had only parts of the Kangyur in their monastery.

46. Derge dialect was also said to be the standard Tibetan dialect taught in primary and middle schools in Kandze TAP.

47. He was educated at the Religious Art Department of Malho Art Institute (Ch: Huangnan Yishu Xuexiao, Zongjiao Yishuxi) in Rebkong. His training lasted five years, and he was eighteen years old when he began his studies.

48. Lopez, " Monastery As a Medium," 61–64. See also Goldstein, *History of Modern Tibet*, 21.

49. (T) *dpe cha ba*. On the definition of this term, see Goldstein, " Revival of Monastic Life," 21.

50. Lopez, "The Monastery As a Medium," 61–64.

51. Goldstein, *History of Modern Tibet*, 24.

52. International Campaign for Tibet, *Forbidden Freedoms*, 45.

53. (T) *dga' ldan srong btsan gling*.

54. According to Pu, *Ganqing Zangchuan fojiao siyuan*, it had more than 1,500 monks and 30 tulkus before 1958.

55. According to our sources, 6 of the tulkus were recognized after 1991, when new tulkus were again recognized after the Cultural Revolution.

56. (T) *thos bsam rnam par rgyal ba'i gling.*

57. (T) *gsang sngags dar rgyas gling.*

58. (T) *ae lba chos 'khor gling.*

59. Nakane, *Labrang.*

60. Li An-che noted that there were 150 monks in the Lower College of Theology (T: *rgyud smad pa grwa tshan*), while our sources stated that there were now about 100 monks. According to Li An-che, there were another 100 monks in the College of Medicine (T: *sman pa grwa tshan*), against 100–200 monks at present. Li An-che gave a figure of 120 monks in the College of the Happy Thunderbolt (T: *kye rdorje grwa tshan*), while the current figure was said to be approximately 100. Li An-che finally noted that there were 100 monks in the College of the Wheel of Time (T: *dus hkhor grwa tshan*) but provided no information on the Upper College of Theology (T: *rgyud stod pa grwa tshan*). Our sources stated that the latter had about 100 monks but did not specify figures for the former.

61. The five subjects on the curriculum were *tsad mar nam'grel, par pyin, dbu ma, mdzod,* and *'dul ba.*

62. Xie, *Guoluo Zangzu Shehui,* 155–57.

63. This includes two monasteries in the United States (Atlanta and New York) and two in Taiwan.

64. Previously, self-study was not practiced in Tibetan monasteries.

65. In addition, new institutions without sectarian affiliations have been set up to teach Buddhism, such as the Institute of Buddhist Dialectics, the Norbulingka Institute, and the Central Institute for Higher Tibetan Studies in Sarnath.

66. Ström, "Between Tibet and the West." See also Ström, *Continuity, Adaptation, and Innovation,* 269–70, 370, on the situation in Sera Monastery, Karnataka, and Sakya College, Dehra Dun.

67. Ström, *Continuity, Adaptation, and Innovation,* 270, 370, 373 (citing interviews with monks at Sera Monastery, Karnataka, and Sakya College, Dehra Dun).

68. Ibid., 373 (citing interviews with monks at Sakya College, Dehra Dun).

69. International Campaign for Tibet, *Forbidden Freedoms,* 44.

70. Ström, *Continuity, Adaptation, and Innovation,* 341–42 (citing interviews at Namdrölling Monastery).

71. Six of these tulkus were appointed to the county People's Congress, two to the prefecture People's Congress, one to the province People's Congress, seven to the county Political Consultative Committee, and one to the prefecture Political Consultative Committee.

72. International Campaign for Tibet, *A Season to Purge,* 52, citing *Xizang Ribao Lhasa* (in Chinese), 1 November 1995.

73. *Daily Telegraph,* 12 November 1999, Panchen Lama "unharmed."

74. *Aba Zhou nianjian 1991–1996,* 359. This source refers to regulations no. 6 and no. 39 of 1991 issued by the State Council.

75. Ibid.

76. Pu, *Ganqing Zangchuan fojiao siyuan,* 4.

77. (T) *krung go bod brgyud mtho rim nang bstan slob gling.*

78. Tulkus who have not received government approval.

79. The document is reprinted in MacInnis, *Religion in China Today,* 8–26.

80. Only Chinese place-names were provided.

81. See Karmay, "Mountain Cults and National Identity," 112–20, and D. Norbu, "'Otherness' and the Modern Tibetan Identity," 10–11.

82. See Barnett, "Symbols and Protest," 238–58; Havnevik, "Role of Nuns," 259–66; and Schwartz, *Circle of Protest* and "Anti-Splittist Campaign," 207–37.

83. Schwartz, "Anti-Splittist Campaign," 207–37, and Human Rights Watch / Tibet Information Network, *Cutting Off the Serpent's Head.*

84. For information about the campaign's implementation in Drepung Monastery near Lhasa, see Goldstein, "Revival of Monastic Life," 15–52. In addition, Tibet Information Network published *A Sea of Bitterness,* a report on the implementation of the campaign in Qinghai, based on interviews with Tibetan refugees in India.

85. As reported by Dr. Charlene Makley, who conducted fieldwork in Labrang during 1995–96, in an open letter to the editors of World Tibet Network News (5 March 2000) after the death of Gungthang Rinpoche on 29 February 2000.

86. See the testimony of Agya Rinpoche at the hearing on religious freedom in China, organized by the Commission on International Religious Freedom and held in Los Angeles on 16 March 2000. Reprinted at http://www.tibet.ca/wtnarchive/2000/3/17.

87. This was formerly one of the main Sakyapa monasteries in the Kham area. Sichuan Sheng Minzu Shiwu Weiyuanhui, *Zangchuan fojiao siyuan ziliao xuanbian,* 51.

88. The Chinese term *fengshui* relates to geomancy, or the idea that spiritual forces in the ground may influence a building in a positive or a negative way. In Tibetan, this is called *sa dpyad.* It traditionally has been important to identify the negative or positive forces in the ground before a new house is built, in order to avoid future problems.

89. Ruo'ergai Xian Renmin Zhengfu Zongjiao Shiwuju, *Ruo'ergai Xian zongjiao gongzuo gaikuan.*

90. In large monasteries, this team should have eleven members, medium-size monasteries have a team of seven members, and teams for small monasteries have three to five members.

91. We were informed in several cases that nuns who adhered to the Nyingmapa tradition practiced as nuns but lived at home.

92. Figures for the Serthar Buddhist Institute are based on information from a Drango County Religious Affairs Department investigative mission that returned from Serthar in March 2000. Investigators concluded that 155 monks and as many as 700 nuns came from neighboring Drango County. According to Germano, "Remembering the Dismembered Body of Tibet," 68, the site had 30–40 Chinese monks and nuns in 1991.

93. International Campaign for Tibet, News Report, 20 June 2001, "Thousands of Tibetan Monks and Nuns Ordered to Leave Remote Encampment."

94. In many areas, county religious affairs were controlled by the United Front department of the CCP. In the changing political climate after 1978, however, most counties established a separate government department for implementing the new religious policies, although local branches of the United Front occasionally still handle religious affairs at the county level.

95. See, e.g., Thar, "*Bla Ma,*" 417–27.

96. See also Goldstein, "Revival of Monastic Life," 15–52.

97. This campaign was reportedly carried out pursuant to State Religious Affairs Department directive no. 62 (1994). In Yunnan, it was based on Yunnan Province Government directive no. 39 (1994) and no. 92 (1996).

98. From the testimony of Agya Rinpoche at the hearing on religious freedom in China, organized by the Commission on International Religious Freedom and held in Los Angeles on 16 March 2000. Reprinted at http://www.tibet.ca/wtnarchive/2000/3/17.

3 / THE DILEMMAS OF EDUCATION IN TIBETAN AREAS

1. Upton, "Cascades of Change."

2. See, e.g., Hansen, *Lessons in Being Chinese,* 159.

3. "Education on the Move," *South China Morning Post,* 21 March 2001.

4. "Racial Discrimination," issued by the Tibetan Centre for Human Rights and Development, 2000, at http://www.tchrd.org/pubs/racial.

5. Hansen, *Lessons in Being Chinese,* 159.

6. Ibid., 169.

7. "Problems Related to Bilingual Education in Tibet," unpublished paper.

8. Upton, "Cascades of Change."

9. *Qinghai Sheng zhi; Jiaoyu zhi.*

10. In the 1940s, three clans—the Kangsai, Kanggan, and Gongmugang (Chinese transcriptions)—each established a primary school, where both Tibetan and Chinese were taught. Zhongguo Shehui Kexueyuan, *Zhongguo shaoshu minzu yuyan,* 309.

11. Kangding Minzu Shifan Zhuanke Xuexiao Ketizu, *Sichuan Zangqu shuangyu jiaoyu yu jiaoxue yanjiu.*

12. The Central Nationalities Institute is now known as Central Nationalities University.

13. Although local government departments in autonomous areas thus have the right to develop their own educational programs and decide on the language of instruction for local schools, it is important to recognize that minority students do not have the explicit right to be educated in their native language.

14. For more information on educational policies and teaching in Tibetan within the TAR, see Bass, *Education in Tibet*.

15. Tibet Information Network (TIN), News Update, "Policy Shift in Teaching Tibetan," issued 6 May 1997. According to TIN, the policy shift was announced on 17 April 1997 by Deputy Secretary Tenzin, during a meeting with the U.S. ambassador to China James Sasser.

16. We did not receive information about this system from the Tibetan areas we visited in Qinghai Province.

17. Third-grade level equals three years of study.

18. *Ruo'ergai Xian zhi*, 642.

19. This type of education is referred to as "first category" (Ch: *yi lei*).

20. This type of education is referred to as "second category" (Ch: *er lei*). In 1985, in addition to the first and second categories, a third type of bilingual education was invented and the names of the two first types were switched. Since then, "first category" has referred to bilingual schools that use Chinese as the medium of instruction and teach Tibetan beginning in the third grade; after six years of primary school, the Tibetan level of graduates would be at the fourth-grade level. "Second category" refers to instruction in Tibetan with Chinese taught beginning in the third grade; upon graduation, these students' Tibetan level is equivalent to that of primary school graduates, and their Chinese level would be at the fourth-grade level. In the third category of education, all subjects are taught either in Chinese or in Tibetan after completion of the third grade.

21. Interview with Kakhok County officials, April 1999.

22. Interview with school staff, April 1999.

23. At the time of our visit, the school's Tibetan-language department had two classes: one taught in Chinese and the other in Tibetan. The mathematics department also had a class taught in Tibetan. In all other departments, Chinese was the language of instruction. According to the headmaster, as of 1999, about 40–50 percent of the students in this college were Tibetans.

24. Interview at Southwest Nationalities Institute, April 1999.

25. Until the first term of 2000, sixty new students were allowed per year. Regulations introduced in the second term of 2000 reduced the annual number of new students to fifty. The reasons for the reduction were said to be the small number of applicants who passed the entrance exam and the difficulties experienced by graduates in finding jobs after the job assignment system ended. Of the students, 10–15 percent received grants of ¥800, ¥600, or ¥400 (US$100, US$75, or US$50). The annual tuition fee was ¥2,000–2,400 (US$250–$300), boarding included.

26. The Ganzi Tibetan School was first established in Derge County in 1984, moved to Tawu County in 1986, and then to Dartsedo County in 1994, where it is now located, near the prefecture seat.

27. The Rokpa Foundation sponsors one class, the 1997 class, for four years.

28. The full name is (Ch) Kangding Minzu Shizhuan Gaodeng Zhuanke Xuexiao.

29. Interview with independent sources.

30. *The Oregonian*, 10 May 2001, "Leaving Tibet: A Long Trek to Freedom," citing information from the International Committee of Lawyers for Tibet.

31. *Ganzi Zhou zhi*, 1644.

32. *Xibu da kaifa, Daofu jiaoyu zenmaban? Zhuazhu jiyu, cujin fazhan, peiyang gao suzhi rencai* (The policy to develop the western region. What will happen to Tawu? Seize the opportunity, promote development, and foster high-quality talents), unsigned article distributed by the Tawu County Education Department, May 2000.

33. This statement does not conform to official statistics claiming a 64.1 percent enrollment rate in the county.

34. In Kandze, we also found evidence of a three-price system by which the children of farmers and herders are exempt from paying tuition fees in primary school, but cadre children must pay ¥60–80 (US$7–10) per year, and the children of migrant laborers (presumably those without residency registration) must pay a fee of ¥460 (US$58) per year. In addition, miscellaneous fees were twice as high for the children of cadres as for the children of farmers and herders, whereas migrant children had to pay six times as much. Total annual school expenses for one migrant child in primary school amounted to ¥760 (US$95). This represents at least half an average annual income in the area and would in practice bar most children without resident status from attending school.

35. *Aba Zhou nianjian 1991–1996*. The source fails to note whether this is per capita income.

36. The entrance rate for primary school in 1992 was reported to be 59.3 percent, with 81,876 pupils in school that year. *Ganzi Zhou zhi*, 1644.

37. Zhongguo Shehui Kexueyuan, *Zhongguo shaoshu minzu yuyan*, 284. According to this source, only 27 percent of school-age Tibetan children in Qinghai were literate in 1982.

38. *Gansu tongji nianjian 1998*, 416.

39. Extrapolating from these figures, about half of all school-age children in Dechen TAP do not attend school. Out of thirty-three children, thirty enter primary school, seventeen of these complete primary school, thirteen go on to junior middle school, and seven complete junior middle school. Only about 20 percent complete nine years of education.

40. *Gansu tongji nianjian 1998*, 416.

41. One way of making it easier for parents to afford the expenses was to let them pay in kind (in meat, flour, or butter) rather than in cash.

42. Paid according to the number of "livestock" (Ch: *shengxu*).

43. According to the unpublished paper "Problems related to bilingual education in Tibet" (1999).

44. *Ganzi Zhou zhi*, 1659. The number of students entering middle school that year was 5,628, of which 2,822 were *minzu* students.

45. Tsolho Prefecture Tibetan Translation Language and Writing Working Committee (Ch: Hainan Zhou Zangyu Wengongzuo Weiyuanhui), "The Tsolho TAP Tibetan Language Working Committee's Request for Assistance to Establish a Project for Promoting the Elimination of Tibetan Illiteracy," dated 25 February 1997.

46. T. Zhang, *Population Development in Tibet,* 105.

47. Special funds for minority education are the Ethnic Minorities Education Aid Special Fund (Ch: Shaoshu Minzu Jiaoyu Buzhu Zhuankuan) and the Border Areas Construction Aid Fund (Ch: Bianjing Diqu Jianshe Buzhu Fei). Project Hope (Ch: Xiwang Gongcheng) is a major Chinese NGO source.

48. Wang, *Minzu pinkun diqu, xianzhang lun jiaoyu.* This book is a compilation of articles written by fifty-two county leaders from minority areas in the poor provinces in China's western region. Several county leaders give detailed accounts about the underdevelopment of educational facilities in their areas.

49. *Xibu da kaifa, Daofu jiaoyu zenmaban? Zhuazhu jiyu, cujin fazhan, peiyang gao suzhi rencai* (The policy to develop the western region. What will happen to Tawu? Seize the opportunity, promote development, and foster high-quality talents), unsigned article distributed by the Tawu County Education Department, May 2000.

50. Special schools for Tibetan children were established in Beijing and other cities in eastern China as early as the 1950s, and critics have asserted that these schools are a drain on TAR education budgets. Some also criticize these schools for contributing to the sinicization of Tibetan students.

51. One of these, a county-level *minzu* primary school, received ¥60 (US$7.50) per month for each student learning Tibetan. According to the staff, the school had two Tibetan-language teachers, and Tibetan was taught from the fourth to the sixth grade only. In the fourth grade, Tibetan was taught four hours per week, and in the fifth and sixth grades, Tibetan was taught only two hours per week. This school has taught Tibetan language since 1986.

52. The language of instruction was Chinese, but according to teachers at the school, Tibetan was taught seven hours per week, Chinese was taught six hours per week, and English was taught five hours per week.

53. Of the total, 314 students were Tibetan and 3 were Han. All were classified as cadre children, with 85 percent coming from herding or farming areas and 15 percent from towns.

54. Language classes at this school included seven hours of Tibetan, seven hours of Chinese, and five hours of English per week.

55. This is a rare example of a bilingual middle school with English in the curriculum. Information from Ma'erkang Minzu Teachers Training School suggests that this was the only bilingual middle school that taught English in the prefecture.

56. For an introduction to the school, see Dai and Zhalo, "Lama Jigmei Gyaincain," 24–25.

57. The English textbook used was a Qinghai publication, "Elementary English—Tibetan."

58. (Ch) Wusheng Zizhiqu Zangwen Jiaocai Xiezuo Lingdao Xiaozu; (T) *zhing chen dang rang skyong ljongs lnga'i bod yig slob gzhi mnyam sgrig byed rgyu'i gros 'cham.*

59. For a detailed description of the compilation and editing of Tibetan-language textbooks, see Upton, *Schooling Shar-Khog.*

60. For instance, we were informed that the Tibetan-language textbooks used in teachers training schools in Ngaba Prefecture were edited by the Ma'erkang Minzu Teachers Training School in cooperation with the Southwest Minzu Institute in Chengdu (responsible for textbooks on politics) and two other teachers training schools in Kandze TAP.

61. Upton, "Beyond the Contents of a Curriculum." In terms of pages, 37 percent are translations from Chinese texts, 46 percent are modern Tibetan, and 16 percent are traditional Tibetan.

62. Ibid.

63. Tibetans live not only in the areas defined as Tibetan autonomous prefectures and counties but also in a number of village districts in neighboring counties. At least eight Tibetan autonomous village districts are located in counties outside Kandze TAP, Ngaba Prefecture, and Mili Tibetan Autonomous County (TAC). Liangshan Yi Autonomous Prefecture has, in addition to Mili TAC, two such Tibetan districts located in two other counties. He'ai Tibetan District is located in Mianning County, and Bao'an Tibetan District in Yuexi County. (Huang and Zhong, *Sichuan Sheng shiyong dituce,* 128, 129, shows the location of the villages.) According to *Sichuan tongji nianjian 1999,* 38, Mianning County has a total population of 304,000, and Yuexi has 231,000. Another five Tibetan autonomous village districts are located in Shimian County, bordering Gyesur (Jiulong) and Chaksam (Luding) Counties in Kandze TAP: Caoke Tibetan District, Wajiao Yi and Tibetan District, Xinmin Tibetan and Yi District, Xianfeng Tibetan District, and Xieluo Tibetan District. Gyesur County in Kandze TAP has at least seven Yi autonomous village districts, and Baoxing County has one Tibetan autonomous village district, Qiaoqi. (Huang and Zhong, *Sichuan Sheng shiyong dituce,* 105.)

64. Interview, prefecture government officials, April 1999.

65. County officials in Lixian confirmed the figure of six middle schools that used Tibetan as the language of instruction, with Kakhok (Hongyuan), Dzoge (Ruo'ergai), Ngaba (Aba), Sungchu (Songpan), Dzamthang (Rangtang), and Barkham (Ma'erkang) each having one school. However, they mentioned only fourteen middle schools that taught Tibetan as a subject, and these were distributed as follows: Kakhok (Hongyuan), two; Dzoge (Ruo'ergai), three; Ngaba (Aba), two; Sungchu (Songpan), three; Dzamthang (Rangtang), two; Barkham (Ma'erkang), one; and Chuchen (Jinchuan), one.

66. With an average of less than 60 students per school, these are probably point schools in herding areas.

67. Apart from teachers training schools, the prefecture also had a health school (1,133 students), an agricultural school (640 students), a school of economics (620

students), and a technical school (343 students), all administered by the education department. At the time of our visit, two county *minzu* teachers training schools were being closed down and were to become senior middle schools in autumn 2000, which means that teachers training will be available only at the Kangding Minzu Teachers Training School. Other senior middle schools at the county level were also being closed, and senior middle school education was to be concentrated in the two former teachers training schools (in Bathang and Kandze), strategically located along the two highways. These would then become key senior middle schools in the prefecture.

68. Interview with the prefecture education department, May 2000. We were told that the prefecture still did not accept foreign English teachers, and especially not American teachers.

69. In Ngaba, Tibetans constituted only 48 percent of the population as registered in the 1990 national census. In Kandze, the corresponding figure was 76 percent.

70. About 75 percent of the Tibetan population of Gansu live in Kanlho, 15 percent live in Pari, and about 10 percent live outside Tibetan autonomous areas.

71. There were 11,025 students in junior middle schools, and 2,049 students in senior middle schools.

72. According to Zhongguo Shehui Kexueyuan, *Zhongguo shaoshu minzu yuyan*, 247, there were twelve *minzu* middle schools: four junior middle schools (50 percent of all junior middle schools) and eight senior middle schools (40 percent of all senior middle schools).

73. The four schools were the Tibetan Middle-Level Vocational School (bilingual), the medical school, the pastoral school, and the teachers training school. The total number of students in these schools was 1,278 in 1998–99.

74. Complete statistics on education from the prefecture government for each county in Kanlho can be found in appendix 4.

75. C. Yang, "Qiandan Zang yuwen jiaoxue zai fazhan minzu jiaoyuzhong de zhongyaoxing."

76. According to the 1990 national census, 83.9 percent of the registered population of Dechen TAP were minorities and only 16.1 percent were Han. Tibetans composed 33 percent of the population.

77. According to the Dechen Prefecture Education Department, Gyelthang County had bilingual (Tibetan-Chinese) primary schools in five village districts: Dongwang (T: *gtor ba rong*), Gezan (T: *skhad tshag*), Nixi (T: *nyi shar*), Wujing, and Xiao Zhongdian. Weixi Lisu Autonomous County had bilingual (Tibetan-Chinese) primary schools in two village districts: Badi (T: *'aba' sde*) and Tacheng (T: *mtha' chu*). Dechen County had bilingual primary schools in four districts: Yunling, Yangla (T: *gyag rwa chus*), Fushan, and Shenping. However, according to the Dechen County Education Department, apart from the Shengping Township district, there were bilingual Tibetan-Chinese schools in three village districts: Benzilan (T: *spam rtse rags*), Yemen, and Yunling.

78. The former had 320 students, and the latter had a Tibetan medicine class with 40 students.

79. According to the Dechen Prefecture Education Department, in 1997 the prefecture had 957 primary schools (362 of them with more than 1 teacher), with a total of 38,257 pupils and 2,337 teachers. There were 25 middle schools in the prefecture, 5 were six-year schools (including both junior and senior middle school) and 20 were three-year schools (junior middle school only). The total number of pupils in middle school was 9,312. In addition, the prefecture had 3 vocational middle schools, with 856 pupils and 74 teachers. These were the Minzu Teachers Training School, the medical school and the Minzu Middle School. Dechen County had 220 primary schools and 5 middle schools, Weixi County had 423 primary schools and 12 middle schools, and Gyelthang County had 314 primary schools and 10 middle schools.

80. According to the 1990 census, Tibetans constituted 20 percent of the registered population of Qinghai.

81. Despite an increase in the population during the years 1990–98, there have probably been only minor changes in the relative sizes of the different ethnic groups as registered in official population statistics.

82. This was the situation in areas such as Semnyi, in Tsochang, and Terlenkha (Delingha), Ulan, Dachaidam, and Mangya, in Tsonub.

83. Interview with the prefecture education department, July 1999.

84. The Tsochang medical school students go to Malho to study Tibetan medicine, and the Malho students go to Tsochang to study Western and Chinese medicine.

85. According to the education department, the prefecture had 232 primary schools, with 27,016 pupils; of these, 82 were *minzu* primary schools, with 11,124 students. There were 28 middle and vocational schools, with 9,440 students; of these, 7 were *minzu* middle and vocational schools, with 1,877 students.

86. These were Gangcha County Minzu Middle School (with instruction in Tibetan), Haiyan County Minzu Middle School (instruction in Chinese), and Qilian County Minzu Middle School (instruction in Chinese). Haiyan County Minzu Middle School also had a Mongolian class.

87. Zhongguo Shehui Kexueyuan, *Zhongguo shaoshu minzu yuyan*, 301–5, gives a different account, stating that 189 primary schools (86.3 percent of the total) and 15 middle schools teach Tibetan. The report claims that Tibetan is used in primary schools in the pastoral regions of the prefecture as well as in *minzu* primary and middle schools. This information accords with the initial statements of prefecture officials but not with the later figures provided by the prefecture government. The report also gives figures for *minzu* schools in the prefecture that are higher than those provided by the prefecture government: 126 as compared to 82 *minzu* primary schools and 12 as compared to 7 *minzu* middle and vocational schools.

88. Ibid., 311–14, provides the following information for 1987: Tsonub had a total of 235 schools, including 169 primary schools, 62 ordinary middle schools, 2 vocational middle schools, and 2 professional schools. Among these, there were 2 Mon-

golian middle schools, 1 Tibetan middle school, and 2 combined Mongolian and Tibetan middle schools. There were 20 Mongolian primary schools and 20 Tibetan primary schools. This is fairly consistent with the information gathered in 1999.

89. The numbers of *minzu* primary and middle schools in each county or district are listed in appendix 4.

90. This accords with information provided in ibid., 311–14.

91. The breakdown is 411 primary schools, 32 middle schools, 2 vocational schools, and 1 college.

92. Both past and current prefecture leaders are Tibetans.

93. Most of these schools were *minzu* schools, of which 1 or 2 were Chinese-Mongolian and the rest were Chinese-Tibetan. The vocational schools were a teachers training school and a medical school.

94. There were 20,096 in primary schools, 4,761 in middle schools, and 726 in vocational schools.

95. The 13 middle schools comprised 11 junior middle schools and 2 complete middle schools that included the senior level (six years). Of the 1,238 students in junior middle school, 834 were Tibetan (67 percent), and of 102 students in senior middle school, only 34 were Tibetan (33 percent). In comparison, the registered Tibetan population in Golok comprised 88 percent of the total.

96. In addition, Jyekundo, like most other TAPs, also had a Tibetan medical school. The prefecture government did not give information about this school, nor were the numbers of students and teachers included in the statistics.

97. According to Zhongguo Shehui Kexueyuan, *Zhongguo shaoshu minzu yuyan*, 290, during the mid-1980s all *minzu* schools in Jyekundo TAP taught in Tibetan language during the first three years of primary school, and Chinese was used beginning in the fourth grade.

98. In several of the schools we visited in Kandze TAP, it was common practice to display detailed information about the staff on a poster on the wall. The information included a portrait photo and gave the age, educational background, ethnic affiliation, and Party membership status of every teacher. In one school, we noticed that of forty-six teachers (twenty-one of whom were Tibetan), nineteen were members of the Chinese Communist Youth League and seven were members of the Communist Party.

99. The staff of this school informed us that during the previous year, the ethnic composition of the students was 79 percent Tibetan and 21 percent others, including Han, Hui, Tu, Mongolian, and Salar. Without exception, all students were required to attend Tibetan-language classes. However, all textbooks and all classes were in Chinese except the Tibetan-language class.

100. The office that sets the minimum scores each year is the students enrollment office (Ch: *zhaosheng bangongshi*) within the prefecture's education department.

101. Teachers in these areas retire at age fifty for women and fifty-five for men, five years younger than in central China.

102. Although 98 percent of the new English teachers were Tibetan, the English-language classes were being taught in Chinese.

103. As of 1999, teachers training in Tsochang was available in Semnyi County. The school then had 443 students in thirteen classes. Six of these were Tibetan classes, with 112 students. Chinese, Tibetan, and English were taught. The Chinese track reportedly had six hours of Chinese and two hours of English weekly, while the Tibetan track had six hours of Tibetan, six hours of Chinese, and two hours of English.

104. See Bass, *Education in Tibet*, 235–37.

105. Note our discussion of dialects and language differences in chapter 1. Some scholars would argue that Tibetan students from places such as Mili, Tashiling, or Namphel would in fact be learning a foreign language, rather than their own native language, when they are taught Tibetan in school.

106. An exception is the Northwest Minzu Institute, where chemistry, management, and computer science have been taught in Tibetan since 1995.

107. For example, fifty students instead of the former annual enrollment of sixty students were accepted to the Tibetan-language courses at Southwest Minzu University, starting in autumn 2000.

108. Kangding Minzu Shifan Zhuanke Xuexiao Ketizu, *Sichuan Zangqu shuangyu jiaoyu yu jiaoxue yanjiu*.

109. Ibid., 23.

110. We collected a number of articles and papers with titles such as "Why Tibetans Don't Speak Tibetan Well"; "A Concern That Tibetans Don't Understand Written Tibetan" (Wei Zangzu shuo bu hao zangyu, Zangzu bu dong zangwen danyou), in Dundrup, *Wo de xinyuan*, 38–44; "A Brief Discussion of the 'Uselessness' of the Tibetan Language" (Qiantan zangwen "wuyong" tan), a hand-written document by a local Tibetan teacher given to us by the Tawu County Education Department, May 2000; and "A Study of Bilingual Education and Teaching in Tibetan Areas of Sichuan" (Sichuan Zangqu shuangyu jiaoyu yu jiaoxue yanjiu), by Kangding Minzu Shifan Zhuanke Xuexiao Ketizu.

4 / IN SEARCH OF TIBETAN CULTURE

1. Although "cultural relics" is the standard translation for this term, "cultural artifacts" would be more accurate.

2. Information Office of the State Council, *Development of Tibetan Culture*.

3. Kangding Minzu Shifan Zhuanke Xuexiao Ketizu, *Sichuan Zangqu shuangyu jiaoyu yu jiaoxue yanjiu*, 7. This source actually refers to the Tibetan autonomous region of Xikang Province. For a discussion of the name Xikang or Sikang, see Watson, *Frontiers of China*, 59–60. After the People's Republic of China was established, the name Sikang dropped out of use, but the formal abolition of Sikang Province apparently was not announced until July 1955.

4. Kangding Minzu Shifan Zhuanke Xuexiao Ketizu, *Sichuan Zangqu shuangyu jiaoyu yu jiaoxue yanjiu*, 8.

5. Shakya, "Waterfall and Fragrant Flowers," 20–24. Tsering Shakya was born in Tibet in 1959 and fled to India with his family in 1967.

6. It should be noted that the recruitment of literate monks as interpreters was not always voluntary. For instance, we met a monk from a monastery in Golok (Guoluo) TAP, Qinghai, who told us that when his monastery was closed in 1958, he and the other monks were sent to a labor camp. After three years in the labor camp, his Chinese was good enough for him to become an interpreter for the local authorities.

7. Interview with one of the key Tibetan news reporters, August 1999.

8. Interviews in villages in Tsolho (Hainan) TAP, near Thriga (Guide) County seat, August 1999. Even viewers who lived very close to Xining, where the Tibetan programs are broadcast, informed us that they were often unable to receive the programs in the village due to poor transmission.

9. This statement seems to contradict the argument that most Tibetans in Mili are actually not Tibetans at all but are Premi. It may also reflect the dispute itself, and the need for people to reaffirm or reject their Tibetan or Premi identity when these identities are questioned.

10. By 1985, 164 feature films, 6 art films, 34 educational films, and 26 documentary films had been translated.

11. According to Zhongguo Shehui Kexueyuan Minzu Yanjiusuo, *Zhongguo shaoshu minzu yuyan shiyong qingkuang*, 283, between 1975 and 1985, nineteen films were translated into Mongolian at the Tsonub (Haixi) station of the Qinghai Province Film Translation and Production Factory. Between 1981 and 1985, two films were dubbed into Tu language by the same translation unit, Huzhu station. In a meeting of the Qinghai Academy of Social Sciences, July 1999, we were told that the Jyekundo (Yushu) station dubbed films into the Kham dialect.

12. Information Office of the State Council, *Development of Tibetan Culture*, 16–25.

13. Among recent academic works are *The History of Tibetan Literature*, compiled by the staff of the Central Nationalities Institute, and the Tibetan-language *The Combined Religion and Politics*, by Dunkar Lobsang Tinley, former professor of Tibetan studies at the Central Nationalities Institute. The Tibet Academy of Social Sciences published *A General History of Tibet* in Chinese and, in Tibetan editions, *The Inference Theory in Tibetan Philosophy* and *A Dictionary of Tibetan Philosophy*.

14. At the horse race festival in Jyekundo TAP, which we visited in July 1999, the prefecture's culture department sponsored a local Gesar storyteller. He was seated in a festival tent and sat in trance for several hours reciting parts of the Gesar epic. Local people visited the tent in large numbers and obviously enjoyed the stories very much. During our fieldwork, we heard mention of other Gesar storytellers.

15. Harris, *In the Image of Tibet*, questions the freedom of expression of mod-

ern Tibetan writers and artists. For example, she writes about the Sweet Tea Painting Association (T: *cha ngarbo rimo tsokpa*), where young Lhasa artists went underground in the late 1980s to avoid government interference, 182, 187.

16. Department of Information and International Relations, *Destruction of Tibetan Culture.*

17. (T) *mtsho sngon bod skad gsar 'gyur.*

18. (T) *kan lho gsar 'gyur* and *nga ba gsar 'gyur. Ngaba News* is a four-page daily and has a circulation of about 2,500.

19. (T) *mtsho sngon slob gso,* (Ch) *Qinghai jiaoyu.* Published by the provincial education department.

20. (T) *rtser snyegs,* (Ch) *Pandeng.* Published by the Qinghai Party School.

21. (T) *tang gi 'tshoba.* Published by the Qinghai Communist Party Propaganda Department.

22. (T) *mtsho sngon khrims lugs gsar 'gyur.*

23. (T) *mtso sngon tsan rig dang 'phrul chas gsar 'gyur.*

24. (T) *gangs ljongs kyi gzhon nu.*

25. (T) *sbrang char.* Published by the Qinghai Minzu Publishing House.

26. (T) *mtsho sngon mang tshogs sgyu rtsal.* Published by the *Qinghai Folk Arts and Literature* editorial committee.

27. (T) *zla zer.* Published by the Kanlho Art and Literature Association.

28. Each issue sells approximately twenty copies in local bookstores.

29. In some prefectures (e.g., Malho [Huangnan] and Tsolho [Hainan]), about one fourth of the books were in Tibetan, whereas in others (e.g., Tsochang [Haibei]), we were unable to find books in Tibetan at all. In Golok, the bookstore was closed, and nobody could tell us for how long or if it was going to reopen in the same location. Judging by the facade, the store appeared to have been closed for a while. In Kandze, we stopped in at bookshops in every county we visited.

30. Shakya, "Waterfall and Fragrant Flowers," 20–24. For a thorough survey of publications in Tibetan, see Stoddard, "Tibetan Publications and National Identity," 121–56.

31. Shakya, "Waterfall and Fragrant Flowers," 20–24.

32. The TAR Writers Association is a province-level organization sponsored by the regional government, not an association of Tibetan writers. Although there is no separate association of Tibetan writers, a number of Tibetan writers are members of the Association of Minority Writers in China. According to news reports from 1990, of the 1,800 members of this association, 30 were Tibetan (Stoddard, "Tibetan Publications and National Identity," 121–56, citing *Lasa Wanbao,* 18 September 1990, and *Bod ljongs nyin re'i tshags par,* 6 October 1990).

33. Shakya, "Waterfall and Fragrant Flowers," 21.

34. Ibid., 22.

35. Biographical information from "Preface," by Dondrup Wangbum, in the English translation of Dawa, *Soul in Bondage,* 5–11.

36. On the works of Tashi Dawa and other young Tibetan authors, see Grünfelder, *An den Lederriemen geknotete Seele.*

37. Upton, "Beyond the Contents of a Curriculum."

38. Shakya, "Waterfall and Fragrant Flowers," 20–24.

39. (T) *dga' ldan rnam rgyal 'phel rgyas gling.*

40. Kangding Minzu Shifan Zhuanke Xuexiao Ketizu, *Sichuan Zangqu shuangyu jiaoyu yu jiaoxue yanjiu,* 246.

41. Ibid., 255–58.

42. According to ibid., 281–82, about 20,000 Mongolians used Tibetan during the mid-1980s. In addition, some Tu, Bao'an, Salar, and Hui people were reported to use Tibetan to "communicate among themselves."

43. Ibid., 301.

44. According to the staff of this office, as of 1999, Kangtsa (Gangcha) County also had a translation office, and Dola (Qilian) and Dashi (Haiyan) had translators but no special offices for translation. The prefecture had twenty-four people working on translation in 1999.

45. Interview with the Tsochang TAP translation office, July 1999.

46. The following documents were received during our visit to Tsolho Prefecture Tibetan Translation Language and Writing Working Committee in July 1999: "Written Application for Editing and Publishing Qinghai-Hainan Tibetan Autonomous Prefecture Ancient Tibetan Books Subsidized by ASIA" (dated 1 September 1998, and including twenty-six titles); "Written Application for Editing and Publishing a Dictionary on Common Foods on the Qinghai-Tibetan Plateau in Tibetan, Chinese, and English by Hainan Tibetan Autonomous Prefecture" (dated 18 September 1998, and "based on the actual requirements to preserve the traditional Tibetan cultural heritage of the Hainan area"); "The Situation in Regard to the Development of the Tibetan Translation Work in Qinghai Province, Hainan TAP," a speech directed to the "leaders" (dated 20 July 1997); and "The Hainan TAP Tibetan Language Working Committee's Request for Assistance to Establish a Project for Promoting the Elimination of Tibetan Illiteracy" (dated 25 February 1997).

47. Interview, July 1999. According to officials in the office, by 1999 the unit was staffed by nine people and had edited sixteen books.

48. For instance, in Tsolho TAP, the culture department published a four-volume edition on the prefecture's cultural history, based on research conducted since 1985. This publication includes famous folk stories and folksongs and was published in both Chinese and Tibetan editions.

49. Source: http://www.columbia.edu/cu/china/yunnan.htm.

50. These are the villages of Wutun, Manduhu, Guomori, and Cashari (Chinese transcriptions).

51. We were told that most *thanka* are made for display in homes, while statues are made mainly for the monasteries. Statues of the Dharma guides (protector deities)

are usually only for monasteries, although Sakyamuni figures can be bought for the home.

52. His name is Lobsum Shangqug, and he is introduced in *China's Tibet* 6 (2000): 43.

53. According to the officials we interviewed, Labrang was a province-level cultural relic from 1961 until 1982, when it became a state-level cultural relic. Of the sites in Sangchu, we were told that the ancient towns of Bajiao and Sangke are province-level cultural relics, while Kecai Monastery, the ancient towns of Madang and Siru, and the Ming dynasty frontier wall of Tumen guan are among the county-level cultural relics.

54. Other important excavations and discoveries were listed as Zongri culture in Tongde County, 1987 (stone utensils, 20,000–50,000 years old); Gonghe County, 1987 (Stone Age utensils); and Layihai culture (approximately 7,600 years old) in Guinan County, 1983. No discoveries of Tibetan culture were reported.

55. The Tsolho Prefecture Culture Department told us that all the song and dance troupes in Qinghai were established around 1964.

56. A book about the 1981 and 1991 festivals was published locally, but we were told it was completely sold out. A new festival publication was expected for the fiftieth anniversary in 2001.

57. Sepa Monastery (Tibetan name unknown) and Samdup Monastery (Ch: Sangzhou Si; T: *'dzomnyog bsam 'grub dgon*). Both are Sakyapa monasteries.

58. Schoolchildren usually wear Western-style clothes, but in some Tibetan-medium schools both the staff and the children tend to dress in *chuba*. Many rural people, especially herders, still use *chuba* for everyday wear.

59. Madsen, "Social Change."

5 / CULTURE AS A WAY OF LIFE

1. See, e.g., Upton, "Home on the Grasslands?" 98–124.

2. Department of Information and International Relations, *Destruction of Tibetan Culture.*

3. Department of Information and International Relations, *Tibet 2000.*

4. Information Office of the State Council, *Development of Tibetan Culture.*

5. Dreyer, "Go West Young Han," 353–69.

6. Ibid., citing *Minzu Tuanjie,* November 1958, "Quickly Develop the Minority Nationality Areas," 7.

7. W. Smith, *Tibetan Nation,* 442, citing "The Rich Frontier Regions Await the Exploration of Our Youth," *Chinese Agriculture and Reclamation,* 20 February 1959. The settlers reportedly reclaimed 330,000 *mu* of land in Tsonub (Haixi) and Tsolho (Hainan).

8. Seymour and Anderson, *New Ghosts, Old Ghosts,* 131.

9. Ibid., 136.

10. Inspection panel's report and findings on the Qinghai project, www.wds.world-bank.org. Although the panel's mandate limited its focus to compliance with the bank's own policies, the panel pointed out a number of problems with the project design. It found that policies on environmental assessment, resettlement, indigenous peoples, natural habitats, pest management, and information disclosure had been seriously violated.

11. *Ruo'ergai Xian zhi,* 124.

12. Longworth and Williamson, *China's Pastoral Region,* 65.

13. Seymour and Anderson, *New Ghosts, Old Ghosts,* 131.

14. Ibid., 150–58.

15. The number of camps was reduced by about one third, and by 1998 there were only nineteen large enterprises (factories and farms) in Qinghai that relied primarily on prison labor.

16. Seymour and Anderson, *New Ghosts, Old Ghosts,* 131.

17. Ibid., 147.

18. Ibid. The grain output of one prison farm alone, the Xiangride Prison Farm in Dulan County, accounted for 13.3 percent of the total grain output of Tsonub in 1989.

19. Ibid., 131.

20. Clarke, "The Movement of Population," 233.

21. *China Daily,* 30 December 1999. Estimates are that more than 1,000 people entered Hoh Xil Nature Reserve illegally in 1999. As a result, the reserve was closed to anyone without a permit as of 1 January 2000. Big-game hunters who can afford it, however, may purchase permits to hunt bharal and argali in Qinghai.

22. Ekvall, *Fields on the Hoof,* 96–97.

23. *Dege Xian zhi,* 196.

24. Marshall and Cooke, *Tibet Outside the TAR,* citing *China Nationalities Economy* 1993, 102.

25. Marshall and Cooke, *Tibet Outside the TAR,* 1523.

26. Clarke, *China's Reforms of Tibet,* and Goldstein and Beall, *Nomads of Western Tibet.*

27. Zhang, *Case Study on Mountain Environmental Management.*

28. Miller, *Rangelands and Pastoral Production.*

29. International Commission of Jurists, *Tibet: Human Rights and the Rule of Law.* Government policy is also cited as the major underlying cause of rangeland degradation by Longworth and Williamson, *China's Pastoral Region,* 333.

30. Tibet Information Network, News Update, 20 September 1991.

31. Ibid.

32. *China Daily,* 24 August 1998, citing Xie Shijie, secretary of the Sichuan Province Chinese Communist Party Committee.

33. Winkler, "Floods, Logging, and Hydro-Electricity."

34. Ibid.

35. *Ganzi Zhou zhi,* 207. The highest density of forest is found in Danba (Rongdrak), where 36 percent of the area is forested, and Chaksam (Luding), where forest covers 30 percent of the county.

36. Xinhua News Report, 4 September 1998.

37. The two prefectures together cover an area of 236,570 square kilometers.

38. Winkler, "Floods, Logging, and Hydro-Electricity."

39. This includes asbestos, iron, magnesium, silica, potash, salt, copper, lead, zinc, gold, rock crystal, natural gas, coal, and petroleum.

40. See especially Wang and Bai, *Poverty of Plenty.* The authors provide a detailed analysis of the economic backwardness of China's five western autonomous regions (Xinjiang, Inner Mongolia, Ningxia, Tibet, and Guangxi) and three provinces (Yunnan, Guizhou, and Qinghai).

41. Ibid., 23.

42. Song and Yao, "Resources Exploitation and Conservation of Qaidam Basin under the Principle of Sustainable Development," unpublished paper, 1998.

43. For those who investigate development projects funded by foreign agencies, it is important to realize that local people are very reluctant to criticize the authorities, particularly to a foreigner. This makes it extremely difficult to obtain accurate information from the beneficiaries of development projects and others who will be affected.

44. Department of Information and International Relations, *Tibet.*

45. Interviews with county government officials, April 1999.

46. Winkler, "Floods, Logging, and Hydro-Electricity."

47. Dundrup, *Wo de xinyuan,* 44–46. The book is a privately published bilingual Chinese- and Tibetan-language publication from Dartsedo, Kandze TAP, Sichuan. It is a compilation of the author's articles written between 1986 and 1991.

48. Passed by the National People's Congress in March 2000.

49. *People's Daily,* 6 October 2000, "Multinationals Marching into Western China."

50. *The Telegraph,* 22 October 2000, "China Planning Nuclear Blasts to Build Giant Hydro Project."

51. *New York Times,* 16 October 2000, "China Plans to Divert Rivers to Thirsty North."

52. *People's Daily,* 15 June 2000, "Plan to Recruit Talent for West China Kicked Off."

53. People's Government of Dechen Tibetan Autonomous Prefecture, Decree no. 1 (1997).

54. The regulations state that specialized personnel coming from outside the prefecture "shall be given subsidies for living expenses and provided with housing by the benefited units" and that those units that make "great achievements in importing capital, technology, and talents shall be commended and rewarded by the government of the same level." In addition, 15–30 percent of the increased profits of that

year may be given to a unit (company or corporation) or individual from outside the prefecture who aids in improving profits for an enterprise in the prefecture.

55. Nanping County has recently been renamed Jiuzhaigou County.

56. Luding and Kangding had about 3,500 hotel beds and 400 persons professionally involved in tourism, according to information from the prefecture's tourism department in May 2000. There are five travel agencies in the prefecture, two of which belong to the department. The tourism department is also in charge of environmental protection.

57. Sichuan Sheng Lüyou Guihua Shijisuo, *Sichuan Sheng Ganzi Zangzu Zizhizhou lüyou fazhan zongti guihua 2000–2015.*

58. From a recent publication, Ganzi TAP Lüyouju Bian, *Shengji xiangrui de difang,* 12. This publication is one of three small glossy books that the department published about tourism. The authors of these publications are all local officials from Kandze TAP. By May 2000, the office had sixteen employees, only three of whom were from outside the prefecture.

59. Makley, "Gendered Practices," 61–95.

60. Peng, "Tibetan Pilgrimage," 184.

61. See Greenwood, "Culture by the Pound," 171–86, and Swain, "Gender Roles in Indigenous Tourism," 83–104.

62. On the importance of tourism as an agent of change, see, e.g., V. Smith, "Eskimo Tourism," 77. This study claims that in the Alaskan Arctic, even mass tourism (introducing four times the total population of a community in three months) has not been a significant agent of cultural change; factors such as land rights, patterns of trade, and government welfare policies have been far more important. For an assessment of marketing culture, see, e.g., Boissevain, "Introduction," 1–26.

63. Peng, "Tibetan Pilgrimage," 198.

64. Cingcade, "Tourism and the Many Tibets," 1–24.

65. Makley, "Gendered Practices," 61–94.

66. Cingcade, "Tourism and the Many Tibets," 5.

67. Schein, *Minority Rules,* 163.

68. Peng, "Tibetan Pilgrimage," 185.

6 / TIBETAN CULTURE ON THE MARGINS: DESTRUCTION OR RECONSTRUCTION?

1. Information Office of the State Council, *Development of Tibetan Culture,* 17.

2. Department of Information and International Relations, *Destruction of Tibetan Culture.*

3. The most famous Tibetan artist is Yadong, who became a national superstar after he won the Chinese MTV prize in 1995. Numerous tapes of Yadong's songs were available everywhere we went, and our impression is that every young Tibetan we met knew the lyrics of these songs.

4. Makley, "Gendered Practices," 61–95.

5. However, the DOE publishes its own Tibetan-language textbooks for all school grades. A report issued by the Tibetan government-in-exile further explains that "Tibetan language, history, and culture constitute a major part of the curriculum in all Tibetan schools." See Rikha, *Tibetan Education in Exile.*

6. Many language minorities around the world are facing similar problems. There are a variety of dilemmas involved in saving such endangered languages and few easy answers to the enormous challenge such rescue missions represent.

7. See Korom, *Constructing Tibetan Culture.*

8. Harris, *In the Image of Tibet.*

9. Ibid. See particularly chapter 6 on "Tibets" in collision.

10. Department of Information and International Relations, Destruction of Tibetan Culture.

11. As previously noted, the majority of monks in Tibetan monasteries in India are new arrivals from Tibet. An important reason for this is that Tibetan exiles prefer to send their children to school, while relatively few choose to join a monastery.

CHINESE AND TIBETAN GLOSSARY

amban ཨམ་བན་ representative of imperial China

Amdo ཨ་མདོ་ region of Tibet

Amnye Machen ཨ་མྱེ་རྨ་ཆེན་ a mountain in Amdo

ani dgonpa ཨ་ནི་དགོན་པ་ nunnery

Animaqing Shan 阿尼玛卿山 Amnye Machen Mountain

ba zangwen wei zhu 把藏文为主 make Tibetan the main language for teaching

Baichunlu 白唇鹿 *White Mouth Deer*

Ba' idurya sngon po བཻ་ཌཱུརྻ་སྔོན་པོ་ *Blue Lapis Lazuli*

baipishu 白皮书 white-covered books (series of white papers on China's ethnic minorities)

Bianjing Diqu JiansheBuzhufei 边境地区建设补助费 Border Areas Construction Aid Fund

bla brang བླ་བྲང་ residence of a tulku (reincarnated lama)

Bod བོད་ Tibet

Bod kyi rtsom rig sgyu rtsal བོད་ཀྱི་རྩོམ་རིག་སྒྱུ་རྩལ་ *Tibetan Literature and Art*

bod kyi rus mdzod chen mo བོད་ཀྱི་རུས་མཛོད་ཆེན་མོ་ *The Great Tibetan Genealogy*

bod mag བོད་དམག་ Tibetan
soldier

bod mi བོད་མི་ Tibetan people

bod pa བོད་པ་ Tibetan people

bod rigs བོད་རིགས་ Tibetan
people; Tibetan nation

Bön བོན་ Tibetan religion pre-
dating Buddhism

btsan po བཙན་པོ་ Tibetan kings
of the Yarlung dynasty

cham འཆམ་ masked ritual
dance performed by monks

chol kha gsum ཆོལ་ཁ་གསུམ་
three regions (of Tibet)

chörten མཆོད་རྟེན་ stupa

chos rgyal ཆོས་རྒྱལ་ religious
king; the king as protector and
patron of religion

chos srid gnyis ldan
ཆོས་སྲིད་གཉིས་ལྡན་ the dual
religious and secular system
of government

chuba ཕྱུ་པ་ traditional
Tibetan costume

chuzhong 初中 junior middle
school

cun 村 village (administrative
unit below district level)
See xiang

danwei 单位 work unit

Daser ཟླ་ཟེར་ Moonlight

dazhuan 大专 vocational
college

deb ther dmar po དེབ་ཐེར་དམར་པོ་
Red Annals

deb ther sngon po དེབ་ཐེར་སྔོན་པོ་
Blue Annals

dgon lag དགོན་ལག་ branch
monastery

dgonpa དགོན་པ་ monastery

dianxiao 点校 point school

difang zhi 地方志 local history

dingyuan 定员 quota (for
monasteries)

diqu 地区 district

Domed མདོ་སྨད་ region of Tibet

dong chong xia cao 冬虫夏草
"winter worm summer grass"
(caterpillar fungus)

draba གྲྭ་པ་ monk

Drangchar སྦྲང་ཆར་ Light Rain

dratsang གྲྭ་ཚང་ monastic college

Drichu འབྲི་ཆུ་ Yangtze River

Dzachu རྫ་ཆུ་ Mekong River

'dzam gling rgyas bshad འཛམ་གླིང་རྒྱས་བཤད་ *On the World* [Grand Exegesis of the World]

Dzayül རྫ་ཡུལ་ place in Kham

er lei 二类 second category, referring to medium of teaching

er pai he zhu 二派合住 "two branches together," referring to monasteries

fahui 法会 Buddhist ceremony

fangzhi 方志 local history

fenlie zhuyi 分裂主义 "split-tism" (separatism)

fenpei zhidu 分配制度 job assignment system

foxueyuan 佛学院 Buddhist college

fuze ziji 负责自己 administered by oneself, referring to monasteries

ganbu zinü 干部子女 cadre children

Gangjongyi Chonu གངས་ལྗོངས་ཀྱི་གཞོན་ནུ་ *Snowland Youth*

Ganzi Zangwen Xuexiao 甘孜藏文学校 Ganzi Tibetan School

gaodeng xuexiao 高等学校 higher-level school or college

gaoji foxueyuan 高级佛学院 higher Buddhist college

gaozhong 高中 senior middle school

gelong དགེ་སློང་ fully ordained monk

Gelug དགེ་ལུགས་ school of Tibetan Buddhism

genyen དགེ་བསྙེན་ candidate monks

geshe དགེ་བཤེས་ highest degree in the Gelugpa system of religious teaching; a person who has obtained this degree

getsul དགེ་ཚུལ་ novice monk

guanli weiyuanhui 管理委员会 management committee

Guoluo Minzu Shifan Xuexiao
Guoluo *Minzu*　果洛民族师
范学校　Teachers School

gyegu　དགྱེས་སྐུ　ceremonial display of a giant thanka on a slope or hillside

hangye　行业　trade

hanyu　汉语　(Han) Chinese language

huizu　回族　Hui *minzu*

huofo　活佛　"Living Buddha" (tulku)

jiaoshi fangwei　教师方位　teaching method

jiaoyuju　教育局　Education department

Jihua Shengyu　计划生育　planned reproduction policy ("one-child policy")

Jimei Jianzan Sili Jigme Gyaltsen Xuexiao　吉美坚赞私立学校　Private School

jin　斤　unit of measurement, one *jin* equals 1/2 kilo

jisu　寄宿　boarding

Jonang　ཇོ་ནང　school of Tibetan Buddhism

Kagyu　བཀའ་བརྒྱུད　school of Tibetan Buddhism

Kangba　康巴　Kham

Kangba daxue　康巴大学　Khampa university

Kangba wenhua　康巴文化　*Khampa Culture*

Kangding Minzu Shizhuan Gaodeng Zhuanke Xuexiao　康巴民族师专高等专科学校　Kangding Minzu

Kangding Zangwen Zhongxue　康巴藏文中学　Kangding Tibetan Middle School

Kangyur　བཀའ་འགྱུར　Buddhist texts (the words of the Buddha Sakyamuni)

Kanlho Sargyur　ཀན་ལྷོ་གསར་འགྱུར　*Kanlho News*

Kham　ཁམས་　region of Tibet

khata　ཁ་བཏགས་　scarf used for greetings and to adorn altars and other objects of spiritual significance

Khawa Karpo ཁ་བ་དཀར་པོ་
name of a mountain in Kham

khenpo མཁན་པོ་ abbot

klu ཀླུ་ spirits of the under
world who often inhabit springs
and waters

klu khang ཀླུ་ཁང་ house where
the *klu rol* festival takes place

klu rol ཀླུ་རོལ་ name of a festival

Kumbum སྐུ་འབུམ་ name of a
monastery

Labrang Tashikhyil
བླ་བྲང་བཀྲ་ཤིས་འཁྱིལ་ name of a
monastery

labtse ལ་རྩེ་ site for ritual
arrows or branches with prayer
flags, often located on a mountain pass, ridge or hillside

Labuleng Si 拉卜楞寺
Labrang Monastery

lama བླ་མ་ teacher (of spiritual
knowledge)

lamrim ལམ་རིམ་ study method
introduced by Tsong-khapa,
founder of the Gelugpa tradition

laodong ke 劳动课 labor class

laogai 劳改 prison labor camp

lha khang ལྷ་ཁང་ temple

lishi xiguan 历史习惯 historical tradition

Liuyuehui 六月会 Sixth
Month Festival

luohou 落后 backward

lungta རླུང་རྟ་ pieces of paper
or cloth inscribed with "wind
horse" symbols

ma bu མ་བུ་ "mother" and
"son," referring to monasteries

Machu རྨ་ཆུ་ Yellow River

Maji Xueshan 玛吉雪山
Amnye Machen

mani མ་ཎི་ mantra or prayer

mani khang མ་ཎི་ཁང་ prayer
house

Meili Xueshan 梅里雪山
Kawa Kharpo Mountain

me tog mchod 'bul
མེ་ཏོག་མཆོད་འབུལ་ flower offering ceremony

Minwei (Minzu Shiwu

Weiyuanhui) 民委（民族事务委员会） Ethnic Affairs Commission

minzu chubanshe 民族出版社 minzu publishing house

minzu gewutuan 民族歌舞团 minzu song and dance troupe

minzu shibie 民族识别 *minzu* identification project

minzu shifan xueyuan 民族师范学院 *minzu* teachers college

minzu tuanjie 民族团结 "unity of the nationalities"

minzu xuexiao 民族学校 minzu school

minzu zhongxue 民族中学 *minzu* middle school

minzuban 民族班 *minzu* education

minzuxue 民族学 *minzu* studies/ethnology

mizong 秘宗 tantra

mkhas pa'i dga' ston མཁས་པའི་དགའ་སྟོན་ *A Feast for Wise Men*

Mönlam སྨོན་ལམ་ religious ceremonies held just after Tibetan New Year

mu 亩 unit of measurement, 15 *mu* equals one hectare

mumin 牧民 herders (nomads)

namthar རྣམ་ཐར་ biographical story; name of Tibetan opera in the Amdo region

nangpa ནང་པ་ believers; literally, "insiders"

Ngaba Sargyur རྔ་བ་གསར་འགྱུར་ *Ngaba News*

ngagpa སྔགས་པ་ practitioner of magic

Ngari མངའ་རིས་ region of Tibet, also known as Tö

nianjing 念经 recite (Buddhist) scriptures

nigu si 尼姑寺 nunnery

nongmu zinü 农牧子女 herder (nomad) children

Nyarong ཉག་རོང་ name of a place in Kham

Nyingma རྙིང་མ་ school of Tibetan Buddhism

Pandeng 攀登 *Climb*

pechawa དཔེ་ཆ་བ་ reader; monk engaged in a philosophical study program

phyi pa ཕྱི་པ་ non-believers, literally "outsiders"

pingdeng 平等 equality

pizhun 批准 government acceptance/approval

Pome སྤོ་སྨད་ name of a place in Kham

puchu 普初 first four years in primary school

puji chudeng jiaoyu 普及初等教育 compulsory primary education

putong 普通 standard

putong zhongxue 普通中学 standard middle school

qiangzu 羌族 Qiang minzu

Qinghai Difangzhi Weiyuanhui 青海地方志委员会 Qinghai Local History Committee

Qinghai jiaoyu 青海教育 *Qinghai Education*

Qinghai keji bao 青海科技报 *Qinghai Science and Technology News*

Qinghai Minzu Xueyuan 青海民族学院 Qinghai Minzu Institute

Qinghai Zangwen bao 青海藏文报 *Qinghai Tibetan News*

quanmin xinjiao diqu 全民信教地区 "area where everyone is a religious believer"

Qunzhong wenyi 群众文艺 *Folk Arts and Literature*

Qutan Si 瞿昙寺 Qutan Monastery

renmin yishu gong 人民艺术宫 people's arts palace

rgya mi རྒྱ་མི་ Chinese people

rgya rigs རྒྱ་རིགས་ Chinese people; Chinese nation

rgyud bzhi རྒྱུད་བཞི་ *The Four-Volume Medical Codes*

rig gnas རིག་གནས་ culture

rig gnas chenmo nga རིག་གནས་ཆེན་མོ་ལྔ་ five great fields of knowledge rig gzhung རིག་གཞུང་ culture

Rongwo Gönba Dechen
  Chökorling
  རོང་བོ་དགོན་ཆེན་བདེ་ཆེན་ཆོས་
  འཁོར་གླིང་ name of a monastery
  in Amdo

rus mdzod thor bu རུས་མཛོད་ཐོར་བུ་
Assorted Genealogies

rus mdzod za 'og ma
  རུས་མཛོད་ཟ་འོག་མ་ *The Brocade
  Genealogy*

ruxuelü 入学绿 entrance rate

saimahui 赛马会 horse race
  festival

sa dpyad ས་དཔྱད་ geomancy

Sakya ས་སྐྱ་ school of Tibetan
  Buddhism

Samye བསམ་ཡས་ name of a
  monastery in central Tibet

san lei 三类 third category,
  referring to medium of teaching

shaoshu minzu 少数民族
  minority *minzu*

Shaoshu Minzu Jiaoyu 少数民
  族教育补 Minority Minzu

Buzhu Zhuankuan 助专款
  Educational Fund

sheshui sengren 社会僧人
  monk without a monastery

sheng 省 province

shengxu 牲畜 livestock

shi 市 municipal area

shuangyu 双语 bilingual

shuyu ziji 属于自己 belongs
  to oneself, referring to
  monasteries

sixiang pinde 思想品德 ideology and morals (school subject)

sixiang zhengzui 思想政治
  ideology and politics

siyuan 寺院 monastery

siyuan guanli jiegou 寺院管理
  结构 monastic administrative
  unit

Ta'er Si 塔尔寺 Monastery
  Kumbum

Tagong Si 塔公寺 Lahgang
  Monastery

Tanggi Tsowa ཐང་གི་འཚོ་བ་ *Life
  of the Party*

Tengyur བསྟན་འགྱུར་ Buddhist texts (commentaries to the Kangyur)

thanka ཐང་ཀ་ image of a deity made of silk, either embroidered or painted

tianzang 天葬 sky burial

Tö སྟོད་ region of Tibet, traditionally known as Ngari

Tongzhanbu 统战部 United Front department (a division of the CCP)

torma གཏོར་མ་ small figure made of barley flour used during religious rituals

Tsang གཙང་ region of Tibet

Tsernyeg ཙེར་སྙེགས་ *Climb*

tsa-tsa ཚ་ཚ་ religious images made of clay

Tso ngön མཚོ་སྔོན་ Qinghai Lake

Tso ngön Böke Sargyur མཚོ་སྔོན་བོད་སྐད་གསར་འགྱུར་ *Qinghai Tibetan News*

Tso ngön Lobso མཚོ་སྔོན་སློབ་གསོ་ *Qinghai Education*

Tso ngön Mangtso Gyutsal མཚོ་སྔོན་མང་ཚོགས་སྒྱུ་རྩལ་ *Qinghai Folk Arts and Literature*

Tso ngön Trimlu Sargyur མཚོ་སྔོན་ཁྲིམས་ལུགས་གསར་འགྱུར་ *Qinghai Judicial News*

Tso ngön Tsenrig dang Trulche Sargyur མཚོ་སྔོན་ཚན་རིག་ དང་འཕྲུལ་ཆས་གསར་འགྱུར་ *Qinghai Science and Technology News*

tuanjie 团结 unite

tuanyuan 团员 member of China's Communist Youth League

tuixiu 退休 retire

tulku སྤྲུལ་སྐུ་ reincarnated lama

Tuzu 土族 Tu *minzu*

Ü དབུས་ region of Tibet

uchen དབུ་ཆེན་ printed Tibetan script

ume དབུ་མེད་ calligraphic Tibetan script

Ü-Tsang དབུས་གཙང་ region of Tibet, including Ü and Tsang

weisheng xuexiao 卫生学校 health school (medical school)

wenhua 文化 culture

wenhua chengdu 文化程度 cultural level

wenhuaju 文化局 culture department

wenyi 文艺 literature and arts

Wuming Foxueyuan 五明佛学院 Chinese name of Buddhist institute in Serthar (Seda) County

Wushengqu Zangwen Xiezuo Jiaocai Bangongshi 五省区藏文协作教材办公社 Five Provinces Teaching Material Office

wu yong 无用 useless

xiafang 下放 rustication

xian 县 county

xiang 乡 village district (administrative unit below the county level)

Xibei Minzu Xueyuan 西北民族学院 Northwest Minzu Institute

xibu da kaifa 西部大开发 Develop the Western Region (campaign)

Xikang 西康 Xikang, pre-1949 name of province in Kham area

Xikang Sheng Zangzu 西康生藏族自治区 Xikang Province Zizhiqu Tibetan Autonomous District

Xinan Minzu Xueyuan 西南民族学院 Southwest Minzu Institute

Xinhua shudian 新华书店 Xinhua bookstore

xiu ziji fuze 修自己负责 be in charge of repairs oneself, referring to monasteries

Xiwang Gongcheng 希望工程 Project Hope

xuexi fangshi 学的方式 study method

xuefei 学费 tuition fee

xuexiao 学校 school

yi lei 一类 first category, referring to medium of teaching

Yizu 彝族 Yi *minzu*

yul lha ཡུལ་ལྷ་ territorial deity

za ju qu 杂居区 area with ethnically mixed population

zafei 杂费 miscellaneous fee (for school children)

Zanghua Yanjiuyuan 藏画研究院 Thanka Research Institute

zangwen 藏文 Tibetan (written) language

zangwen zhongxue 藏文中学 Tibetan middle school

zangyu 藏语 Tibetan (spoken) language

zangyu xuexiao 藏语学校 Tibetan school

Zhang qui'er 障恰尔 Chinese transcription of the name of a Tibetan-language journal (T: *sbrang char*)

zhaosheng bangongshi 招生办公室 students enrolment office

zhen 镇 town, or township

zhengxie 政协 Chinese People's Political Consultative Committee

zhongdian wenwu baohu danwei 重点文物保护单位 key historical and cultural site under state protection

Zhongguo zangyuxi gaoji foxueyuan 中国藏语系高级佛学院 High-Level Tibetan Buddhist Institute of China

zhonghua minzu 中华民族 Chinese nation

zhongxin xuexiao 中心学校 key school

zhongxue 中学 middle school

zhongzhuan 中专 vocational middle school

zhou 州 prefecture

zhou wenhuagong 州文化宫 prefecture cultural palace

zhou wenhuaguan 州文化馆 prefecture cultural house

Zhuqing Si 竹庆寺 Zhuqing Monastery

zhuxuejin 助学金 scholarship, grant

zi ren ding de 自认定的 self-appointed

ziran baohuqu   自行还俗
  nature reserve

zixing huansu   自行还俗
  return to secular life (for a
  monk)

zizhiqu   自治区   autonomous
  region

zizhixian   自治县   autonomous
  county

zizhizhou   自治州
  autonomous prefecture

zongjiao yiwu   宗教义务   religious work (for merit)

zongjiao huodongchang   宗教活动场   religious site

zongjiao huodongdian   宗教活动点   religious site

zongjiao renyuan   宗教人员 religious personnel

zongjiaoju   宗教局   religious affairs department

REFERENCES

Local histories *(fangzhi)* and yearbooks are listed according to their place-names.

Aba Zhou nianjian 1991–1996 (Ngaba Prefecture yearbook 1991–1996). Aba Zhou Difangzhi Bianzuan Weiyuanhui (Ngaba Prefecture Local History Editorial Committee), ed. Chengdu: Sichuan Minzu Chubanshe, 1998.

Aba Zhou zhi (Ngaba Prefecture history). Aba Zangzu Qiangzu Zizhizhou Aba Xian Difangzhi Bianzuan Weiyuanhui (Ngaba Tibetan and Qiang Autonomous Prefecture County History Editorial Committee), ed. Chengdu: Sichuan Minzu Chubanshe, 1994.

Abu-Lughod, Lila. "Writing against Culture." In Richard G. Fox, ed., *Recapturing Anthropology: Working in the Present*, 137–62. Santa Fe, N.M.: School of American Research Press, 1991.

Anderson, Benedict. *Imagined Communities: Reflections on the Origin and Spread of Nationalism*. London: Verso, 1983.

Banister, Judith. *China's Changing Population*, Stanford, Calif.: Stanford University Press, 1987.

Barnett, Robert. "Symbols and Protest. The Iconography of Demonstrations in Tibet, 1987–1990," 238–58. In R. Barnett and S. Akiner, eds., *Resistance and Reform in Tibet*. London: Hurst, 1994.

Barth, Fredrik. "Enduring and Emerging Issues in the Analysis of Ethnicity," 11–32. In Hans Vermeulen and Cora Govers, eds., *The Anthropology of Ethnicity: Beyond Ethnic Groups and Boundaries*. Amsterdam: Het Spinhuis, 1989.

Bass, Catriona. *Education in Tibet: Policy and Practice since 1950*. London: Tibet Information Network and Zed Books, 1998.

Boissevain, J. "Introduction," 1–26. In J. Boissevain, ed., *Coping with Tourists. European Reactions to Mass Tourism*. Providence, R.I.: Berghahn Books, 1996.

Brown, M., ed., *Negotiating Ethnicities in China and Taiwan*. Berkeley, Calif.: Center for Chinese Studies, Institute of East Asian Studies, University of California, Berkeley, 1996.

Bushell, S. W. "The Early History of Tibet: From Chinese Sources," *Journal of the Royal Asiatic Society*, vol. 12, part IV (1880), 435–542.

Cheung, Siu-woo. "Representation and Negotiation of Ge Identities in Southeast Guizhou," 240–73. In M. Brown, ed., *Negotiating Ethnicities in China and Taiwan*. Berkeley, Calif.: Center for Chinese Studies, Institute of East Asian Studies, University of California, Berkeley, 1996.

China Exploration and Research Society. *Buddhist Monasteries of Ganzi Tibetan Autonomous Prefecture, Western Sichuan, China. A Project for Architectural Conservation Funded by the Getty Grant Program*. Los Angeles: China Exploration and Research Society, 1992.

Choedon, Dhondub. *Life in the Red Flag People's Commune*. Dharamsala, India: The Information Office of H.H. the Dalai Lama, 1978.

Cingcade, Mary L. "Tourism and the Many Tibets: The Manufacture of Tibetan 'Tradition,'" *China Information*, vol. 13, no. 1 (Summer 1998), 1–24.

Clarke, Graham. *China's Reforms of Tibet and Their Effects on Pastoralism*. IDS Discussion Paper no. 237. Brighton, England: Institute of Development Studies, 1987.

———. "Research Design in the Use of China's Census and Survey Data for Rural Areas and Households," 217–40. In E. B. Vermeer, ed., *From Peasant to Entrepreneur: Growth and Change in Rural China*. Wageningen, Netherlands: Pudoc, 1992.

———. "The Movement of Population to the West of China: Tibet and Qinghai," 221–57. In Judith M. Brown and Rosemary Foot, eds., *Migration: The Asian Experience*. Oxford: St. Martin's Press, 1994.

Clifford, James. *The Predicament of Culture*. London: Harvard University Press, 1988.

Corlin, Claes. *The Nation in Your Mind: Continuity and Change among Tibetan Refugees in Nepal*. Ph.D. dissertation, University of Gothenburg, 1975.

Dai, Kui, and Zhalo. "Lama Jigmei Gyaincain and His Private School," *China's Tibet*, no. 1 (2000), 24–25.]

Dai, Qingxia. *Zang-Mian yuzu yuyan yanjiu* (Research on Tibeto-Burman languages). Kunming, China: Yunnan Minzu Chubanshe, 1990.

Dari Xian zhi (Darlak County history). Dari Xian Difangzhi Bianzuan Weiyuanhui (Darlak County Local History Editing Committee), ed. Shaanxi, China: Shaanxi Renmin Chubanshe, 1993.

Dawa, Tashi. *A Soul in Bondage, Stories from Tibet*. Beijing: Chinese Literature Press, 1992.

Dege Xian zhi (Derge County history). Dege Xian zhi Bianzuan Weiyuanhui (Derge County History Editorial Committee), ed. Chengdu, China: Sichuan Renmin Chubanshe, 1995.

Department of Information and International Relations of the Tibetan government-in-exile. *Tibet. Environment and Development Issues.* Dharamsala, India: DIIR, 1992.

———. *Destruction of Tibetan Culture through a New Socialist Culture,* 2000. *(www.tibet.can/wtn.archive/2000/7/20).*

———. *Tibet 2000: Environment and Development Issues.* Dharamsala, India: DIIR, 2000.

Deqin Xian zhi (Dechen County history). Deqin Xian zhi Bianzuan Weiyuanhui (Dechen County History Editing Committee), ed. Kunming, China: Yunnan Minzu Chubanshe, 1997.

Dolkar, Sonam, ed. *Zongjiao zhi* (History of religion). Beijing: Zhongguo Zangxue Chubanshe, 1994.

Dreyer, June Teufel. "Go West Young Han: The Hsia Fang Movement to China's Minority Areas," *Pacific Affairs,* vol. 48, no. 3 (1975), 353–69.

———. *China's Forty Millions. Minority Nationalities and National Integration in the People's Republic of China,* Cambridge: Harvard University Press, 1976.

Dundrup, Tsering (Zeren Dengzhu Derong). *Wo de xinyuan* (My dream). Dartsedo, Kandze Tibetan Autonomous Prefecture, 1995.

Dwyer, Arienne. "The Texture of Tongues: Language and Power in China." In William Safran, ed., *Nationalism and Ethnoregional Identities in China.* Boulder, Colo.: University of Colorado Press, 1998.

Ekvall, Robert. *Religious Observances in Tibet. Patterns and Function.* Chicago: University of Chicago Press, 1964.

———. *Fields on the Hoof. Nexus of Tibetan Nomadic Pastoralism.* Prospect Heights, Ill.: Waveland Press, 1983.

Epstein, Lawrence, and Wenbin Peng. "Ritual, Ethnicity, and Generational Identity," 120–38. In Melvyn C. Goldstein and Matthew T. Kapstein, eds., *Buddhism in Contemporary Tibet, Religious Revival and Cultural Identity.* Berkeley, Calif.: University of California Press, 1998.

Fei, Xiaotong. *Towards a People's Anthropology.* Beijing: Foreign Languages Press, 1981.

Gansu tongji nianjian 1998 (Gansu statistical yearbook 1998). Zhongguo Tongji Chubanshe (China Statistical Publishing House), ed. Beijing, 1998.

Ganzi TAP Lüyouju Bian (Kandze TAP Tourism Department), ed. *Shengji xiangrui de difang* (A place which is holy, pure, and lucky). Dartsedo: Ganzi TAP Lüyouju Bian, 2000.

Ganzi Zhou zhi (Kandze Prefecture history). Ganzi Zhou zhi Bianzuan Weiyuanhui (Kandze Prefecture History Editorial Committee), ed. Vols. 1–3. Chengdu: Sichuan Renmin Chubanshe, 1997.

Geertz, Clifford. *The Interpretation of Cultures.* New York: Basic Books, 1973.

Germano, David. "Re-membering the Dismembered Body of Tibet, Contemporary Tibetan Visionary Movements in the People's Republic of China," 53–94. In Melvyn C. Goldstein and Matthew T. Kapstein, eds., *Buddhism in Contemporary*

Tibet, Religious Revival and Cultural Identity. Berkeley, Calif.: University of California Press, 1998.

Gladney, Dru. *Muslim Chinese: Ethnic Nationalism in the People's Republic.* Cambridge: Harvard University Press, 1991.

———. "Representing Nationality in China: Refiguring Majority/Minority Identities," *The Journal of Asian Studies,* vol. 53, no. 1 (February 1994), 92–123.

———. "The Question of Minority Identity and Indigeneity in Post-Colonial China," *Cultural Survival Quarterly* (Fall 1997), 50–54.

Goldstein, Melvyn C. *A History of Modern Tibet, 1913–1951. The Demise of the Lamaist State.* Berkeley, Calif. University of California Press, 1989.

———. "Change, Conflict, and Continuity among a Community of Nomadic Pastoralists," 76–111. In R. Barnett and S. Akiner, eds., *Resistance and Reform in Tibet.* London: Hurst, 1994.

———. *The Snow Lion and the Dragon: China, Tibet, and the Dalai Lama,* Berkeley, Calif.: University of California Press, 1997.

———. "The Revival of Monastic Life in Drepung Monastery," 15–52. In Melvyn C. Goldstein and Matthew T. Kapstein, eds., *Buddhism in Contemporary Tibet: Religious Revival and Cultural Identity.* Berkeley, Calif.: University of California Press, 1998.

Goldstein, Melvyn C., and Cynthia M. Beall. "The Impact of China's Reform Policy on the Nomads of Western Tibet," *Asian Survey,* vol. 29, no. 6 (1989), 619–41.

———. *Nomads of Western Tibet: The Survival of a Way of Life.* Berkeley, Calif.: University of California Press, 1990.

Goldstein, Melvyn C., and Matthew T. Kapstein, eds. *Buddhism in Contemporary Tibet: Religious Revival and Cultural Identity.* Berkeley, Calif.: University of California Press, 1998.

Greenwood, D. "Culture by the Pound: An Anthropological Perspective on Tourism As Cultural Commoditization," 171–86. In V. Smith, ed., *Hosts and Guests: The Anthropology of Tourism.* Philadelphia: University of Pennsylvania Press, 1989.

Grünfelder, Alice. *An den Lederriemen geknotete Seele. Erzähler aus Tibet: Tashi Dawa, Alai, Sebo.* Zurich: Unionsverlag, 1997.

Hansen, Mette Halskov. *Lessons in Being Chinese: Minority Education and Ethnic Identity in Southwest China.* Seattle: University of Washington Press, 1999.

Harrell, Stevan. "Anthropology and Ethnology in the PRC: The Intersection of Discourses," *China Exchange News,* vol. 19, no. 2 (1991), 3–6.

———. "The History of the History of the Yi," 63–91. In Stevan Harrell, ed., *Cultural Encounters on China's Ethnic Frontiers.* Seattle: University of Washington Press, 1995.

———. "Introduction," 3–36. In Stevan Harrell, ed., *Cultural Encounters on China's Ethnic Frontiers.* Seattle: University of Washington Press, 1995.

———. "The Nationalities Question and the Prmi Problem," 274–96. In M. Brown, ed., *Negotiating Ethnicities in China and Taiwan*. Berkeley, Calif.: Center for Chinese Studies, Institute of East Asian Studies, University of California, Berkeley, 1996.

———, ed. *Cultural Encounters on China's Ethnic Frontiers*. Seattle: University of Washington Press, 1995.

Harris, Clare. *In the Image of Tibet, Tibetan Painting after 1959*. London: Reaction Books, 1999.

Havnevik, Hanna. "The Role of Nuns in Contemporary Tibet," 259–66. In R. Barnett and S. Akiner, eds., *Resistance and Reform in Tibet*. London: Hurst, 1994.

Heberer, Thomas. *China and Its National Minorities: Autonomy or Assimilation?* Armonk, N.Y.: M. E. Sharpe, 1989.

Huang, Zheng, and Zhong Tian. *Sichuan Sheng shiyong dituce* (Practical map of Sichuan Province). Chengdu: Chengdu Ditu Chubanshe, 1998.

Human Rights Watch/Tibet Information Network. *Cutting Off the Serpent's Head: Tightening Control in Tibet, 1994–1995*. New York: Human Rights Watch, 1996.

Information Office of the State Council of the People's Republic of China. *Tibet— Its Ownership and Human Rights Situation*. Reprinted in *Beijing Review*, September 28–October 4, 1992.

———. *National Minorities Policy and Its Practice in China*. Beijing: Information Office of the State Council of the People's Republic of China, 1999.

———. *The Development of Tibetan Culture*. Reprinted in *Beijing Review*, July 3, 2000, 16–25.

Ingold, Tim. "The Art of Translation in a Continuous World," 210–32. In G. Pálsson, ed., *Beyond Boundaries: Understanding, Translation, and the Anthropological Discourse*. Oxford, England: Berg, 1993.

International Campaign for Tibet. *Forbidden Freedoms: Beijing's Control of Religion in Tibet*. Washington, D.C.: International Campaign for Tibet, 1990.

———. *A Season to Purge: Religious Repression in Tibet*. Washington, D.C.: International Campaign for Tibet, 1996.

International Commission of Jurists. *Tibet: Human Rights and the Rule of Law*. Geneva: International Commission of Jurists, 1997.

Kangding Minzu Shifan Zhuanke Xuexiao Ketizu (Dartsedo Minzu Teachers Training College Task Group). *Sichuan Zangqu shuangyu jiaoyu yu jiaoxue yanjiu* (A study of bilingual education and the medium of instruction in Sichuan Tibetan areas) Chengdu: Sichuan Daxue Chubanshe, 1996.

Kangding Minzu Shizhuan Bianxiezu (Dartsedo *Minzu* History Editing Board), ed. *Dangdai Ganzi* (Contemporary Kandze). Beijing: Dangdai Zhongguo Chubanshe, 1994.

Karmay, Samten. "Mountain cults and national identity in Tibet," 112–20. In R. Barnett and S. Akiner, eds., *Resistance and Reform in Tibet*. London: Hurst, 1994.

Keesing, Roger. "Theories of Culture Revisited," 301–12. In R. Borofsky, ed., *Reassessing Cultural Anthropology*. New York: McGraw-Hill, 1993.

Korom, Frank J., ed. *Constructing Tibetan Culture: Contemporary Perspectives.* Quebec: World Heritage Press, 1997.

Lamb, Alastair. *The McMahon Line: A Study in the Relations between India, China, and Tibet, 1904 to 1914.* London: Routledge & Kegan Paul, 1966.

Lemoine, Jacques. "Ethnologists in China," *Diogenes*, no. 133 (Spring 1986), 83–112.

Longworth, John W., and Gregory J. Williamson. *China's Pastoral Region: Sheep and Wool, Minority Nationalities, Rangeland Degradation, and Sustainable Development.* Wallingford, U.K.: Cab International, 1993.

Lopez, Donald S. "The Monastery As a Medium of Tibetan Culture," *Cultural Survival Quarterly*, vol. 12, no. 1 (1988), 61–64.

MacInnis, Donald, ed. *Religion in China Today.* New York: Orbis Books, 1989.

Madsen, Richard. "Social Change, Cultural Conservation, and Economic Development." Paper submitted to the Leadership Conference on Conservancy and Development, Yunnan, China, 1999.

Makley, Charlene. "Gendered Practices and the Inner Sanctum," *Tibet Journal*, vol. 19, no. 2 (1994), 61–95.

———. *Embodying the Sacred: Gender and Monastic Revitalization in China's Tibet.* Ph.D. dissertation, University of Michigan, 1999.

Marshall, Steven D., and Susette Ternent Cooke. *Tibet Outside the TAR: Control, Exploitation, and Assimilation. Development with Chinese Characteristics.* The Alliance for Research in Tibet (CD-ROM), 1997.

McKhann, Charles F. "The Naxi and the Nationalities Question," 39–62. In Stevan Harrell, ed., *Cultural Encounters on China's Ethnic Frontiers.* Seattle: University of Washington Press, 1995.

Michael, Franz. *Rule by Incarnation: Tibetan Buddhism and Its Role in Society and State.* Boulder, Colo.: Westview Press, 1982.

Miller, Daniel. *Rangelands and Pastoral Production on the Tibetan Plateau in Western China, and Nomads of the Tibetan Plateau Rangelands.* (*http://www.tew.org/rangelands/index.html*), undated.

Minority Rights Group. *The Tibetans: Two Perspectives on Tibetan-Chinese Relations.* London: Minority Rights Group, 1983.

Nakane, Chie, ed. *Labrang: A Study in the Field by Li An-che.* Tokyo: University of Tokyo, Institute of Oriental Culture, 1982.

Norbu, Dawa. "'Otherness' and the Modern Tibetan Identity," *Himal*, May/June 1992.

Norbu, Jamyang. *Warriors of Tibet: The Story of Aten and the Khampas' Fight for the Freedom of Their Country.* London: Wisdom Publications, 1986.

———. "Dances with Yaks: Tibet in Film, Fiction, and Fantasy of the West." In *Tibetan Review*, January 1998, 18–23.

Pang, Keng-Fong. "Being Hui, Huan-nang, and Utsat Simultaneously: Contextualizing History and Identities of the Austronesain-Speaking Hainan Muslims," 183–207. In M. Brown, ed., *Negotiating Ethnicities in China and Taiwan.* Berkeley,

Calif.: Center for Chinese Studies, Institute of East Asian Studies, University of California, Berkeley, 1996.

Peng, Wenbin. "Tibetan Pilgrimage in the Process of Social Change: The Case of Jiuzhaigou," 184–201. In A. McKay, ed., *Pilgrimage in Tibet*. Richmond, Surrey, U.K.: Curzon Press, 1998.

Pu, Wencheng. *Gan Qing Zangchuan fojiao siyuan* (Tibetan Buddhist monasteries in Gansu and Qinghai) (in Chinese only). Xining: Qinghai Renmin Chubanshe, 1990.

Qi, Yan. *Tibet—Four Decades of Tremendous Change*. Beijing: New Star Publishers, 1991.

Qinghai Sheng zhi; Jiaoyu zhi (Qinghai Province history; history of education). Qinghai Sheng Difangzhi Bianzuan Weiyuanhui (Qinghai Province Local History Editorial Committee), ed. Xining: Huangshan Shushen, 1996.

Ran, Guangrong. *Zhongguo Zangchuan fojiao siyuan* (Tibetan Buddhist monasteries in China). Beijing: Zhongguo Zangxue Chubanshe, 1994.

Richardson, Hugh E. *Tibet and Its History*. Boulder, Colo.: Shambhala Publications, 1984.

Rikha, Tashi, ed. *Tibetan Education in Exile: Current Status Report 1998*. Dharamsala, India: Department of Education of the Tibetan government-in-exile, 1998 *http://www.tcewf.org/publications/csr/index.html*).

Rock, Joseph. *The Amnye Ma-chen Range and Adjacent Regions*. Rome: Istituto Italiano per il Medio ed Estremo Oriente, Serie Orientale, 1956.

Ruo'ergai Xian Renmin Zhengfu Zongjiao Shiwuju (Dzoge County Religious Affairs Department), ed. *Ruo'ergai Xian zongjiao gongzuo gaikuan* (A brief introduction to the conditions of religious work in Dzoge County). Unpublished document, 1989.

Ruo'ergai Xian zhi (Dzoge County history). Ruo'ergai Xian Difangzhi Bianzuan Weiyuanhui (Dzoge County History Editorial Committee), ed. Chengdu: Sichuan Minzu Chubanshe, 1996.

Schein, Louisa. *Minority Rules: The Miao and the Feminine in China's Cultural Politics*. Durham, N.C., and London: Duke University Press, 2000.

Schwartz, Ronald D. "The Anti-Splittist Campaign and Tibetan Political Consciousness," 207–37. In R. Barnett and S. Akiner, eds., *Resistance and Reform in Tibet*. London: Hurst, 1994.

———. *Circle of Protest: Political Ritual in the Tibetan Uprising*. London: Hurst, 1994.

Seymour, James D., and Richard Anderson. *New Ghosts, Old Ghosts: Prisons and Labor Reform Camps in China*. Armonk, N.Y.: M. E. Sharpe, 1998.

Shakya, Tsering. "Tibet and the Occident: The Myth of Shangri-La," *Lungta*, special issue on Tibetan authors (1991), 20–23.

———. *The Dragon in the Land of Snows: A History of Modern Tibet since 1947*. London and Seattle: Pimlico, 1999.

———. "The Waterfall and Fragrant Flowers: The Development of Tibetan Literature since 1950," *Tibetan Bulletin,* vol. 5, no. 3 (July–August 2001), 20–24.

Sichuan Sheng Lüyou Guihua Shijisuo (Sichuan Province Travel Planning Office), ed. *Sichuan Sheng Ganzi Zangzu Zizhizhou lüyou fazhan zongti guihua 2000–2015* (Sichuan Province, Kandze Tibetan Autonomous Prefecture tourism plan 2000–2015). Chengdu: Sichuan Sheng Lüyou Guihua Shijisuo, 1999.

Sichuan Sheng Minzu Shiwu Weiyuanhui (Sichuan Province Ethnic Affairs Commission), ed. *Zangchuan fojiao siyuan ziliao xuanbian* (Selection of sources about Tibetan Buddhist monasteries). Chengdu: Sichuan Sheng Minzu Shiwu Weiyuanhui, 1989.

Sichuan tongji nianjian 1999 (Sichuan statistical yearbook 1999). Zhongguo Tongji Chubanshe (China Statistical Publishing House), ed. Beijing, 1999.

Smith, V. "Eskimo Tourism: Micro-Models and Marginal Men," 55–82. In V. Smith, ed., *Hosts and Guests: The Anthropology of Tourism.* Philadelphia: University of Pennsylvania Press, 1989.

Smith, Warren W. "The Nationalities Policy of the Chinese Communist Party and the Socialist Transformation of Tibet," 51–75. In Robert Barnett and Shirin Akiner, eds., *Resistance and Reform in Tibet.* London: Hurst, 1994.

———. *Tibetan Nation: A History of Tibetan Nationalism and Sino-Tibetan Relations.* Boulder, Colo.: Westview Press, 1996.

Stoddard, Heather. "Tibetan Publications and National Identity," 121–56. In R. Barnett and S. Akiner, eds., *Resistance and Reform in Tibet.* London: Hurst, 1994.

Ström, Axel Kristian. "Between Tibet and the West: On Traditionality, Modernity, and the Development of Monastic Institutions in the Tibetan Diaspora." Revised version of a paper published in Frank J. Korom, ed., *Tibetan Culture in the Diaspora: Papers Presented at a Panel of the Seventh Seminar of the International Association for Tibetan Studies, Graz 1995.* Proceedings of the seventh seminar of the International Association for Tibetan Studies, Graz, 1995, vol. 4, Ernst Steinkellner, general editor. Vienna: Verlag der Österreichischen Akademie der Wissenschaften, undated.

———. *Continuity, Adaptation, and Innovation: Tibetan Monastic Colleges in India.* Ph.D. dissertation, University of Oslo, 2001.

Swain, M. "Gender Roles in Indigenous Tourism: Kuna Mola, Kuna Yala, and Cultural Survival," 83–104. In V. Smith, ed., *Hosts and Guests: The Anthropology of Tourism.* Philadelphia: University of Pennsylvania Press, 1989.

Teichman, Eric. *Travels of a Consular Officer in Eastern Tibet.* Cambridge: Cambridge University Press, 1922.

Thar, Tsering. "The *bla ma* in the Bon religion in Amdo and Kham," 417–27. In Samten G. Karmay and Yasuhiko Nagano, eds., *New Horizons in Bon Studies.* Osaka, Japan: National Museum of Ethnology, 2000. *Tianzhu Xian zhi* (History of Pari County).

Tianzhu Zangzu Zizhi Xianzhi Bianzuan Weiyuanhui (Pari Tibetan Autonomous

County History Editing Committee), ed. Lanzhou: Gansu Minzu Chubanshe, 1994.

Tibet Information Network. *A Sea of Bitterness.*

Union Research Institute. *Tibet: 1950–1967.* Hong Kong: Union Research Institute, 1968.

Upton, Janet. "Home on the Grasslands? Tradition, Modernity, and the Negotiation of Identity by Tibetan Intellectuals in the PRC," 98–124. In M. J. Brown, ed., *Negotiating Ethnicities in China and Taiwan.* Berkeley, Calif.: Institute of East Asian Studies, University of California, Berkeley, 1996.

———. *Schooling Shar-Khog: Time, Space, and the Place of Pedagogy in the Making of the Tibetan Modern.* Ph.D. dissertation, University of Washington, 1999.

———. "Notes towards a Native Tibetan Ethnology: An Introduction to an Annotated Translation of dMu-dge bSam-gtsan's 'Dwags po'i mi rigs kyi gnad don skor' (On the question of the Dwags po' nationality) and 'Dwags po'i mi rigs kyi skor la lta stangs bshad pa' (A discussion of [my] views on the matter of the Dwags po nationality)," *The Tibet Journal,* vol. 25, no. 1 (Spring 2000), 3–26.

———. "Beyond the Contents of a Curriculum: Toward an Ethnographic Reading of Tibetan-Language Textbooks in the People's Republic of China." Forthcoming in the proceedings of the eighth Conference of the International Association for Tibetan Studies.

———. "Cascades of Change: Modern and Contemporary Literature in the PRC's Junior-Secondary Tibetan Language and Literature Curriculum." Forthcoming in *Lungta.*

Verdery, Katherine. "Ethnicity, Nationalism, and State-Making. Ethnic Groups and Boundaries: Past and Future," 33–58. In Hans Vermeulen and Cora Govers, eds., *The Anthropology of Ethnicity: Beyond "Ethnic Groups and Boundaries."* Amsterdam: Het Spinhuis, 1994.

Wagner, Roy. *The Invention of Culture.* Chicago: University of Chicago Press, 1975.

Wallerstein, Immanuel. *Unthinking Social Science: The Limits of Nineteenth-Century Paradigms.* Cambridge: Polity, 1991.

Wang, Xiaoqiang, and Nanfeng Bai. *The Poverty of Plenty.* New York: St. Martin's Press, 1991.

Wang, Xiuyun, ed. *Minzu pinkun diqu, xianzhang lun jiaoyu* (County leaders in poor minority areas discuss education). Beijing: Minzu Chubanshe, 2000.

Watson, Francis. *The Frontiers of China.* London: Chatto & Windus, 1966.

Wellens, Koen. "What's in a Name? The Premi in Southwest China and the Consequences of Defining Ethnic Identity," *Nations and Nationalism,* vol. 4, no 1 (1998), 17–34.

Winkler, Daniel. "Floods, Logging, and Hydro-Electricity: The Impact on Tibetan Areas." In WTN-L World Tibet Network News, issue ID 99/01/27 (1999).

Xie, Haining. *Guoluo Zangzu shehui* (Golok Tibetan society). Beijing: Zhongguo Zangxue Chubanshe, 1994.

Yang, Chunjing. "Qiandan Zang yuwen jiaoxue zai fazhan minzu jiaoyuzhong de zhongyaoxing" (A tentative study on the importance of teaching in the Tibetan language for developing national education), *Xizang yanjiu* (Tibet studies), vol. 59, no. 2 (1996).

Yang, Jiaming. *Dege Yinjingyuan* (Derge Sutra Printing Academy). Chengdu: Sichuan Renmin Chubanshe, 2000.

Zhang, Rongsu. *A Case Study on Mountain Environmental Management: Nyemo County (Tibet)*. ICIMOD Occasional Paper no. 13. Katmandu, Tibet: ICIMOD, 1988.

Zhang, Tianlu. *Population Development in Tibet and Related Issues*. Beijing: Foreign Languages Press, 1997.

Zhongguo Shehui Kexueyuan Minzu Yanjiusuo (China's Academy of Social Sciences, Institute of *Minzu* Studies) and Guojia Minzu Shiwu Weiyuanhui Wenhua Xuanchuanci (State Ethnic Affairs Commission, Culture and Propaganda Office), eds. *Zhongguo shaoshu minzu yuyan shiyong qingkuang* (Conditions and use of China's minority *minzu* languages). Beijing: Zhongguo Zangxue Chubanshe, 1994.

INDEX

www.ingramcontent.com/pod-product-compliance
Lightning Source LLC
Chambersburg PA
CBHW030644270326
41929CB00007B/199